PRIVATES

STONEWALL INN EDITIONS
Michael Denneny, General Editor

Buddies by Ethan Mordden
Joseph and the Old Man by Christopher Davis
Blackbird by Larry Duplechan
Gay Priest by Malcolm Boyd
Taking Care of Mrs. Carroll by Paul Monette
Conversations with My Elders by Boze Hadleigh
Epidemic of Courage by Lon Nungesser

GENE HOROWITZ

PRIVATES

ST. MARTIN'S PRESS · NEW YORK

Grateful acknowledgment is made for permission to reprint from the following:

Tennessee Williams, *A Streetcar Named Desire*. Copyright © 1947 by Tennessee Williams. Reprinted by permission of New Directions Publishing Corporation.

W.B. Yeats, "Brown Penny." Reprinted with permission of Macmillan Publishing Company from *Collected Poems* by W.B. Yeats. Copyright © 1912 by Macmillan Publishing Company, renewed 1940 by Bertha Georgie Yeats.

James Joyce, *Dubliners*. Copyright © 1916 by B.W. Huebsch. Definitive text copyright 1967 by the estate of James Joyce. Reprinted by permission of Viking Penguin, Inc.

"Hi Lili, Hi Lo" By Bronislau Kaper and Helen Deutsch, Copyright © 1952. Renewed 1980 Metro-Goldwyn-Mayer Inc. Rights Assigned to CBS Catalogue Partnership. All rights controlled and administered by CBS Robbins Catalog, Inc. All rights reserved. International copyright secured. Used by permission.

Design by Victoria Hartman

Library of Congress Cataloging-in-Publication Data

Horowitz, Gene, 1930–
Privates.

I. Title.
PS3558.0693P7 1986   813'.54   86–3659
ISBN 0-312-64716-6

ISBN 0-312-01496-1 (pbk.)

For Stan Herman,
who long ago touched my life
with the joy of his love

As I Lay With My Head in Your Lap Camerado

As I lay with my head in your lap camerado,
The confession I made I resume, what I said to you and the
*   open air I resume,*
I know I am restless and make others so,
I know my words are weapons full of danger, full of death,
For I confront peace, security, and all the settled laws, to
*   unsettle them,*
I am more resolute because all have denied me than I could
*   ever have been had all accepted me,*
I heed not and have never heeded either experience,
*   Cautions, majorities, nor ridicule,*
And the threat of what is call'd hell is little or nothing to me,
And the lure of what is call'd heaven is little or nothing to me;
Dear camerado! I confess I have urged you onward with me,
*   and still urge you, without the least idea what is our*
*   destination,*
Or whether we shall be victorious, or utterly quell'd and
*   defeated.*

—From *Drum-Taps*, **Walt Whitman**

PRIVATES

PROLOGUE

"**A**aron Lebow calling, fresh from his overnight at Our Lady of the Vapors. Come for a drink, Willy. At seven-thirty. I bought the new Boulez *Parsifal*. I'll play some for you and then we'll go for a pleasant dinner to Bobby Van's. Come. I need you, Willy."

"Did you go to the doctor before or after the baths?"

"Before."

"And?"

"Later, Willy. When you get here. More important, did you hear from Victor? He's where now?"

"En route, probably. From Albuquerque to Dallas. According to his itinerary, tonight he stays at the Fairmont Hotel. Tomorrow night he'll be next to me in bed. I can't wait. This trip I've missed him more than usual. I've missed you too all week."

"I'm glad. That's what friends are for, to be missed when they're gone. And Victor? He's found good things for the museum?"

"He found a collector, an Indian collector who's willing to sell. A Navaho living in Albuquerque."

"So he'll come home happy. And if he's happy, you'll be happy and Saturday night the two of you will give a happy party. All week I've been looking forward to it. A May Day party in the Hamptons . . . you're so . . . irreverent? Is that the word I want?"

1

"Vehr vehst."

"You know, Willy, honey. You always know what I want. You're my writer-in-residence. In advance I'm hiring you to be my official biographer. So, better be here at seven-thirty, promptly. I need you."

"In advance of what, Aaron?"

"Never mind that now. Just come and you'll hear."

"I'll come, but I've got an advance for you, too. I need you, too. Tonight I'm burning up with needs. While you've been feeding and watering in New York all week, I've been having hot flashes and palpitations and my work's been shit. Must be my menopause. It's starting, Aaron. I'm fifty."

"So come earlier. I'll happily kiss you where you're burning. Just don't tell Victor."

Good dumpling Aaron! At sixty-one, he lived alone in an H-shaped, heavily mortgaged house up on the high ground moraine overlooking the potato fields of Bridgehampton north of Montauk Highway. From his bedrom picture window he could see a dirt road leading across a potato field and into a thicket of tall scrub oak and even taller pitch pine. Hidden inside that thicket was our house, Victor's and mine. Hidden, too, even from Aaron's overview, was our little glacial lake. Our house sat close to its eastern shore. It was made of glass and cedar shingles and filled with Navaho rugs and Indian artifacts, simple cedar end tables and sofa platforms made by me out of leftover lumber from when the house was built in 1970. Aaron's house was brick. It was filled with *chochkes* of value purchased from pieces of life he had lived in London and Paris and Rome after World War II. He had decided to take his discharge from the army in Europe, ending up in Rome and working for Orson Welles. "Rome in the late forties, Willy . . ." he often told me when he was in his cups, nostalgically reviewing the ups and downs of his early free fall life. "Rome, then . . . it never ends in my head. Even though Orson had no money and never paid me, I'd do it all over again. Not that I regretted coming back to America when I did. It was time. The fun was over by 1950. *Moi, je ne regrette rien. . . ."* He played scenes of regretting nothing, not even never having had a long-term live-in lover. He had, instead, the honor of having become the English-language film voice of Marcello Mastroianni. When he returned to America he also had a profession: voice-over/dubber/director of foreign-language films. He had more than enough money to spend on clothes and books and recordings and fine china and antiques and works of art he predicted would someday become valuable, "a lot more valuable than a lover would be in the long run. Cheaper, too . . ." For as long as I had known him—twenty-seven years, exactly; exactly as long as Victor and I had been lovers; Aaron had followed Victor into the William Tell bar the night Victor and I met—for all that time not one piece of his adored Futurist Italian art had increased in value. *"Nu,"* he would say, if some one of his party acquaintances had the effrontery to confront him with the possibility that the work might be junk, "so I made a few mistakes." Those scenes he played as an overweight vamp, lifting one sloping, round shoulder forward seductively. "I revel in mistakes. Success is too time-consuming. . . ." His doubts he shared with us, "because, in spite of everything, you love me." To us he talked art and books and music. At parties he talked Broadway musicals, the rising mortgage rates in the Hamptons, and how to cope with frozen pipes in the winter— "Wrap them, my dear. Wrap them tenderly." To me he also confided his mazy movements through the tangled undergrowth of a now often-rejected fatty's solitary gay existence in New York City and the Hamptons. "I know this year of their Lord, 1980, it will get harder for me out there, Willy"—he handed me my Scotch; we raised glasses, his was almost empty; we clicked, sipped—"but last night, for some inscrutable reason, I was among the chosen at the baths. An exhilarating night it was." He looked anything but. He looked wilted, enervated, pensive. But he would rally. He always rallied, eventually. "And this morning, when I dragged myself over to the office, some more

3

good fortune. There's a chance I'll get the new Zeffirelli film to dub. If I do I'll have to go to Rome in June."

Oddly, he didn't seem happy about the prospect: a very bad sign indeed. "What did the doctor have to say?"

"Nothing." He rose quickly from his leather club chair. I was in a sister chair on the other side of his fireplace. "I absolutely need another drink." He left for the kitchen, and when he returned he immediately went across the room to the closet where he kept his stereo equipment. "Why don't I play the Prelude. I listened to it already. Heavenly. Please don't feel betrayed, Willy darling, but I ached for a fix of purity. Of course that you never need."

"Stop the acting, Aaron. What did the doctor say?"

"I'm giving a terrible performance. Not from the heart . . . He said I have a *petite tache*."

"Where?"

"In the left lung. A tumor . . . and after I gave up cigarettes. All that struggle for nothing."

"You gave them up just two months ago."

"Two months, three months, what's the difference? There's a tumor and I have to go back next week for tests. That's all he said. That's all I know. And about that which I know not of . . . let me be silent? Yes, Willy darling?" He readied the stylus. "Music time now. *Shah.*" He waited for the opening string strains before returning to his chair. It was our habit that when we listened to music together we listened in silence. Over the years, habit had hardened into law. Aaron knew I could be counted on to honor it—as well as the plea in his sad gray eyes that I cease and desist. Anyway, what was there to ask? Did he have pain? Was he losing weight? It didn't seem so. And his skin . . . yes, it did look sallow, but that was from the baths. . . . I tried to sink into the music, to still the flurry of cross-current thoughts, to imagine Victor in an airplane on his way from Albuquerque to Dallas. I felt staccato stabbings start up in my heart. I missed him . . . too much. I would miss Aaron if . . .

4

looking over at him, I saw that he had his eyes closed, that he was smiling. I closed my eyes, thinking of the deaths I had already lived through, my mother's and father's, both sets of grandparents . . . and now friends would begin to drop away. Irreplaceable, the friends one loses at fifty. Irreplaceable, Aaron Lebow, who had followed his friend Victor Friedman into the William Tell and who had followed that same Victor, and his lover William Howards, out to the Hamptons when, by accident, out driving one April Sunday in 1957, they had made a wrong turn onto a dirt road and discovered a hidden lake inside a thicket of tall scrub oak and even taller pitch pine. As if it were the proverbial yesterday—in the mind it was and always could be—I remembered us at Monte's Italian restaurant on Mac-Dougal Street in the Village near our West Fourth Street walkup apartment that Sunday night excitedly telling Aaron about the hidden lake. For the next decade, while I was going from teaching high school English to having my first and second and third novels published, and Victor was going from an American Indian assistant curator's job at the American Museum of Natural History to becoming co-curator of a modest-sized folk arts museum, summers we rented make-do cabins in the vicinity, inviting Aaron out almost every weekend, patiently putting some money together, applying to the Veterans Administration for a loan for the rest, finally persuading Mr. Buettel, the farmer who owned the land, to sell us a sliver. That was in the late sixties. Our house was finished in 1970. Aaron moved into his house in 1972 . . . yesterday. Inside my head, a fifty-year-old's collection of yesterdays and, now, today, an addition: the day Aaron told me about his tumor.

I'd heard nothing of the Prelude and it was concluding and Aaron was leaping to his feet, light on his toes, always, saying we should leave, it was getting late, he was tired, "but I think we should go in two cars tonight, anyway, Willy. I may have to leave. I may . . . get sticky. Maudlin . . . you know how I can get. So, don't you add to it. Nothing more about my *tache*.

5

There's nothing sensible I can say about it. It's there and that's that."

Aaron, in his bright yellow VW Beetle, followed me in our gray Jeep down Scuttlehole Road and out onto Montauk Highway. Light traffic this Thursday night. Aaron had no trouble turning just after I did. I had no trouble getting into first. Usually I did. Usually I stalled. It was Victor who loved the Jeep. Not I. Ever since my army days I had fought a battle with the stick shift, having believed then that if I mastered it, I would be sent directly to Korea. During his Korean War army years Victor had been stationed in Europe, in Bavaria. He enjoyed driving a Jeep up and down those mountain roads. He enjoyed driving so much that, usually, I let him do all our driving. Out of Manhattan to our house. Over to Gristede's in Southampton. To Catena's fish market. To Palma's liquor shop. To the Green Thumb in summer. I was happy to let him drive the Jeep—or whatever car we drove in together—and wherever. On vacations . . . from Milan up to Lake Como . . . through the Brenner Pass and on up into the Alps . . . from Edinburgh to London to Land's End and back . . . from Denver down to the Grand Canyon . . . I've always been content to let Victor drive, not bothering to subject that contentment to very much analysis. No need to. Lovers who have been together for twenty-seven years find out what works for them, just as people who live alone find out what works for them. Like buying a yellow Beetle worked for Aaron. "At my age I need something to call attention to me before I retire to my bed. . . ."

Bobby Van's had the makings of a crowd. That brought a smile to Aaron's face. He loved to *yenta* in crowded restaurants, loved to outflank and maneuver for the seat at the table with the most commanding view. So did Victor. I had gotten used to sitting with my back to the crowd and to watching the eyes of my nearest and dearest make visits to nearby tables or up to the entrance whenever the door opened. Aaron chose a choice table facing the bar. The waitress, being a particular admirer of the

6

sound of his voice and the bushiness of his eyebrows, willingly submitted. "I need another Scotch."

So did I.

Aaron launched into a description of a dinner he had had that week at La Grenouille. "An old friend took me. An admirer from way back when. It was his eightieth birthday, but he insisted on taking me. We had a thing in Rome in the forties. Nothing eternal." He sipped, his gaze drifting toward the bar for a languid cruise, even as he went on to ask me what I thought of the Prelude. "I couldn't concentrate." He expected me to say more, to say a lot. About *Parsifal* I usually did. Not tonight. Tonight I wanted him to talk, to tell me what and all he knew. But he was equally determined. He found another subject to leap to momentarily while he regained his balance. He asked about Victor's Indian collector. I didn't have any more to add to what I had told him earlier. "If he calls you later, Willy, tell him not to take any wooden nickels." He even ha-ha-ha-ed, straining to keep our conversation neutral, desultory, to keep it circling out, further and further away from the forbidden center of his tumor. I nodded, studying him. He just wanted to look and to be left alone. I gave in, launched the topic of my week-long writer's block. "It started as soon as I dropped Victor at La Guardia. I can trace it to the sinking feeling I had when I got behind the wheel of the Jeep, waved to Victor and the fucking thing stalled, right there in a yellow sea of honking taxicabs. Victor was so embarrassed he didn't even wait to see me emerge triumphant. I did, but I paid a price. My head's frozen and I have to finish my article by next week. I've got an advance. My agent has it placed in a nongay magazine—'Gay Sensibility—If It Exists, What Is It?' What I'd really like to be doing is working on my novel . . ."

"Tell me about the party plans, Willy. How many of each do you have? Straights, gay, otherwise?"

"Half and half. We always aim for half and half."

"Maybe you should do thirds."

"Victor and I don't know any thirds. We're not into that."

7

"Should I do one of my famous dips?"

"Thanks a lot, Aaron, but no thanks."

The waitress came for our orders. For me, house salad, broiled scrod, baked potato. Aaron wanted chicken Kiev. "I'm feeling my Russian heritage tonight, gloomy. The butter will cheer me up."

Quietly, we chomped through our salads. Aaron ordered yet another Scotch. When his chicken arrived, he drank more than he ate. He poked a hole into the center of the cutlet and watched the butter ooze out all over the rice. "I suddenly don't feel much like eating, Willy. Maybe you won't mind if we leave sooner than later?"

"I won't mind."

Nor did he want any coffee or dessert. "The baths, Willy. Drained the sap right out of me—not that you would know of such things. No need for you to, either. You've got Victor. Victor's got you. That should be more than enough. Maybe in the next life I'll try your way. In this one it's too late to change." He gestured for the check, and then he reached across the table to take hold of my hands. He lifted them. Suddenly, there were tears in his eyes, but he was smiling—for me. "I want to tell you . . . thank you . . . for all our times together."

"And to you, too."

He nodded, let go of my hands, covered his eyes, brushing them, swallowing hard, struggling for control. "I don't feel we'll have . . . many more times . . . together. I don't feel it in my bones. But I'm not so afraid. Not yet, anyway. Not so special, dying. Everyone does it, even an old gay man." He stared off toward the bar. By then every stool was occupied. At least he would have some diversion while we waited for the check to arrive.

We divided the bill in half. That was another of our habits together—extra drinks notwithstanding—that and his dramatic, eye-lifting passage down the length of the bar, of any bar we happened to be leaving. Bobby Van's was no exception.

8

A light rain had begun to fall. We zipped up our down jackets. We wore matching green ones, sister jackets. Arm in arm we crossed Montauk Highway. I walked him to the door of his Beetle. He took hold of my hand, squeezing it. "You were a good *boychik* tonight. You obeyed your old mother. Do one more thing for me. Don't tell Victor about me until he gets home. He'll worry . . ."

I hugged him close. He went soft, his dumpling weight sagging. But as soon as I tightened my grip, he straightened, determined. "A momentary lapse. By Saturday I'll be perfect. All I need is a party to go to. Mother's milk, a party . . ." He moved me back to arm's length, leaned close for another cheek-to-cheek. "Maybe you'll follow me back . . . just in case?"

The rain had steadied to a downpour, but I waited next to the Jeep until I saw Aaron's outside house lights go out. For tonight, at least, he was safe.

I ran up onto the deck and around to the sliding door entrance to the kitchen. Inside, I made my rounds: the lamps above the butcher block; the end table lamps in the living room; on into the den for the gooseneck above Victor's desk, across the room to my desk and my gooseneck. I stopped there, looked down at the page in the typewriter: notes . . . under the heading "Causal vs. Casual Sex." There was pitifully little typed beneath it. I should sit down. I should try to work. Nearly ten. Nearly nine in Dallas. I stared at the phone, sending thought waves through it. Now, Victor. Now . . . usually, when he's off, scouring the countryside for curious Indian artifacts to bring back to his museum, he telephones me every night from . . . wherever. Something to count on, his calling. Sooner or later, he would. So, while I waited, why not a page or two?—but not on the magazine article. No. All evening, the engines in my mind had been spinning out threads of thought from another source, from the novel I'd been trying to prod into life for over a year now, a novel whose parts and pieces had steadfastly refused to be sewn into a web of connection. I wanted the book to be about Victor and myself, about our meeting, our lives together, the building of our house . . . I had always envisioned that as its central metaphor. Aaron would begin it because he had been there at the beginning. But, then what? For a year now, the scenes I wrote had remained inert: a pile of pages I couldn't seem to shape into matter that might matter to anyone else, especially that legendary reader out there always hungry for a good read. Nevertheless, I kept at it because . . . because that's what I enjoy doing and because if I don't do it I won't have a product to sell in a year or two. This past March, however, something I thought of then as having no particular importance unpredictably and unsuspectingly began to change the collecting pile of pages into a promise: I received a letter in honor of my fiftieth birthday from a long-ago army friend, Sam Tolan.

The letter was filled with a lot of old memories and some new facts. Sam recalled for me our years together at Fort Hood, Texas, our fateful—"prophetic" he called it—accidental meeting one Sunday in Dallas, "the day I took you to the Blue Bonnet bar and we had run out of Saturday night gin and we had beer and you got drunk and told me all about your father's uncle Vladimir, after whom you'd been named, who had had his stomach ripped open by a Cossack's saber on the streets of a city named Minsk during a pogrom at the beginning of this appalling century. Everyone, you told me, referred to him as V'lodya. Ever after that's what you were to me, V'lodya, or, sometimes, Willhee? Won't-hee? *Recuerdo?* . . ." I had read his letter so often pieces of it had become stuck in my head. *Recuerdo* . . . I surely did. I remembered the Blue Bonnet and that used-to-be Dallas a decade before John Kennedy was assassinated there, a Dallas without a Fairmont Hotel in it. In the years that had intervened since we last saw each other in 1953, we had maintained a sometimes correspondence. His birthday letter was meant to bring us both up to date. He had finally managed to get mortgage money from the Veterans Administration to buy an old Victorian rehab in the Western Addition section of San Francisco, "... I described it to you in a letter years ago, the same letter in which I wrote you about breaking up with a Zachary and so it would become necessary for me to look around for another letter of the alphabet to fall in love with. (There are no letters left now.) The house shared a back garden wall with a now-defunct synagogue, the garden then in ruins and filled with a riot of rotting cacti. I saw the connection to the synagogue as a good omen evoking your spirit. Mother is here visiting me now. She wishes to be remembered to you. How is that nice young Jewish boy from New York? she asked. Not so young anymore, I told her, when she asked after you. We grow old, V'lodya, *n'est-ce pas?* So how about coming out here for a visit before it gets to be too late? I long for the sight of you, my lady. Twenty-seven years since last we saw each other. . . ." Unlikely, a visit now. Then, in '53, I never wanted to leave Sam.

His birthday letter had gone unanswered. I kept putting it off, waiting for the propitious moment, perhaps for the day of *his* fiftieth birthday in June, but I kept the letter close, in the kneehole drawer of my desk. Every time I needed a clip or a pen or pencil or carbon or more typewriting paper, I had to see it there, to think about it and about the twenty-three-year-old green-eyed, Texas-tanned Samuel Tolan still very much alive in my memory. One morning, opening my kneehole drawer, looking down at the envelope, I suddenly said out loud, "Why, of course, Sam has to be in the book. But how? Why?" And then, if Sam is in it, who else from the past should be in it and what other pieces should the story include? How much should I tell? When should I tell it? Should I tell about the night in the William Tell, about a month after being discharged from the army, I was standing near the door of the bar, getting ready to leave because no one seemed to want me, getting my head ready for the subway ride back to Brooklyn where my mother was all too quickly dying of cancer, when suddenly the door was opened and in rushed a string of stalwarts? I remember how, at that very

11

moment, I was deep in thought, thinking about other places, of Fort Hood and Dallas, of a person there, Sam. I was missing him, missing him too much . . . when Victor passed by, followed by Aaron . . . Aaron had always been a character in the book. Tonight, how he would be now, and why, had recharged the engines secretly whirring away in my head ever since I had received Sam's letter. I took it out of the kneehole drawer. Tomorrow morning, first thing, before "Gay Sensibility—If It Exists, What Is It?" I would answer it. . . . Ten-thirty. Nine-thirty in Dallas. Where are you, Victor? Long past my bedtime. I retrace my rounds. The goosenecks, off. The end table lamps in the living room, off—and then the lamps above the butcher block. Darkness. The rain splashes against the kitchen sliding doors. I lean against them, looking out and up to where I know Aaron's house would be if I could see it. No lights on there either. Sleep, Aaron, sleep.

In the darkness I make my way up the wrought-iron spiral staircase. Habit guides my steps. The rain on the roof beats down in wind-driven bursts.

I undress quickly, rush into bed, shivering. The sheets are cold. I reach over to touch Victor's pillow, to smooth it, shooting my thoughts Dallasward. His twin bed is pressed up against mine. Early on we had made that choice: in Manhattan, in Bridgehampton, separate twin beds but never separated, even when the family came, so that, whenever the need came upon us, all we had to do was roll over. The need came upon us still, at least two or three times a week. The need was upon me now, but less for sex than to feel him put his arms around me, to reassure me and to be reassured himself that for another night, another week, another year we were here together in our house along the shores of a glacial lake at the edge of a potato field in Bridgehampton.

I had a book to read, Justin Kaplan's *Walt Whitman*, but the sounds, the darkness, were soothing. A stand of hollow-trunk sassafras out back of the house near the woodpile groaned, creaked in a gust of wind. The baseboard heater tapped on. Downstairs the refrigerator began its automatic defrost cyle. I re-smoothed Victor's pillow, conjuring up the feel of his silky hair, the shape of his broad shoulders turning off to sleep, at peace beneath his warm quilt in the bed pressed up close to mine . . .

The shrill ring of the telephone next to my head startled me. I jumped up, fumbling for the receiver.

"You were asleep. What time is it there? Eleven?"

"Yes. I didn't feel like reading. It's raining. You know how that sounds on the roof. Like a lullaby."

"I called earlier, before I left Albuquerque. Did you hear from Aaron about his doctor's appointment?"

"I had dinner with him. We went to Bobby Van's. He . . . has no news from the doctor. Not until next week. He sends his love. You're in Dallas?"

"I am . . . at the Adolphus Hotel."

"The Adolphus? Weren't you supposed to be at the Fairmont? What made you switch?"

"Didn't you tell me you used to stay there with your army buddies?"

"I never did. Sam Tolan . . . he did—but is that why you changed hotels?"

"No. By chance I did. On the flight over from Albuquerque my seatmate happened to mention the fact that the Adolphus has just been refurbished. Very dee-luxe is how he put it. A Texas cattleman. A little the way Rock Hudson was in *Giant*. High-heeled boots, but very polished. A Stetson. Weather-tanned skin. Salt of the earth."

"Oh."

"Oh, what, Willy?"

"Oh . . . I get the picture. You painted it vividly."

"It sounded like your 'Oh' meant more. I know your sounds. Is anything wrong?"

"Wrong?" Suddenly, my *kishkas* were erupting. I tasted scrod and bile rising past the esophagus and on up into my throat.

13

"Nothing's wrong. It's just that . . . I'm fifty. Fifty can't stand surprises in the middle of the night. It also happens that earlier I was thinking about Sam Tolan and Dallas . . . synchronicities are striking at my 'heartes roote.' My oldest memories seem to be in a state of some agitation tonight. They feel young again . . . not like my skin or my eyes—but none of that has anything to do with the Adolphus. It's been redone, you said, so it wouldn't match my memory of it anyway. . . . In my day in Dallas I sometimes stayed at the Baker Hotel. It was diagonally across from the Adolphus."

"Gone. Torn down. The cattleman mentioned it. He thought it was a hotel they should have saved too."

"My first weekend pass after basic I stayed at the Baker. A bunch of us, *landsmen* from New York City, went up to Dallas together. Must have been June . . . June 1951 . . ."

"The same June I was on my way to Europe."

"The June I was wilting and wasting away in Texas, expecting at any moment to be sent to Korea . . ."

"You couldn't draw, Willy." He laughed. Our private joke about how his captain had come into his mess hall at Fort Dix to hand out orders, but asking, first of all, if there was anyone among them who could draw. He needed someone who could draw. Victor could. Victor had studied drawing in college. The captain changed his orders on the spot. From Korea to Germany . . . "He had a thing for me. That part I never told you before."

"No, you didn't, but it comes as no surprise. Just look at yourself in the mirror. You're beautiful."

But his sigh was a sure sign he wasn't listening. I knew his sounds too. His head was on the boat to Europe. "How I pitied the poor fuckers from my platoon that ended up going to Korea. Who even remembers Korea today? No one. The war everyone forgot . . ."

Remembering the separate parts we played in that long-ago-forgotten war, we let silence reign. At my end, the raindrops on the rooftop comfort me. Through thousands of miles of telephone wire I study the cameo of Victor's near-perfect Roman-coin profile. I see a pensive smile lift his ripe upper lip, see his hand pinch the thin ridge of his straight, narrow nose. And, then, another sigh, from deeper down, from where nostalgia lives, from where it suddenly leaps out at you from the darkness. On his smooth, broad forehead then, furrows. And, yes, there goes his hand up to his eyebrow. He worries a wild, curling gray strand of it between his fingers. His smile fades.

So does mine. My turn to sigh.

Next, he will be rubbing circles at the back of his head. His silky brown hair is thinning back there. It's graying. "I remember I almost didn't come back from Europe. A sergeant was after me to re-up, go to officer's training. I came damn close to staying."

"I'm glad you didn't. We wouldn't have met."

"And what if you had stayed in Mexico with Sam Tolan after your discharge?" But more than asking a question, the slow hiss of his breath escaping indicates he needs no answer. He is balancing the ifs. Will it be favorable?

Another silence. This one I fill with my own equivalent of a wild hair. Starting at my lips, I slide my fingers down the chin of my beard, poke into it, fluff it, smooth it. A grizzled gray thicket, my beard. So are my thoughts in the darkness of our bedroom without him next to me. "I remember a bar . . . across from the Adolphus, but down a ways, in the opposite direction from the Baker, the Blue Bonnet. Sam and I used to go there a lot."

"After dinner I can check to see if it's still there."

"Not on my account, Victor, honey . . ." and then, unchecked, an unforgivable question slides through my lips. "Is the cattleman staying at the Adolphus too?"

Victor's sigh was so loud it kicked me in the head, re-opening the wound in my *kishkas*. I saw his usually welcoming dark

15

brown eyes rolling to a dead stop, his lips pursing, making a tiny telltale sound of annoyance.

I was leading us into a rat's alley. "Sorry, Victor. Scratch the last remark. *Mea culpa.* Accept my apology? Please?"

"No apology needed." I heard the rattle of ice cubes, and then his sipping, his determined crunching of ice.

We needed an immediate thaw. Go back to Go, William Howards. "Did the Indian decide to sell?"

"He sold me enough for a show. For the autumn. And your work? Is it going any better since my last call?" He wanted a thaw as much as I did.

"Not really. Circuits all over my brain are shutting down, going dead forever. I feel them popping off. Thousands of them every second."

"Maybe we should have skipped the party this year. I was going to suggest that before I left. You've had it all to do yourself, plus your work . . ."

"I've looked forward to it. It's ours, Victor, our tradition. It gives us . . . continuity. Year after year . . ."

"Yes . . . well, at least on Saturday morning I'll be there to help. My plan for tomorrow night is to take a cab from La Guardia to Jamaica station and catch the 4:06, if my plane's on time. If not, I'll call you from the airport. Okay?"

"Okay . . . and about the cattleman, I'm sorry, Victor. You do . . . whatever you want to do."

"What I want to do is get home to you. This trip has tired me out more than most. As you said before, it's being fifty. I don't enjoy traveling as much anymore. It's too . . . lonely. I miss you."

I nodded. I smiled. Did he see? Was he listening for my smiling sound? "And I miss you too. Very much."

"Good. This call we only got our wires crossed once. Your trouble is you think you hear something and immediately you jump to a conclusion. No need to, Willy. Okay?"

"Okay." I nodded again, but I wasn't smiling this time. I was . . . hearing something . . .

16

"Okay . . . so go back to sleep now. Get a good night's rest and finish your article tomorrow so we can enjoy the party."

"I'll try."

"Okay, then, Willy?"

"Yes. Okay . . . I love you, Victor."

"And I love you. Good night . . ."

Disconnect. Darkness. The rain on the rooftop. I listened, tense, disturbed by the tangled thoughts rushing through my head, thoughts of then and now, of Victor and Sam and Aaron, and of others, others further back, all the way back to Brooklyn, stored thoughts of my mother and father, of Jerry Saperstein and Harlan Royce, of City College and Amelia del Viso, thoughts hermetically sealed in steel bins at the bottom of my brain . . . the mind, the mind, shooting off rockets of remembrance when it should be resting. The Nostalgies at fifty: the knife of memory slicing deep into the center of another time; the tin can, age, banging out its tin-tin truth behind lidless eyes. We grow old. We grow old. . . .

Eventually, I slept . . . and I dreamed . . . of crossed wires . . . of cattlemen who looked like Rock Hudson.

The next morning heavy rains—a nor'easter—beat against the clerestory glass in the living room. Coffee cup in hand, I watched the wind whipping through the tender trees down along the lake shore. On the phonograph, the Mozart flute and harp concerto comforted—but there was work to be done, no matter how soggy my thoughts about gay sensibility and the human condition might be this morning. I shut off the phonograph. Discipline at seven A.M. a necessity.

At my desk I studied notes . . . gay cooking—gay clothing trends—gay bar sexual freedom and its affect on heterosexual singles scene . . . I picked up Sam's letter, tapped its edge against my chinny-chin-chin, considering . . . later. For now, begin . . . perhaps with a prototypic bar, perhaps the Blue Bonnet or the William Tell—but that was ancient history. *Nu!* So what? Is there nothing to learn from history? Let us consider the first gay bar and bath house in ancient Greece . . . I sharpened pencils. And then I had to shit.

And then I returned, readied my fingers above the keyboard, my eyes . . . watching the rain beat down on the empty rows of our summer vegetable garden. Chickenwire enclosure needed mending, had rusted through the winter . . .

For the next five hours I typed . . . words. "Words without thoughts never to heaven go . . ."

At one the rains stopped. So did I. I wolfed down a yogurt. I had miles of chores to see to before I could allow myself the luxury of anticipating Victor's arrival.

I drove to Southampton, to the Uncommon Market, to order another platter of assorted cheeses and exotic salamis. Then, over to Palma's to set a time for a Saturday-morning delivery . . . and an extra bottle of vodka, an extra Scotch, Dewar's. Victor hated cheap Scotch at parties. And then Gristede's for our dinner things, and, sure, why not, some more mixers. Eventually, at parties yet to come, they'd get used up . . . and I needed more carbon paper and another ribbon and then I needed more money from Tinker National Bank.

Back at the house I telephoned Aaron. No answer. I set a flank steak steeping in a marinade of Victor's devising.

On the tape deck I started one of my homemade tapes of an old Met broadcast of *Salome* starring our favorite aging soprano, Leonie Rysanek . . . music to sweep to, to dust to, to Lemon Pledge rattan furniture to.

I skipped my usual four-thirty tea time. Visions of Victor coming closer—no call; he had made the train connection—rushed me into the shower. I washed my flyaway, long hair. Wet, the gray seemed less conspicuous.

Vigorously, I terry-toweled.

I oiled. I scented. Carven Vetiver. Too much of it. I clipped my toenails and fingernails. I scanned the western horizon from our bathroom window. A glorious sun promising a glorious sunset. We'd go down to the dock for a sit-out, for a lollygag, for a reconnect. I'd be patient. I would not ask about the cattleman. Remember, William Howards! I pointed a finger at my reflection in the steamed mirror: patience and trust. I combed and brushed and center-parted some semblance of order into my ordinarily unruly hair. About the unruly features showing above the unruly beard . . . nothing much to do with them. The nose? Dominant; a kind word. But the eyes had a certain call in them, a hooded intensity, however much their gray had faded. And the body? Small-muscled, lean, leaner than most at fifty, trim, tennis-toned. Not bad. Not great. Never that, but, once upon a time, more than a few had followed after it with their eyes, searching out my secret part, my privates. Not bad, those. Enough to satisfy, Victor had assured me long ago. And what should I wear to the train station that would satisfy? What would be alluring? Catch his eye? I settled for black corduroys, a bright red plaid flannel shirt, a gray down vest.

Before I left, I tried Aaron. Home. He had gone to the beach for a walk. To clear his head. Would he like to come to us for dinner? "And be a third? Never. You just welcome him home in your own inimitable way. I'm . . . fine. I'm listening to the rest of *Parsifal* . . ."

Only one more chore remained: the post office.

I hightailed it out to the Jeep, pausing to hail the sun.

And then, of course, the Jeep stalled. I was too anxious, expectant, too hot on for my Victor. Patience!

Among the pieces of mail only one stimulated: the monthly newsletter from EEGO—the East End Gay Organization for Human Rights, a group that Victor and I had helped to establish back in 1976 when the Southampton Village Board had suddenly decided to curtail parking at the gay beach. Forty of us had gone to a board meeting, had stood up and been counted, Aaron among us: his first official act of coming out, and at the age of fifty-seven. We even won. Aaron had been thrilled . . . the rest of the mail was junk and bills.

Fifteen minutes to train time. Leaving the post office parking lot, I stalled twice.

And then, a solitary, rain-slicker-hooded figure pacing the platform informed me that the train would be from twenty minutes to a half hour late. I began pacing—in the opposite direction. A bad sign. Our wires and, therefore, our moods may not mesh. What then, O Horatio?

The train whistle began blowing at seven-thirty—only twelve minutes late.

Usually, our greeting after any separation is a kiss, a modest kiss, the meeting taking place out of doors and we being grown-up American men, men aware, all too often painfully aware, that the laws and customs of our land have not been cast with our kind in mind. Some compromises were necessary, even reasonable. But, being Americans, we would not stoop to any cheek-to-cheek, European dissimulations. No earlobe shit either. No kisses to the wind. No nouvelle cuisine *ooow*s or *ummm*s. Full on the lips for us—but modestly. So, when Victor stepped down from the train and I reached to relieve him of a valise and he wasn't smiling and his kiss went amiss, landing somewhere in the thick hair cascading down my shoulder, I froze—at the very same moment he was thrusting a recording at me, its thrust meant for my free hand but missing by far, its point stabbing into my tender privates, into their tenderest portion, the testes.

A silent scream! Pain beyond the telling of it.

He sees. He takes his valise from me, takes hold of my shoulder, trying to get me out of the way of the anxious hordes pushing down the steps of the train. "I'm sorry, Willy." He manages to turn me out of the path of the throng. "It's the Shostakovich you've been asking for. I carried it all the way back from Dallas."

An offering. Why? Even doubled over as I am by pain, I think that, and then, I worry that I am unable to thank him properly. But my struggle is with essentials, with one step, another step—and I see that he is walking right on by me. I clutch my Dallas Shostakovich, thinking my troubled thoughts.

20

I see Victor waiting at the Jeep . . . on the passenger's side! I have a vision of all our *usually*s suddenly unraveling. "You drive, Willy."

Starting the Jeep is no problem. I'm dependable when it comes to turning a key. It's going from neutral to first that causes trouble. It's expecting Victor to wince, to make comment—neither of which he did either time I stalled. Nor did he even turn to smile encouragingly. He was busy studying other faces and other cars rushing past us.

Usually, as soon as we came out from under the railroad trestle and turned onto the open road for home, Victor, especially when he was driving, would reach over for my hand. When I successfully made it into third, I reached for his. His began rolling down the window, and then it busied itself with stuffing *Art News* and *Car and Driver* into his overstuffed shoulder bag.

I let well enough alone—but it was a struggle. I concentrated on the open road, leaving only the corners of my bemused eyes for his shiftings. The landscape received his attention next, as well it should, the rose-blue evening light sharpening the green up on the high ground where Aaron lived, darkening the potato fields on either side of us. String-of-pearl clouds over in the west had lowered to just above the tree line. Victor leaned forward to study them. I was in his way, but he was smiling. I was a left-handed twelve o'clock driver. I had a free hand for him. He was ready for it. He lifted it, kissed it. "Sorry about the blow to the balls."

"All in a day's work. No lasting damage."

He held fast, but his smile was gone. He was in and out. Unsteady. Unsure. And when we got home . . . would he or wouldn't he want to go down to the dock? Would he or wouldn't he tell me about what was wrong? Something was, and that—I could guess what—plus what I would soon tell him about Aaron would take more than one Scotch to sort through before we could reconnect.

But Victor wanted a sit-out and the sunset. Walking from the Jeep, he stopped, stopped me, even loaded down as we were, for a kiss, leaned against me, hooking his chin over my shoulder. "Let's drop all this shit and go down to the dock. . . ."

The light on the still surface of the lake reflected the darkening sky. The sun was visible between the puffs of cloud that seemed to rest now on the line of treetops over on the western shore. Spears of yellow-blue-red stabbed up and down, into the sky, down into the water: a seamless sight. Silent, we lollygagged. We sighed, as if in unison. We sipped some Scotch.

I have hold of his hand, holding it loosely, resting it between us on the ledge made by our side-by-side Samsonite chaises. But a peripheral glance shows me the too-busy beat of his eyelids. He isn't at rest. Neither am I. "What is it, Victor? What's wrong?"

"Nothing." He hunches higher in his chaise, frees his hand to worry some wild hairs in his eyebrow.

I plunge into my beard. Before this night concludes, his *nothing* will turn out to be something. I know the signs. "Nothing?" A question! Mine—which is how it usually begins when he comes home from being in the "field" and feels guilty about . . . something.

"Not yet, Willy. We came down here to watch the sunset."

"It's set."

"All right. So I don't mean *nothing*. But can't you wait? I'll get to . . . what's wrong. I always do. You make sure I do."

"You make sure I have to. Even so, between my question and your eventual answer we waste hours. Why not talk now? Tell me now? Get it over with?" Usually, usually before we fall asleep, I . . . we . . . would get it over with, but, just as usually, my initial appeal would fail. He expected me to ask questions before I could expect him to tell me about what I called his "traveling salesman" stories. There, in his eyes, beneath the busy beat of his eyelids, sat the rock-solid monument to this survival habit of ours. "Tonight I can't wait. What I want to talk about isn't us. It's Aaron." For that he shifted his gaze from the horizon to me, listening attentively while I told him what little

22

I knew. "He wouldn't let me ask him anything more. Last night he acted as if he expected the worst. He seems to want time to prepare himself for that, but in his own way . . . which is what worries me. Remember how he always used to say he had a supply of pills on hand for any emergency? He hasn't said that for a while."

Victor started up off the chaise, "I'll go call him."

I pulled him back down. "I think he'd rather have you wait. I asked him for dinner. He refused. He wasn't going to interfere with your homecoming. But he also doesn't want you to question him—not before the party. There you won't have a chance. In that way he's like you . . . always putting off answers."

"Give me a break, Willy. For Christ's sake. Haven't I been traveling all day? I'm tired . . . and now this about Aaron . . . let up, will you?"

"Sorry." I was. But more than that, I felt the uneasiness of the past week mounting again. Why did we have to perpetuate this children's game of ask and tell? A waste of time. A loss of precious time at our age. A loss made all the more pointed and painful by news of Aaron's tumor. Lost time is never found again; only in memory. "You're right. You should call him."

Standing, he paused, expecting me to follow him back up to the house. He wanted me nearby, the anxious, little-boy expression on his handsomely aging face asking me to come with him, as if he might need help in the bathroom.

And yes, I wanted to be near him, to help him, just as he helped me whenever I had fears to face.

Walking together back up to the house, Victor drew me close. "We'll talk later. I promise. You won't have to ask me to, either."

Aaron wasn't at home.

We should start dinner, Victor suggested. He'd take care of the salad. The potatoes were baking in the toaster oven. All that remained was for me to light the fire in the kitchen fireplace. I removed the flank steak from its marinade, dried it.

23

The kindling needed some coaxing. Still wet from the rain. I'd forgotten to lay in a dry supply. I fanned it with the *Southampton Press*. When it caught I went into the living room, turning on the lights, switching on the stereo receiver. Connecticut Public Radio. A Mahler something.

"Mahler's Fourth?" he asks, looking up briefly, smiling when I nod. I take up my vigil at the fireplace. He resumes tearing up the lettuce. And then there is a cucumber, a tomato, scallions to cut up, the dressing to measure out. He enjoys doing, discovering, using his hands, instead of having to use words. And I enjoy watching him while I wait for the fire to burn down enough so that when I put the steak on it will sear and cook, not sear and char. Victor's salad proportion is four parts oil to one part vinegar with lots of garlic slivers he will remove just before pouring. Usually, he throws things together with unfailing instinct. This night his butcher block activity is marked by more than ordinary fastidiousness. But this night, whatever can go wrong does.

When I test the potatoes, they seem underdone. Therefore, I leave the steak on too long, making it overdone. And then, of course the salad dressing is too vinegary, the lettuce too wet, too sandy. My fault! Earlier, I had rushed that job, wanting to get to my shower. But I hadn't rushed the wine. I had remembered to open it in plenty of time for it to air. An Italian red we liked, usually dry, full-bodied, but with lots of character. This night it was a plain and simple dud, a fact which did not prevent us from nearly finishing it.

Victor tried Aaron's again. Still no answer. "He didn't want to come here, but he didn't want to stay home alone either. He's been that way for as long as I've known him, and that, as you know, is a long time."

"Exactly one month longer than you've known me."

"You always remember those things." He pushed back from the butcher block, went into the living room. The Mahler was ending—not well. Sluggish conducting and a lousy soprano solo-

24

ist neither of us recognized. Victor asked if, maybe, I'd like to listen to the Shostakovich?

What I would have liked was for him to tell me his traveling salesman story, but I didn't say that. Patience, William Howards! Trust! Loyalty! Besides, he had brought this Shostakovich all the way from Dallas. I readied the turntable.

The Shostakovich Fourteenth is not music to talk through. We stretched out together on one of the living room platform sofas to listen. Only once did we break the silence—when I had to get up to turn the record over. A gripping performance: Rostropovich conducting, Vishnevskaya and Reshetin soloists. Throughout its fifty minutes both of us gave ourselves up to it, forgetting Aaron, Victor's *nothing*, the dishes in the sink.

The tone arm banging against the center post rapped me back to reality.

Too late to call Aaron.

Too late to do the dishes. "In the morning . . . let's just go upstairs, Victor. . . ."

We undressed by half moonlight. Shadowy. Romantic. Perfect light for smoothing things over.

Getting into his bed, Victor shuddered. "Cold sheets."

"I've got a fire laid. Should I start it?"

"No. Don't bother."

"Want me to get in bed with you to warm things up?"

Nothing. Silence—and then a sigh. I got into my bed. Usually, in bed, our hands come together: Do we sense sex signals or are we seeking simple comfort before we have to set off alone into sleep? Our hand habit holds. He wants my fingers. And then he wants us facing each other, wants us up close, as close as our separate quilts will allow . . . but then all he does is stare at me. In spite of his earlier promise, he is not going to face the moment of his truth without some prodding.

His eyelids were too busily beating again. Maybe something much more than a cattleman was at stake—or was it Aaron? I

25

leaned up on my elbow. "How many times this trip?" I tried for glib, but it came out nag.

He rolled onto his back, letting go of my hand.

"Am I on the right track? At least answer that."

"Yes."

"Well, we're making progress."

"Don't try for laughs, Willy. Laughs aren't your best thing."

"Neither is gloom. I thought we had enough with Aaron, but, if you insist, I can add to it. What makes this trip any different from some of your other trips? Will you answer that much, at least?"

"I'll answer everything. Just give me a chance."

"All night I've been giving you a chance. You've even had the chance to ask me a question. I would have enjoyed that. 'How did your work go?' you might have asked, for example. Or, 'Read any good books lately?' But maybe all that really matters to you tonight is that on your way from Albuquerque to Dallas you met a cattleman who, later, asked you up to his recently refurbished room at the Adolphus Hotel for some hot sex. Is that it?"

"No. That's not it."

"Well, then what's all the disturbance about tonight?" My turn to sigh and roll away onto my back.

But then he wanted my hand back—and took it. He wanted us facing each other again—and pulled me closer. He sat up, staring off through the darkness, a sure sign that he was ready to begin. Usually, he didn't like watching my reactions to his traveling salesman stories. But this night was different. His gaze shifted back to me unflinchingly. This was not going to be an ordinary sex story. This was going to be harder to make light of, to joke about. Usually, I managed to persuade myself that his traveling salesman stories were just that, jokes, stories about sex, not love. Once he told them, they were done with, quickly forgotten, good for a laugh, before we settled back into the habit of each other's arms. We had only ourselves to fall back on, to trust. There were no marriage manuals for our kind, no lawyers

26

anxious to take on our cases. We grew up knowing we would always be outlaws. We had to make our way ahead on our own. When our lives began to spin into free fall, we reached out for any handle to hold onto, a hand, for example . . . if that happened to be close. "So, Victor, honey, here we are. We've come full circle. We're back to *nothing*. You promised to talk, so talk, already. It's time." But the sound of my voice was not jocular. Sticks around, stabbings into, my heart caused a dying fall. What if, now that he was readying himself for a speech, he said what I didn't want to hear? What if, instead of a one-night stand, the cattleman had turned into someone more important? That was always a possibility, always a risk.

"Yes. It's time for the cattleman. You figured that one out. You see through telephone wires. He did stay at the Adolphus. We had drinks and dinner together. He told me all about his wife, his three sons and how great they were, how he loved them all, but how once in a while he just liked to try something different. Made him appreciate what he had all the more. I told him not with me he wasn't going to try. Not that I wasn't tempted. I was. But I said no. For the usual reasons . . ."

"Which are what, Victor?"

"You've heard them before."

"Tell me again. Maybe this time I'll understand them. Maybe this time so will you so that maybe the next time you won't have to tell me what I know you're going to go on to tell me next."

"If you know, Willy, why is it necessary for me to tell you? It hurts you. It hurts me . . ."

"Because I believe in the possibility of change . . . at any age."

"I wish I did. I wish I could have had sex with the cattleman, with someone I sat next to on an airplane, had dinner with, got to know. But that means coming home and having to face you with . . . reality. I'd rather—but you know what I'd rather . . ."

Yes, I did know. I also knew the wild, weary feelings of anger and resignation charging through my bloodstream. Natural enough, what I felt. Natural enough, what he felt under such tempting circumstances. "Yes, I know what you'd rather—and is that what you did?"

"I went out looking and I found. Not in a bar—the Blue Bonnet *is* gone. The cattleman remembered it . . . but bars aren't a good place for me. They remind me of our meeting. I stay out of them. All I did was walk. I thought of those stories you used to tell me about Saturday-night downtown Dallas, about those cars cruising the corner in front of the Baker Hotel. The Baker's gone, but the cars aren't. Probably the only thing the same from the Dallas you used to know, those cars. . . . I got picked up by a pickup truck. A cowboy type. In jeans. We never even exchanged names. He just drove to some safe place he knew and blew me. That's all he wanted. That's all I wanted. I was back in my hotel room within a half hour. I don't think I could even tell you what he looked like, and by the time I got up this morning it was as if he never existed. But when the train arrived in Bridgehampton, when I saw you see me, saw you waving and smiling, I choked up. You looked so . . . happy. Your hair was all shiny in the sun. Your beard puffed and combed. Your face so welcoming. I could even smell the Vetiver . . . and before the night was over I knew I'd be spoiling all that. Hard not to hate yourself. I did. And not just for what I knew would happen later but for all the other times like it. I froze when you took hold of my valise and then even my gesture of atonement missed its mark." He leaned lower, closer, smoothing the quilt just above my prick. And, with a will all its own, it stirred, reacting to that familiar touch. He withdrew his hand instantly. That's not what he was about. Not this night. But what he was about I was not prepared for. I couldn't have been. "Doing that I feel as if I'm using you, deceiving you. That's too easy, Willy. Kiss and make up. You're too trusting and all I do is abuse your trust. You're understanding. You believe I'll change. But I haven't. After all these years I haven't changed anything. Tonight that's all I've been thinking of. You've done all the accommodating. You've rolled with the punches."

28

"That's my choice . . . because I'd rather . . . for reasons you know."

"But where does that leave you now? That's what I've been realizing tonight, even before you told me about Aaron. That only added to what I was feeling about you. All these years, what have I been doing to you inside? In that private place where everyone's alone? And what will it do to you in the future? Here we are, both of us fifty, both of us near the end of it all. Tonight I thought maybe . . . before it was too late . . . we should . . . separate. Maybe that would give you a chance to find someone else, someone who wouldn't go on hurting you, someone . . ." He leaned closer again, fell forward, his head coming to rest on my shoulder.

Usually, after such confessions, I could be counted on for a few hundred words of brave consolation, words about how nothing was forcing us to stay together, about how it was always a matter of free choice—was it ever, could it ever be, free?—and how, if the balance between us ever swung to unfavorable and stayed there, then, yes, maybe it would be right to separate, look around, start all over again with someone else, always saying those things because I felt secure in the belief that it wasn't really what he or I wanted. Tonight, those words rose up, but I didn't feel secure about any of my old beliefs. I felt as if I were falling through all the empty space my head could imagine. Another habit kept rising into thought, a habit deeper down than resignation, a habit so deep it felt like instinct, the instinct to survive, to survive in one piece, to stay whole even if it meant being alone. He was right: Why should I be the only one making accommodations? Here I lay, his head resting on my shoulder, my heart running riot, a fifty-year-old graybeard loon, a deluded loon, deluding himself into believing that sweet reason could lead us to a newer, a more honest way of life together. But here I lay, nearer my end than my beginning, just another one of time's fools. Therefore, fuck the expected words. Fuck the familiar soothing phrases. I'd let my exploding *kishkas* take charge.

I touched his cheek, lightly traced the outline of his lips, went

29

up the thin ridge of his nose and up into his eyebrows, the pads of my fingertips barely skimming, barely lingering, barely brushing against the wild hairs there, moving up across the tense furrows of his forehead. My fingers knew their way around and I knew what I was up to. I knew that deep-down instinct to survive included this solution to our current dilemma. It had worked before, touching, teasing together the threads of our oldest sensations into a tissue of connection stronger than his words of separation were, stronger than my words of conciliation might have been. Sex could save us. Two, sometimes three, times each week of every month of every year of our lives together it had smoothed over every problem we had so far faced. But, tonight, as my fingers slid into his hair, I felt him stiffen.

My hand retreated.

He raised himself off my shoulder, moved back into his own bed.

Silence.

"Do we sleep on it, Victor? Is that it?"

"Sex isn't the answer. I'm . . . tired . . ." I saw him smiling, a sad ironic smile, his eyelids slowing down, ". . . and we've got the party to get through tomorrow night."

"Maybe we should call it off."

"We can't. I don't want to. I just want . . . to sleep on it."

"I don't. I don't want to go to sleep angry. I don't want to . . . separate. Not after twenty-seven years. Not without a fight. I didn't . . . expect what you said."

"I didn't expect to say it. It just came out. And that's why I don't want us to talk anymore. I can't. I won't." He rolled away from me, onto his side.

Usually, after other arguments, after a while, he or I or both of us at the same moment would roll back around ready to offer some touch of peace before sleep. I listened for a sign, for a stirring. None. Nothing—only the slowing, deepening, regular sound of his breathing.

Neither did I stir from my pillows. This night had nothing

30

usual about it, except for the wind gusting and then the groaning and creaking from the stand of hollow-trunk sassafras out back of the house near the woodpile. The upward-tilting half moon appeared in the corner of a facing window. Sun for tomorrow. Sun to match the color of Victor's courage in saying what he had. Maybe by morning it would tilt down, spill its rain, make a gray to match the color of my fear that he might be right. I turned on my side toward sleep, hoping it would come fast, that I might rush into it and stay there if all that Victor and I had to face in the morning was the prospect of our ending.

But the next morning daze and habit swept us along. The roots of affection and love planted young are too tough for any sudden frost to destroy overnight. Victor prepared our grapefruit halves: he ate his in chunks; I liked mine sectioned, ready for scooping. I did the toast and coffee, set out plates, napkins, silverware, butter and jam: my morning chores. I turned on the stereo. "Morning Pro Musica." Vivaldi. The "Seasons." Winter . . .

Sitting at our usual places at the butcher block, we ate in silence, staring out at a swooping flight of gulls about to land on the lake, at a squadron of Canadian geese hovering high, honking, deciding: Would they go? Would they stay?

After breakfast Victor had the plants to water.

I began the dinner dishes.

And then the liquor for the party arrived and with it came the renewed realization of how much effort it was going to require for us to get through to the end of this day.

Victor called for a truce, "at least until after the party." He opened his arms for me. I welcomed them, lingered inside them, straightening the straps of his Big Smiths, settling the collar of his corduroy shirt. Always in a rush getting dressed. Always something out of place. Always a quick stride. A sudden movement. A sudden stillness, stopping to study a bird at our kitchen window feeder or bending toward a budding flower or selecting a shell from among the hundreds when we walked a winter beach. An outside man, Victor Friedman, with still so many undiscovered inner complexities; still a challenge to me after so many years, a challenge, perhaps, about to be . . . withdrawn. Leaning back, still inside his arms, I see confusion in his half-mast eyes. What will we do? "A truce, Willy?"

"Yes." Our kiss has peace in it, peace for now, at least, and for the rest of this day.

All day we puttered, losing ourselves in preparations, inside ones and outside. Outside, raking the path from the parking area up to the deck, cutting back some sharp juniper ends, collecting brittle twigs and blowing leaves. We stopped for a yogurt-and-cut-up-banana lunch. And when it was time to go to Southampton for the food, Victor never hesitated about who would do the driving.

The strong afternoon sunlight on the fields of budding green potato plants dazzled the eyes; a cloudless sky; a fresh, clean bite in the air; all of that an irony not lost on either of us. We stared out at the passing scene and said nothing.

At five-thirty—the official beginning time for the party—we went down to the dock, Scotch in hand. At parties we hosted two Scotches were allowed. Our truce had held. My anger had turned to mush. I sipped. I smiled. So did he—and then the first carload appeared. Debbie and Donna and with them two extras—"Patsy and Michelle, this is Victor and Willy."

"Welcome." The next carload contained another gay group from our organization: three men, two more women, from Wainscott.

We had set the bar on the butcher block. Help yourself.

Platters of food were at hand everywhere.

Upstairs was not off-limits, but not encouraged.

By six o'clock we had at least thirty of the expected sixty.

See-through clouds above the line of pine trees over on the western shore promised a spectacular sunset.

Victor went mingling one way, I another. The mounting noise

level canceled out our carefully chosen music coming from the tape deck. The smoke level we could control: no ashtrays inside the house. Outside, clam shells were strategically placed on railings and down at the dock. A party honoring May Day demanded some outdoor activity. A party mixing gays and straights—a fresh batch of both were headed toward me for hellos—needed the vivid air, needed an expansive perspective.

Some Sag Harborers—painters, writers, editors—strolled the deck, enjoying the perfect light. Chuck Peale surprised me from behind, "Which is which, Willy? How can I tell gay from straight without a scorecard?" "Have another drink and it won't matter. They won't bite, not unless you like that. . . ."

Aaron arrived. Victor got to him first. A long, leaning-against-each-other-embrace. Even from my hemmed-in corner across the living room I could read the signs of their silent clutching—but then Victor was moving Aaron out to arm's length, was opening Aaron's denim jacket, revealing its fur lining. "From Fendi's, my dear." Aaron's actor's cigarette basso boomed louder than any surrounding sound. "The last time I was in Rome. I've been saving it for May Day. Outrageous. I know it. Obscene—but fun . . . and I don't have children to send through college as some here do—meaning no offense, of course. We all do what we do in the name of love and life. . . ." Victor turned him in my direction.

We met mid-throng. "You told him, Willy. You should have waited until after the party. . . . You all right? You look worse than I feel." "I'm fine. Just the day. So much to do—and I better go see about the ice. Mix, Aaron. Go. Some nice numbers here for you." "Something, Willy, something is not right. I can see. Your nose is growing even bigger. You're lying to me, lying to your mother. Not nice." "I'm not, Aaron. Go mix. Go eat, drink, and be merry." "I'll drink. You eat, Willy. You're skin and bones." "Victor likes me that way . . ." I broke his hold by waving to a new contingent from East Hampton. "I have to go, Aaron . . ." Admen. PRs. An agent and his wife. A publishing power and his newest "friend." Seven o'clock. Another hour and

33

a half to go. The sun would set. Everyone would come crowding back inside. More ice. More mixers. Open more wine. Replenish the food platters.

On the same instinct schedule, Victor and I met in front of the refrigerator. He was being pursued by one of his oldest, most indefatigable pursuers, an anthropologist from Victor's Natural History apprenticeship days. Always out on a dig, that one, whether in front of or behind my back. But nothing to fear there: Victor knew him too well. Just then my presence, armed as I was with a bag of ice, cooled the digger down. A blandishment. No time for smart repartee. There was work to be done. More red. More white. More vodka and Scotch. We offered. We put out. Victor took hold of my hand for a still-point moment. We drifted apart. I pushed back into the livid, sunset-colored living room. Let there be . . . electric light. "Come away from that wall switch, Willy"— Gloria Pasternack, Sapphic poet, one of my nearest and dearest in EEGO had me in hand —"and jump, jump into the whirl of your own devising." "Unseemly, Gloria. I'm a host here. But you, you jump for me. You've got someone to jump for. I can see it in your eyes. You've got a target . . . she's married. To him with the diamond earring and the walrus mustache. The one without the hair." "More's the pity. Her loss. I'm good. You've heard how good I am. I'll search further. There are others. You've brought a great group together. Provocative. Tell Victor how much I love the party the next time you see him. . . ." I did see him. A glimpse. Through a sudden opening in the crowd. Being re-pursued, re-fondled by the digger. People just can't keep their hands off him. Drawn to him. To his Roman profile. To his Greek torso. As I was . . . and am. But Willhee? Won't-hee? let me stay drawn? That is the question! Will-I? Won't-I? let myself be? Should I? Should he? The press of people pressed closer. It felt . . . good. Familiar faces talked to me. I felt surrounded by . . . family. Gay brothers and sisters, any of whom I could have turned to in that overflowing room who would have understood if, suddenly, I were to say, Hey, listen,

Victor and I, we're having a crisis. Oh? which variety? one would have surely replied, Temporary? Longstanding? Terminal? Any one of them would have understood, but not one of them could have helped us. No one there, no couple, had been together for as long as we had, could know how much of our lives were invested in each other's being. Aaron would come closest. Gloria would say, I'm always surprised people can live together at all . . . if they're honest every day. Better try the open market, she would tell me. And half-a-hump Chuck Peale, who had just then sidled up to me and was just then saying something totally unhearable above the crash and bang of words and laughter everywhere around us, what would he have to say to me? Oh, cruising, was he? Well, no harm in that, is there? We all do that, Willy. Us straights. You bents. We're all out looking for it, for pointless, mindless sex. That's the point, isn't it, Willy, its pointlessness? Because it's never enough. It never satisfies enough. There's always more to want. Half-a-hump Chuck Peale had said just that to me many times when he wasn't drunk. In the end, he'd said, friendships matter more, last longer. . . . Sam's words too, words suddenly rising from the bottom of my brain, "Friendships matter more, last longer. You'll see I'm right, V'lodya. . . ." Chuck had hold of my chin, was eyeing me quizzically, "You drunk, Willy?" "Not at all." I was in fact still nursing the second of my allowable Scotches. But my vital signs, they were fading fast. I felt myself slipping into a lollygagging stasis, a still figure in the center of a swirling circle, an eye in the hurricane of my own imaginings. Sam was calling to me, calling for me to come back to the party, a party at the home of Oveta and Owen Murchison in Electra, Texas. Sam had taken me there and then let me loose . . . a still figure in the center of a circle of people, none of whom I knew—but I knew Aaron's hand on my shoulder. I knew he was pulling me by the collar of my Burgundy corduroy big shirt, knew he was pulling me back beside, then behind, the sharp-edged fronds of our most major Yucca plant. "You're not well. I saw it before. I

35

recognize the symptoms. Different from mine. For me, death. Life-threatening, yours. Wake up, Willy. It's me. Victor told me something's wrong. Stay calm. Use your head. We'll talk next week. In New York. You'll take me to the doctor. You're listening?" I was. Aaron said, "I'm going, not alone. Do you hear? I found someone who finds fatties irresistible. Cancer or not, this has been a lucky week. At the baths. Here. My wheel of fortune is on the move. Maybe sideways." His kiss was quick but concentrated. "Don't put on the outside lights until I've made my getaway. I don't want him changing his mind. And let me tell you, this has been a great party." He left, trailing one of Chuck Peale's straight friends.

On my side of the room the departees I handled all agreed: A great party!

I moseyed on over to the lakeside sliding glass door to share the rest of the good-byes with Victor: a grouping, *en famille*.

Nine by the time the last of the stragglers had been dispatched.

Usually, post-party, viewing the wreckage, Victor would suggest a Scotch before the cleanup began in earnest. That habit held, but the cleanup he thought we should delay. "We'll talk first. You want that, I know."

I didn't, but there was no turning back now. The terms of our daylong truce were being abrogated unilaterally. A hello to arms . . .

We sat at the butcher block on our customary stools. I lined some bottles up between us: the line of scrimmage. "Okay. Shoot, Victor. I'm as ready as I'll ever be. What's your pleasure."

"What's yours? Last night you were angry."

"I'm not now."

"Maybe you should be. You give in too easily. You always do. You always have."

"So, what you're saying is that I'm damned if I'm understanding and damned if I'm not. I love you, Victor. I do now. I always have. What else can I tell you that you don't already know,

36

haven't already heard? What else do you want from me that you don't already have?"

"Nothing." He added more bottles to the line of scrimmage. "That's the problem, isn't it? What you have you're not so sure you want. You're not so sure any more it's enough or it's really what you want. That's it, isn't it, Victor?"

He didn't flinch, didn't turn away. Inside me, the knives of time passing stuck deep. He watched me closely, started to, stopped, began again to say, "Don't you ever feel like sucking and fucking with someone else? A Chuck Peale, for instance?"

"Sure I do. Lots of times I feel like it. But I don't feel like it long enough to do it. I take a deep breath. I wait for the feeling to pass. I know it will. I know it can. I did have a life before Victor Friedman. I wasn't a virgin when we met, remember. I could compare. I wanted you. I still do. Maybe not in the same way as when we met, but enough, more than enough."

"What if I don't? What if that's why, when I'm away, I do what I do? Maybe that's why I said what I did last night. It's wrong for me to keep on doing this to you. It's wrong for you to take it."

I sipped some Scotch, looked out over the rim of the glass. Not knowing what to say or do next, I sipped some more. He was moving us out onto a murky, no-holds marshland. No solid ground to set my case down on was anywhere in sight. Unblinkingly, he met my stare. A dumb stare it had to be. I felt dumbfounded and . . . weary, confused, and, most of all, defeated. The balance had shifted against me, had been shifting against me probably for some time now, but I hadn't stopped to read the scales. I'd been too busy believing they would shift back to center, to the center of how we felt for each other, without having to tamper with the habits of our life together. Wrong! And now, what was there left for me to do except break through the barricade of bottles between us, take hold of his hands, tug them, shake them, make them and him understand that we couldn't, shouldn't give up. Not now. Instead, my hands slipped

37

off the butcher block. "You want me to stay angry enough for me to say . . . to agree with you . . . that we should . . . end us."

"I didn't say *end*, Willy. I said separate. There's a difference. Maybe we need to shake things up. Break our old habits."

"Habits . . . helped. I thought ours did."

"Your habits helped you. Mine didn't do so good. I'm the same as I've always been, except that now I realize I am."

"Why can't I be part of that realization? Why can't I be with you when your old habits break up and new ones begin? Don't I have a right to be?"

"Habits can't keep us together, Willy. Feelings have to."

"Most people have to work out a balance between habits and their feelings."

"We're not most people. You always say that. Gay or straight we're not. Most people don't last twenty-seven years together."

I nodded, unable to think of anything else to say. He had me memorized, chapter and verse. A flutter of fibrillations marked the moment. I pushed my palms against the edge of the butcher block. I stood up. "You're wrong to give up on us, Victor. You're wrong not to keep on trying. You've got more than half of your life invested in me. That should matter."

"It matters more than anything else in my life ever will. I know that."

"So?"

"Sew buttons, Willy. I have to do this. I have to try to help myself, whatever the consequences. Like you always say, life is all about risks . . . and cleaning up afterward." He reached for some bottles. "We've got a lot of that to do now." His usually winning smile did not persuade one out of me.

During that sleepless night the only plan I kept coming back to was that maybe what I should do was go visit Sam Tolan in San Francisco. At least it was another place to be, a place away from Victor. He wanted a separation. Three thousand miles should be enough.

As usual, Victor went for the Sunday *Times*. We had our usual breakfast, went into the den to read, and it was then that I told him about going to Sam's. "It may not help anything. It might even hurt, but he did ask me out there."

"Why do you have to go away? You've got your work to do. You can work on the novel, stay out here. I'll stay at the apartment, come out weekends—if you want me to."

"That's not changing anything, is it, Victor?"

"Why Sam Tolan?"

"He used to be a friend."

"Aaron's a friend. Sam Tolan was more."

"You aren't taking any risks if you eliminate the chance of losing."

He nodded.

I sought the safe, familiar harbor of my desk and typewriter. A letter to Sam, asking, not a telephone call. A letter would take longer. Victor might change his mind. I might. Maybe Sam had.

> Sunday,
> May 4, 1980
> Dear Sammy for star,
>   Well I declare, you'll be saying, slapping your cheek, if it isn't Miss Ida Flare! and, yes indeed, it is an unconscionably long time between letters. . . .

Without at all intending it to, my letter struck an antique sound, all very old-shoe Sam from the days of his teaching me to go slow, to breathe some weary into the spaces between the words. . . .

> Your recent birthday letter put me in mind of a similar fact: on June fourth you too will turn fifty. Your kind invitation that we might celebrate together has resulted in my writing to say yes, subject, of course, to your renewed approval. Would an arrival on your fiftieth be too sticky? Please feel free to decline, to change the date, or whatever. As to your house, I

39

do indeed recall your long-ago description of its rotting garden and the wall it shared with a now-defunct synagogue. We Jews do not easily forget walls. Genetic imprint, doncha know. Of course, age does make us forget what's stored up inside which is why I'm happy I so long ago got into the habit of writing things down. Just the other day a fugitive thought of you led me to an old army journal and to an entry dated June 23, 1951, the very day I spoke to you in the Dallas Greyhound bus terminal. Well, Stella, honey, many more such moments have been recorded. When and if I get out there, we'll take "world enough and time" to remember some. I, too, long for the sight of you, my lady. If my proposal meets with your approval, soon we shall see each other. We used to be Stella and Blanche, "sisters in desperate straights." Who are we now? . . . Most abundant love, V'lodya

Sam's delighted response followed fast, but there were not many other delights the rest of that month of May.

I went with Aaron to his doctor that Tuesday. Further X rays revealed a sizable tumor in his left lung, and the right one riddled with holes from emphysema. Aaron agreed to have the doctor set in motion the necessary mechanics for a Sloan-Kettering operation the following week. In the cab we took to his dubbing studio, he struggled for a one-liner. "Not the immortal Lebow I longed to be . . . and no more Rome. *Addio.* You'll excuse me if we don't have our heart-to-heart today. . . ."

The tumor proved inoperable. Before they closed him up, they implanted it with atomic pellets to monitor its advance, or diminution. They would try a series of out-patient radiation treatments. (Before I left for San Francisco, Aaron was back out in Bridgehampton, a suitably gentle, but humpy, male nurse in attendance.)

On the home front, Victor and I entered a limbo-like state. We existed together. Friends had us for drinks and dinner. We reciprocated. No one suspected any problem. Not even Aaron. He was otherwise occupied. Together, Victor and I visited him on weekends. During the week I saw him every day. One of those afternoons, over his teacup, he said, "Passed, hasn't it? Just a phase . . . but it's good you'll be going to the coast. He'll miss you. Absence and all that. I'll miss you too. A phase . . . it'll pass. So will I. . . ." He put his teacup down on the end table next to his bed, reached for my hand, squeezing it, the force of his fingers telling me not to respond. No need to. He knew he was right. I knew he was right. No need to talk any more about it. . . .

As we did each spring, Victor and I worked together, pruning the shrubs along the lake shore, cutting back the limbs of the trees growing out over the dock. Working alongside him, I wondered where I would be at sunset time this summer.

As we usually did, we restacked the winter woodpile, raked up pine droppings and hidden batches of persistent oak leaves. We repainted what had peeled, nailed and neatened what the winter had rusted over or worked loose.

Evenings, weather permitting, Scotch in hand, we even went down to the dock for sit-outs at sunset. Down there, mostly we were silent.

With the lengthening of evening light, I cooked steaks outside in the crumbling brick fireplace. Every summer I promised Victor to read up on how to regrout. I said nothing about that now when he came to join me outside.

After dinners we listened to Mahler and Mozart and *Les Nuits d'Eté.*

We went ahead with the already-planned, customary Decoration Day weekend visit of my sister, brother-in-law and whichever, if not all, of my three nephews and their families might want to come. (Only the youngest, still unmarried, came.) Nothing went amiss. My sister never asked about the why of my now-imminent trip to San Francisco. She never even thought to question her often-stated belief that Victor and I were as married as she and my brother-in-law were. During the fifth of our annual Decoration Day weekends together Victor and I had decided to tell them all. They were not surprised. (Neither had Victor's family been when we told them, although that was harder. We didn't see them as often as my family. Afterward, we didn't as much either. I think they thought I was responsible for Victor's being gay.)

I provided the cover story for my departure, a story for family and friends: I had further research to do on my "Gay Sensibility" article; San Francisco was the place to do it. Who could disbelieve that? (A lie, of course. I had shelved my article for the duration. At this juncture in my life what could I say about anyone's gay sensibility when I couldn't cope with my own.)

All of us that last weekend before my departure went en masse to visit Aaron. He was out of bed, sitting up in his easy leather chair. A colorful print caftan covered the tilt of his body, perked up his pale. I assured him I would write lots of letters, that I would be home in time to join him on the beach for a game of Scrabble. When we embraced, he whispered, "See to it. I will need you then more than ever. . . ."

In New York, Victor took me to Barney's and Bloomingdale's for some last-minute purchases to add to his gifts of a summer-weight blazer he knew I needed and a pair of buttery, thin, out-of-my-price-range gray flannel pants. He added a sleeveless cashmere pullover, an argyle on a field of gray, "to match your beard. It can get cold in San Francisco."

We even had sex. A "Four Last Songs" kind of sex: fingers sadly lingering on familiar sweet spots; long thoughtful caresses; a weepy, warm but weary passion, passion about the end of things, nothing mindless nor swept away. After sex, the night before I was to leave, he stayed in my bed, holding me tightly, saying, "We have to see what happens, Willy. We have to try . . . this." I said nothing. I had talked myself into believing he was right, that the only possibility for our ever being able to go ahead together again was for each of us alone to go back to *before* . . . wherever that might lead us.

Victor drove me out to JFK in the Jeep. Catatonia kept my

surface composed. He talked on nervously about all the work that lay ahead for him at the museum. "You'll miss the opening of the new exhibit. It'll be the first you have, ever, but maybe—" *But maybe* stopped him dead: "but maybe you'll be back before it's taken down," he had been about to say. I saw that conclusion in his eyes.

My feelings I managed to keep in deep freeze until we reached the security checkpoint. He kissed me, a long, warm, full-on-the-lips kiss. Tears sprang into my eyes. He saw them, pushed me forward. The security officer looked at me suspiciously, some kind of kook, kissing a man that way, but he took charge of my shoulder bag anyway. The process was under way. No turning back now.

Once through the metal detector frame, I did turn back, though, ready to wave, but Victor was gone. I clutched my wristwatch: his fortieth birthday present, an Omega railroad watch with easily read Arabic numerals. The attached note had read: "Vision goes first after forty. Love lasts longer. . . ."

I had a window seat. During the flight, declining a headset, food, a "beverage," I stared down at the cloud cover, my fingers stroking the smooth face of my Omega. I dozed. I dreamed that my head was coming to a rolling boil. I woke. The plane was in some minor turbulence above the Rockies. I dozed again. I awoke again to ". . . approaching San Francisco International Airport. Please fasten your seat belts, ladies and gentlemen."

As if still dreaming, I let myself be pushed off the plane and into the crowd, disappearing in it, wanting to. But at the baggage claim, there was my valise and on my shoulder there was my loaded-down shoulder bag. The boil in my head had come to a bubble.

My Omega said eleven-forty-five A.M.

I hailed a cab. Soon I would be seeing Sam Tolan for the first time in twenty-seven years. When the cabbie asked me "Where to, mister?" the bubbles in my head burst. I went blank. I plunged into my shoulder bag, passed a bottle of celebratory

43

Scotch for Sam, threaded between books and unread magazines, a hairbrush, a long comb, my wallet, address book, memo pad, in case I came up with some brilliant, fleeting thought midair, reached the bottom where my glasses had managed to fall. Only when I put them on did I see down there as well the envelope of Sam's letter. On it I had oh-so-cleverly written the street crossing to which I should tell the taxi driver to take me. "The corner of Bush and Gough, please." By then, in a word, I was in a state.

Off we raced, my heart pounding, my thoughts erupting, a fireworks display of them dizzying my view. My life, as they say, was passing before me. I forced myself to settle back, clutching the stem of my glasses as if to a lifeline. Perhaps an old-shoe Mantra might help . . . "Da, da, damyata, da, da, damyata" . . . from my City College, *Wasteland* years . . . I saw Amelia del Viso and me lounging between classes out on the sun-warmed, cascading stone steps of the Lewisohn Stadium amphitheater softly chanting, "Da, da, damyata" . . .

Grinding gears brought me briefly back to reality. Daly City. The cab crested a graceful hill, hovered, descended. In the distance, a cityscape: brilliant, cloudless blue sky, skyscrapers, a Sphinx-like spire. I grabbed for my Omega. My eyes filled up with . . . Victor. Victor down at the dock. Victor, bareassed, leaping into the lake, swimming off, his arms lifting, slicing cleanly through the water, his head turning up, a breath, a sudden stopping, a call for me to come in, to join him. . . . "Da, da damyata" . . . control . . . calm . . . center—but on what? Reels of memory were unraveling, pictures, scenes, faces, flashing on and off and on again. Sam's. Sam's whisper . . . "Just go where the will wills you to go. Lollygag, V'lodya. Let go." . . . A railroad siding. Was it hell? Hot enough to be. Furnace hot. The troop train is screeching to a stop. Light the color of lead out there beyond the grime-streaked window my head has been lolling against this last hour watching the dawn break over nothingness. Land as flat as a *latke* for as far as the eye can see. An arrival is at hand. WELCOME TO FORT HOOD, TEXAS. Coming down the aisle, a column of yahooing *Soldaten*, a stampede advancing, led by a dark-faced sergeant who, seeing me seeing him, stalls the stampede next to our seats—we are a band of bewildered New Yorkers who have banded together for safety. But we are badly outnumbered. And the sergeant wants me. He leans in among us, leaning low, leaning lowest over me, screaming into my face, "Get yo fuckin' ass up and movin'. On the double, soldier! Hee-yah?"

"Hee-yah?" What is that?

My recoil provokes satanic snarls. He pulls me by my khaki tie, lifting me to my feet, shoving me out into the aisle where the poised maelstrom waits, whooping it up.

"Now you jes reach on up there. Take holt a yo fuckin' duffel bag, soldier!"

I reach. I sway. How had I let such a moment come to pass? All it would have taken was a word, a three-letter word. I'm gay. *Oy vay.* I was too young to die, a mere twenty-one-year-old stripling. The sergeant offers his unwanted help. He leans in on me, pulls the duffel bag down onto my head, squeezes on past. Other bodies follow. I am pinioned there, a narrow-shouldered, raw youth. The stampede, yahooing again, whooping again, presses on, squeezing past. One body presses longer than is necessary, lingers an extra second, grazes firmly. Looking over my aching shoulder I spy a comely face glancing back, a face in absolutely no perplexity. Lots of *talk* in those green eyes glancing back. A fair-haired number glancing back. A cruise? Could it be? On a troop train? At dawn? Why, I never!

I let my duffel bag fall where it may, drag it after me, joining the stampede in hot pursuit out into the cab of the car, down the steps, a bump, a bump, a bump . . .

"Bush and Gough, mister."

Once again I plunge to the bottom of my shoulder bag in search of my wallet, dropping my glasses down into the well of the cab. Without my glasses how will I know what bill to pull from my wallet? My kingdom for a rhinestone-studded neck-strap holder for my glasses.

Out of the cab, I stand motionless. The dazzling sunlight has blinded me, rendered me eyeless at the corner of Bush and Gough. *"Da, da, damyata"* . . . I see outline, no detail. I see the numbers on Sam's house. A two-story Victorian with a Mount Everest of white steps to climb.

The air thins. My heart pounds. My stuffed shoulder bag drags me earthward. A fool to have come. A fool to be pressing a bell that will open a door into a lost past.

I lean against the door, listening. From the back of the house, back where the garden must be, where the synagogue wall waits, wailing for me, I hear footfalls start up, hear them come closer, their sound louder, my heartbeat matching them, faster, faster. The door opens. I fall in . . . against a remembered body. Tall. Strong. A hand at my elbow holds me up, guides me inside, relieves me of my valise. The door closes behind me. Arms encircle me. A breath at my ear, "V'lodya, honey, you've made it back to Moscow, and not a second too soon, let me tell you." He presses me close, as close as we are able, what with my shoulder bag scrunched between us. But it is not that that separates us. It is something else, something I can't make out. My eyes have remained unfocused. Gently I urge him back, hoping for some distant sight at arm's length. "Sammy," I say, "Sammy for star . . ."

He turns his head, bringing his left ear close up to my mouth. "Say what?" He hasn't heard me.

"Happy birthday!" His hearing, my vision: we are fifty. " 'O my dear, O my dear . . .' "

That he hears. That he recognizes. That brings a smile to his face. In the murky light of the corridor at least that much I can see. "Yeats," he says, linking his arm through mine, starting me down the corridor, his fingers hooking onto my belt loop. One of our habits whenever we walked together out of eyesight, his fingers hooking onto my belt loop, and then he saying or my saying "lines" to each other. "Still so slim, Willy, honey. However do you manage that?" But he wants no answer. We are on the move.

The something that had separated us moments before, I see now, is his stomach. Far more substantial than the lean, tall, muscular Sam of my young memory. Not fat. No. But a beginning, a bulge, which his buttoned-up cardigan sweater controls. I lean closer, the way we used to walk, let him lead me forward even as my mind keeps racing back, back to all those times he led me down dark deserted early A.M. streets of downtown Dallas. Bubbles of memory from then float through my mind. I feel lightheaded. Off balance. I lean back against the corridor wall. Close my eyes, remembering.

"Unconscionably dark. You just hang onto my arm." But he knows it is more than that. His hand on mine, squeezing mine, tells me so. He could always read my mind. "Been looking all over everywhere for the right lights. Something in the line of electrified Japanese lanterns. Something kind on the age lines, doncha know. The Blanche Dubois kind." He starts us moving once again.

A sharp left out of the corridor. We enter a sliver of a room filled with fiery light. Sunlight through stained glass slivers dangling in front of the top part of the far wall's single narrow window. Windblown spears of orange yellow ruby light advance across the waxed surface of an oak table, retreat as the wind dies down. In front of the window, a lectern. Elaborately carved wooden knurls adorn its sides. On it a book is open, a passage marked in red. Before I can find my glasses to read it, Sam has propelled me forward again and out into the kitchen.

A perfect square of a room. High ceilings. Dazzling light. No rest for my tired eyes. At dead center, a circular oak table. A venerable table with a four-claw base and polished to a velvet-grain sheen. Straightbacked armchairs, four of them carefully, invitingly, placed, promise some rest. But not yet. Sam is turning me to witness his handiwork, his homemade oak cabinets

47

hung above the sink and stove, framing the prodigious refrigerator, a side-by-side GE, the very same refrigerator Victor
and I bought in white. Sam's is in brown. I reach behind me for a
chair, feeling the weight of my shoulder bag, the trip, the years.
Sam does not let go of me. He aims me toward the back wall, a
wall of windows, mullioned panes, each of them spotlessly
clean. A hip-high dado offers a fingerhold. Sam's hand at the
small of my back steadies me.

And then, there is the synagogue wall. A Jewish star of faded
stained glass shards hangs suspended by its apex point inside a
frame of crumbling brick. A miracle, I suppose. The Lord's work.
I lean my cheek inside a mullioned pane, my beard a soft
cushion. The glass is cool against my forehead. My gaze lowers,
goes where it will, lollygagging down the synagogue wall to its
base. There the garden explodes. Blooms. Buds. All colors. All
shapes. All sizes. Fleecy fern fronds lifting on a sudden gust, a
whipping green froth. But the low-hanging spikes of the yuccas
resist, click and clack. Stripling trees sway, bend, do not break,
supported as they are by thoughtful wrappings and guy wires
from their tender limbs to stakes. A young willow slithers,
wildly waving above descending tiers of cacti. A menacing variety of cacti. Blistery bulbous ones. Prickly ones. Dangling ones,
armed with spiny, spidery tentacles. Sphericals. Cones. Needle-
studded domes. Below them all a row of dwarf jades. And then
come the flowers. Begonias. Azaleas. Peonies all abloom:
creamy, lemony, pink, and red puffs. Hanging fuchsias above
beds of anemones and, all along the base of the synagogue wall,
roses and brilliant blood-red geraniums.

Sam's hand slides down my blazer's back, reaches in under its
side pleat, searching for a belt loop to hang on to. "Mary, Mary,
quite contrary. I know I am, Willy, honey. But what I've done
out there I'm proud of." His fingers crawl in under the edge of
my argyle sweater.

Voluptuous, the sight of his garden. Voluptuous, the touch of
his searching fingers. The past is in them. They haven't forgot-

48

ten their old habit. Neither have I. "Sammy," I sigh, remembering our young time together, "Sammy for star . . ."

"Say what?" His good left ear grazes to a stop in front of my mouth.

"Sammy for star . . ." The sound of the past is what I hear inside my head.

Attached now, he pulls me closer. Our cheeks meet. Silent, we stare out.

And then Sam lowers his chin onto my shoulder.

That chin! How he used to raise it, rocklike, defiant, daring any no-account sergeant to just mess with him. Just better not, that's what. Lay 'em all to whaleshit's what he'd do. . . .

My gaze shifts sideways for a close-range view . . . and, finally, there he is, in focus. The chin, fleshier; a network of tiny veins blues the slopes of his fast-flaring nostrils. Hard at work, those nostrils now. The nose has spread some. Not quite so neat and narrow, but, still, the well-honed centerpiece of his strong-featured face. Still a handsome face. Beguiling, still. But his full lips are paler now, the Texas sun glow of his skin muted. The skin itself gone slack. No dry wind to tone and toughen it. Rounder now the angles of his face. Only his hair still matches my memory of it. A wheat-flecked blond. Slippery, a shock of it always managing to slide free from under the edge of his garrison cap and down onto his brow, always managing to highlight the green flash in his eyes. So much *talk* in those green eyes then. Quiet now, at rest as they stare up from my shoulder and out at his growing garden.

My jet-weary eyes close. A rush of young-Sammy memories rise up from the deeps.

"V'lodya," Sam whispers, "here we are, together again."

My mind pulls free of the present moment. The Sam at my side is the young Sam of my memory, the Sam brushing past my back, glancing back . . .

CHAPTER

1

C ould it be?
 A cruise? On a troop train? At dawn? Why, I never!

But I am quick to follow, inspired by the sight of those glancing green eyes. I let my duffel bag drop where it may into the aisle behind me. It forces a yahoo to stop short. I join the stampede. These are not New Yorkers. These are another breed. Southern. Texan. During the night, the train had screeched to a stop. I woke, looked out: Texarkana. Soldiers waiting to come aboard. Green Eyes was one of them. A lean, strong Texan. Had to be.

Just in time I arrive in the cab of the car, in time for his descent. He lifts his duffel bag dramatically high—does he see me watching? is that why?—lets it drop onto his broad, big-boy shoulder, steps down smartly, smartly steps off and away into the gray heat haze of this Texas dawn. Was it real, that glance back? "Do I wake or sleep?"

In hot pursuit, I drag my bag after me, raising eddies of dun-colored dust.

He pulls far ahead.

I lag, losing heart. I scan the vast flatland. Gray for as far as the eye can see. I stop altogether. Immediately I am being pushed from behind, pushed to the right, into a line of soldiers slowly snaking its way across the open field.

50

At my left, in another line, far ahead, there is Green Eyes. Four lines are inching forward toward four desks. Human forms wave in the heat haze far off. The Final Solution is at hand. Yet another Final Solution at yet another railroad siding. And shouting too from sergeants and officers rushing up and down each line, pushing us into order. At my very own ear, my very own sergeant shouting into it, "Pick that fucker up, soldier!"

Ignoring his command, I moved around him, still dragging my duffel bag after me.

A hand the size of my chest grabbed hold of my wilted khaki shirt, lifting me. "You fuckin' deaf, soldier? I tole ya to pick the fucker up!" He did not let go. He expected, he demanded, a reply.

But after three days and nights of a troop train, after passing from the northeast sanity of Fort Devons, Massachussetts, to this . . . this *cauchemar*, I was beyond caring. I was inside a dun-colored whirlwind. I was Job. I was coming unglued. I curled my index finger, pointed it to the center of my sweaty forehead, "Is it me you've been calling a soldier, Sergeant?"

Not amused, he let go of me long enough to grab up my duffel bag and drop it down onto my shoulder.

I buckled, but I didn't drop.

"You jes better carry that thar sonofabitch all the way up to that fuckin' desk yonder. Ahm gon' be watchin', *soldier!*"

He did, and, of course, wouldn't cha know it, the very same sergeant—Heebler, lately returned from Korea, born in Baton Rouge, Louisiana—somehow arranged it so that I became a member of his platoon, D Company, Eighty-first Reconnaissance Battalion, First Armored Division, Fort Hood, Texas. He arranged it by further pushing me . . . into another line. . . .

Dear Mom and Dad,
    Here I am in Texas, assigned to a company called D for Dog. Aren't you proud of me?
                                                        Love. . . .

Dear William,
    Didn't I warn you? Once you left City College without saying a word to us first, I warned you. A leave of absence you

51

called it. The army called it eligible. Now you'll have to make the best of it. You yourself always quoted it to me, What's done cannot be undone. So, now, whatever you do, don't make it easy for them to send you to Korea. They are all *meshuganah*. No sooner does one war end, another begins. Your father says I don't understand. Your father believes in Harry Truman. Good for him. I believe in keeping my son alive. If only you had listened to me this once. But now it's nevermind, done. I'll send you your favorite pinwheels. I'll bake this afternoon.

Love, Mother

Basic training began this way: A for Able, B for Baker, C for Charlie, and us, D for Dog, were marched up to the battalion motor pool to hear a speech from our commander, a Colonel Something-or-other. I couldn't hear, what with his screaming into a microphone. Not that I cared much; lost among this military mob, pressed round by anonymous bodies at seven-fifteen A.M. Slumped, bowed down, the fierce sun broiling the air, drying the lining of my lungs with each labored breath.

And then, suddenly, Sousa exploded. First lesson: marching, battalion review, arms linked. Then company by company. Finally, platoon by platoon. All morning, marching. All morning me, searching. Searching for Green Eyes. Yes. He was out there somewhere. I screwed my mind to that thought: He was out there somewhere and I would find him . . . and then I could collapse.

"To the right flank . . . harch." I looked for him.

"To the left flank . . . harch." I looked.

"Parade rest," "Atten-hun," "About face," I kept looking.

During cadence count—"One, two, three, four, I just want to go to war"—I didn't sing out in unison. Not those words. Never. I mouthed them, too busy looking out. Which my very own sergeant Heebler, marching alongside me, finally saw. "You ain't singin', How-itz." His Cajun accent made *z* of my *d*s.

"How-*ards*, Sergeant. I'm a How-*ards*."

"You a piece a shit, How-*itz*. Soon's ya learn that, better off ya gonna be. So sing out, hee-yah?"

"I can't say what I don't believe." The platoon was leaving the motor pool by then, heading back toward our barracks, otherwise Heebler might have stopped us on the spot. His beefy hand seemed ready to pluck me out of my rank. "Company commander's gon' hear 'bout that line, How-itz. You can rest yo ass on it. . . ."

That afternoon at "Fall out," Heebler held me fast, told me to follow him over to the orderly room. I was on report.

He ushered me into the company commander's office, got me placed on the right spot, called me to "Atten-hun."

I drooped, swayed. It had been a busy day.

Ordered to salute, as Heebler had, ever so smartly, my fingers slid down my sweat-smeared forehead.

On the command of "Parade rest" I grabbed for the CO's desk to steady myself. After all, I was brand new at this game.

"You certainly are a fuck-up, Howards." The captain spoke quietly. Blondly crew-cut, bull's eyes bulging, he managed some self-control, even smiling before the kill. I seemed to amuse him: an authentic Sad Sack, I supposed, in a fatigue uniform five sizes too big. A bag of bones and a big Jewish nose. Shorn. Forlorn. Defenseless. No Bill of Rights to stand on. "But you'll learn. You'll learn fast. Like it or not, you'll go to war if you're sent. And when you get there, you'll want to know how to protect yourself. So, Private Howards, my advice is you better shape up and *damn fast*." His smile had faded. "I get another report on you from Sergeant Heebler here and you will have had it. I'll put you in the stockade and you'll never get out, understood?"

"Yes."

"Sir, Howards. Yes, sir. You say 'sir' to an officer. Say it."

I idled, taking as much time as I deemed safe. I stared back into his bulging eyes. Fuck him! Fuck Heebler! Fuck the whole fucking army. I scanned the ribbons pinned to his heart. "Sir."

"*Yes*, sir, Howards."

"*Yes*, sir, Howards, Captain."

"Heebler . . ." He swiveled away and around. "Take him out of my sight, but you watch the shit out of him."

"Yes, sir!" Heebler's salute was beautiful to behold. I fell back gracelessly, pirouetted more than about-faced.

End of day one, basic training.

Heebler haunted my every day.

To rifle handling I never brought enough *slap*. "*Slap* the fucka, How-itz. Beat it, like ya beat ya meat."

Marching, my corners were never cut sharply enough.

At inspections, my boots didn't reflect his face. Neither did my brass. The window next to my wall locker was never cleaned cleanly enough. The blanket pulled over the pillow on my cot was never pulled taut enough. A half dollar dropped on the other blanket never bounced. And my face? *Oy vay!* "You usin' a fuckin' pick to shave, How-itz? Got blood all over yo big fuckin' Adam's apple. Better jes wiz-en up, How-itz-ah. Company commander see you this way I get it rammed up ma ass. Yo gon' be hurtin' iffen ah do. Hee-yah? And open yo eyes wide. Look like two pissholes in a snowbank . . ."

Day after day, inspection after inspection, week after week, Heebler watched "the shit out of me," even following me into the latrine, on occasion . . . following orders. For that most private of all private functions, no privacy—with or without Heebler's surveillance. There were always other eyes to avoid. Three commodes faced three commodes. Squeeze—one, two, three, four. Plop—one, two, three, four: six faces pretending to see nothing, to hear nothing, to smell nothing. Six heads trying not to think, being trained to forget how to think for eight weeks of basic training to be followed by eight weeks of advanced basic training. We had tanks to do after we did every other weapon man was heir to. Heebler kept reminding me to be proud I was in an armored division, "best kind a fuckin' part in the army, How-itz. Better believe it." I tried to make him believe I believed it.

At night, sitting on my cot, shining my boots, Noxon-ing my brass, Heebler hardly ever failed to sweep down the barracks aisle without stopping to watch me. Not the others. Me. I longed for "Lights out." The others would stop their shining to watch Heebler watch me. I felt an aloneness only a Green Eyes might relieve. But even then, even if I found him, or another, even if I found "an asshole buddy," even then I would always have to "have a care." For two miserable years I would. Surrounded always, in the shitter, in the shower room, in the mess hall, in the barracks at night before "Lights out"—but always alone.

Some nights, after Heebler left, I would kneel before my footlocker, reach inside it, to the furthest corner, on the bottom tier where, under the alien long john's—rolled according to the rules of the manual for footlocker storage—I could feel the sharp edges of my books. A stack of hidden friends. A collected Yeats. *Ulysses.* A Wallace Stevens sampler. *Four Quartets.* A pound of Pound's *Cantos.* They had all seen City College service—but they weren't army issue. I had to have a care for them too. Nights when Heebler was duty sergeant sometimes he would catch me at the foot of my footlocker. He would flick the barracks lights on and off and on, announcing "Lights out," and then he would use the intervening minute to come stand behind me for a final taunt, "Gettin' to ya, ain't it, How-itz? Comin' round to soldierin', aincha? Might as well. Be easier on ya iffen ya give in." Some nights when the lights went out I would close my foot locker, lean my head down on its cover, thinking, filling the noisy, busy darkness with comforting images from my other world, the world of family and friends where I could be . . . myself . . . sometimes. Even in that world I was only a *sometimes. . . .*

About four weeks into basic, at the completion of a rifle range day, a ghastly sweltering day it had been—and still was, even worse at four P.M. than at six-thirty A.M.—the entire battalion, company by company, A and B and C, came marching up the battalion street on their way to the motor pool. We followed, the D for Dogs. The colonel was there, ready to instruct us on marching for review in a division parade. On Saturday morning that's what we would be doing, "and I expect our battalion to be the best." The stirring sounds of Sousa readied us, rallied us to perform feats of perfection—"and that's what we want," the colonel boomed above the music, "perfection from every single one of you. . . ." Next the division's theme song was played, "the *Kerryowen*, men. When you hear that, stand tall and proud. . . ." We were kept at attention. The only shade in that treeless motor pool was under one's own helmet liner. Beads of sweat salted my lips, brought tears to my eyes. My helmet liner slid lower onto my forehead. I'm blind. "Where am I?" "Let's step out smartly. Let's get it right the first time. The sooner you get it right, the sooner you'll be dismissed. Listen to the music . . . left, right, left, right. Straighten those ranks. Company commanders get those ranks straighter . . . eyes right! Eyes left! . . ." When nothing worked, Colonel Bradley instructed us to link arms, "get the feel of the fellow next to you." Really, Colonel! Isn't that a little much?

Not that I minded. I grabbed hold of Private Lyman Seward on my right—he was from Lubbock, Texas, had an oxleg for an arm. On my left was V-chested Private Stewart Parsons from Lima, Ohio. Firm fellows, both of them. I had fun, forgetting myself, feeling free for a few minutes. "Afoot and light-hearted" until Colonel Bradley called *"Halt!"* and sprung a new activity on us, another piece of chickenshit army which we were going to begin that very afternoon and repeat every afternoon thereafter at four P.M.: "Rain or shine you will be assembled here at the motor pool. You will march four miles. Company commanders will accompany their companies and keep precise records of time for each soldier under their command. You can run. You can quick-step. You will be expected to improve your time.

56

Those not improving will be placed on extra duty. Do I make myself clear?" He waited for an answer. Battalion silence is an awesome sound. "Good. Fatigue uniforms will be worn, minus shirts, T-shirts and helmet liners. Shirts, T-shirts and helmet liners to be retrieved only upon completion of four miles. The course has been marked out. Completion is mandatory. Company commanders will enforce the rules. Every member of every company will be forced to march four miles . . . no matter how long it takes. . . . Today, A Company will lead off . . . followed by B, C, D, and Headquarters. Tomorrow the order will be reversed and will proceed in that order every day until the end of basic training. . . . Company commanders! Take over. . . ." A round of calls rang out, from the colonel then the captains, and down to our own Sergeant Heebler. He put us at ease, "Smoke if you got 'em. . . ." a kindness which our Captain Quarles instantly countermanded, "*Parade rest!* We'll do it right, right from the start. We will remove shirts, T-shirts, helmet liners now. We will be ready when it's our turn to start out. . . ."

Now that was just the plainest piece of chickenshit army. Waiting that way under a Texas sun in June? Well it just about sucked my capillaries dry. And when we did start out, I did not quick-step, as Captain Quarles commanded. I did not run either. I ambled, trying to lose myself in the horde, but Heebler quickly caught on. Whenever he could he hovered nearby, urging me to go faster, faster. I tried leaping, doing something that looked more like a *grand tour jeté* than anything human. That first forced four-miler I finished in one hour and thirty-five minutes flat, the platoon record. I was last, and Heebler had to wait up at the motor pool for me . . . liked to kick my ass all the way back to the barracks.

There, Captain Quarles awaited us, assigning me to extra duty for the rest of the day: "Until 'Lights out' you will go into each barracks of Dog Company and clean out every single butt can as soon as a butt is dropped into it. Sergeant Heebler here will follow you on your rounds. You will stop only for chow. Am I understood, Private Howards?"

"Yes, sir, Captain Quarles, you *are* understood."

The next afternoon's forced four-miler I started off like a house on fire. Heebler made fuckin'-A sure I did. But out there on the march he had other responsibilities. I was not the only fuck-up in our platoon. A few others felt faint that afternoon. Must have been 110 degrees. Seared the lungs. Left alone, I plodded, kicking up the dun-colored dust. Others quick-stepped past me. Some ran and raced away. I gamboled, falling back, musing on my outcast fate. I would probably spend another evening with the butt cans. So be it! Better that than an early death. Better to walk and wonder about man's inhumanity to man. Better to glance and prance at one's will. . . .

Thus preoccupied, I did by chance barely glance up in time to see Green Eyes go by. Shirtless, helmetless . . . Godlike. The lift of his chin caught my idling eye first thing: a rock. Out of my way, it said. Don't fuck with me, you callous fuckers, it said, for I have a rendezvous with destiny . . . and the sun glinted on his wheat-wet hair, made sparkling diamonds of the beads of sweat trickling down the sleek contours of his handsome, strong face. His arms swinging like pistons, he pulled away from the pack of his B Company buddies. My badly blunted will caught fire: I would endeavor to keep his pace.

Every day thereafter I contrived to seek him out. No matter the order of our departure I would tangle myself up among B Company's camerados, managing—an act of will it was indeed—to slooch in behind Green Eyes and follow his lovely behind. Perfect, those globes, straining the seat of his fatigues. Orbicular harmony. Smoothly synchronous. One rising. One falling. One rising . . . World upon World . . . world without end . . . inspirational. Such loins. Long . . . firmly muscled. Ah, D. H. Ah, Lorenzo: loins shaped in your image . . . but if only he would lower his guard once, let his chin thaw. If only he would deign to turn around, glance back!

He didn't—or wouldn't. Perhaps he didn't want to. Perhaps it was all over between us. Because even the once, pushing my lungs and legs and heart to follow him to the finish line, rushing to retrieve my belongings and report my astounding time to an astounded Heebler, even then, managing to walk near him from the motor pool and closer still, almost matching him step for step, down the cinder path behind the row of battalion barracks, even then he didn't shift his far-seeing gaze nor lower the cleft of his defiant chin. What if he wasn't gay?

That afternoon, frustrated beyond caution or caring, when we arrived at the B for Baker barracks he seemed to live in, I called out, but softly, only semi-demi-seductive, "Hello there."

He seemed not to have heard me. He bounded up the back steps, pulling open the screen door without so much as a consoling pause. The door whined, slammed. He disappeared into the darkness behind it.

Well, "Let me not to the marriage" of sisters Green Eyes and V'lodya any further impediments intrude.

> *The guests are met, the feast is set:*
> *May'st hear the merry din.*

(My journal entry includes the Coleridge lines as epigraph for the description of the events which follow. Prophetic, my invoking a wedding scene and an albatross simultaneously.)

"June 23, 1951, 10:00 A.M. Sunday morning, Inside the Greyhound bus terminal, Dallas . . ."

What, pray tell, has brought me inside at so early an hour? Air conditioning is only part of the answer. Despair, disappointment, and the desire to get the fuck out of Dallas as soon as humanly possible—they matter much more.

But how had it fallen out that I was in Dallas in the first place?

The "basic" phase of basic training having concluded after

59

Saturday-morning inspection on June 22, and having passed said inspection—e'en I, Dog Company fuck-up, had passed—the entire First Armored Division was then granted weekend passes. What to do? What to do? I hovered near my cot, milling alone, debating the issue, when several of my recently revealed Dog Company fellow Jews sought me out, suggesting we go up to Dallas together, "We can put on our horns," Arnie Weintraub offered, "they'll like that up there. It's a big city." I knew Arnie casually from the good old City College cafeteria days. I used to wave to him. We had also been in a Basic Philosophy class together. Ergo, Arnie's logic was unassailable. Besides, he had been my seatmate all the way down from Fort Devons.

We were five horny Jews. Not one among them, however, my kind. Being big-city boys we put an inordinate amount of trust in mass transit and bought round-trip bus tickets: Killeen–Dallas–Killeen. (Killeen, the gateway to Fort Hood, had a 1950 census population of 5,212. Mostly people hung out in air-conditioned chili parlors.)

We arrived in Dallas at dusk. Arnie reasoned that one hotel room would be more than sufficient, "to shower in afterward, after we make out. One at a time we can go up and shower." The Baker Hotel had a single left. Arnie registered. We waited outside. From there we followed the crowd to the nearest package store. I bought a night's supply of Gordon's gin. Melvin, Stanley and Kenny bought rye. Arnie, the assimilator, bought bourbon. The owner of the store instructed us in local folkways. Bottles must stay inside brown paper bags at all times, even when you stop on the street for a swig, even when you pour inside a bar. Soft drink set-ups cost a buck, "and there's beer. Lone Star's good. Pearl too, and Slitz. . . ." (*Schlitz*. In those days before assassinations and Jack Ruby the only *sch* sound Texans seemed able to wrap their tongues around was *Sheeeet!*)

Under cover of darkness our group dispersed nervously. It was every man for himself, each of us stepping off smartly, each of us basically trained for war; each of us with our own bottle and ready to fight our separate battle, each in his own way eagerly seeking a bed of peace to fuck in for a few hours during this Saturday night in Dallas.

My Gordon's secure and snug in my armpit I moseyed up and down those busy streets, stopped to stare into shop windows—a New York City technique—but always on the lookout for a *talking* pair of eyes. A horde of khaki-clad bodies streamed by. We were everywhere—but we were not alone. There were cowboys too, hundreds of them, all done up in starched denims, shiny high-heeled boots and big-brimmed Stetsons. Dallas belonged to them. Their war cries let you know it. Their territory: they were as ready to fight for it as any fuckin' foreign soldier. Throughout that long, hot night whooping erupted all around me, whooping and fistfights and broken bottles everywhere—but nary a woman. Not a one worth fighting over, leastways, so the boys and cowboys did the fighting, drinking from their brown paper bags first of all, flinging them into the middle of streets when finished. Cruising cars crunched cracked glass as they turned that wild corner between the Adolphus and the Baker hotels. (That was the center of downtown Dallas in those days long ago.)

I walked and walked and walked, up and down and back again, on the lookout for a pair of glancing eyes. Any pair would have served, any pair belonging to a face that flashed some human intent. I walked all through that Saturday night, looking.

I ended up dozing on a bench in Jefferson Square, a tiny park squeezed between the railroad station and the *Dallas Herald*. When I awoke, hung-over and disconsolate, it was Sunday morning. . . .

And there had been no Mr. Right-for-a-night. No "glancing green eyes." Probably he hadn't deigned to come up to Dallas.

So . . . the best thing for me to do was to head back down to Fort Hood, pronto. I'd go to the bus terminal and take the next bus out. . . .

Not far from the men's room, slouched the length of a gracefully curved Art Deco wooden bench, there he was, sleeping it off. How angelically he slept . . . how pale and wan. I moseyed closer, fairly floating over the dirty marble floor of the terminal. I would seize the moment. I would awaken and take him . . . to . . . the Baker Hotel. I would be bold. I would resuscitate the fading art of my youthful and sometimes-successful New York seductiveness, however shitty I now felt and knew I looked. A bad morning for resuscitation. But what more could I lose? What is there after a night of nothing?

Standing before him, I dug in with my bootheels, into the un-yielding marble, arms akimbo, thumbs hooked into my khaki belt holds, readying myself for speech. His eyes opened. I led off with, "Back at the fort . . ." His cool green gaze stopped me instantly, wilting my will, but, having come this far, I would push on determinedly. It was now or it was never. "You may not have noticed me . . . behind you . . . during the four-milers. You're so . . . intense." He wasn't about to help me, wasn't about to let down his guard, to "come out" to me here in the middle of this great hall bus terminal. Even at ten A.M. of a Sun-day, any one of those nearby dead-eyed drifters could be a spy. Can't be too careful, can one! And we were, after all, in uniform. "I've been . . . inspired . . . by . . ." Rejection: that was it. Re-jected, without even a chance to get to *Go*. He wanted to be left alone. It was all there in his eyes, all the classic signs: vague disdain; a generalized, patronizing pity for those less fortunate than himself; a plea that I allow him to preserve his right to privacy. By love possessed, I had probably misread the "talk" in his eyes. It didn't always "take one to know one," did it? "I've been inspired by . . . your . . . pace."

"Is that what you came over here to tell me?" A breathy basso, easily projected, like an opera singer or an actor, its sharp edges softened by the slow flow of its southern legato. Lovely. Beguiling. "Is that why you called out to me that day after the four-miler? 'Hello there' you said. I heard you distinctly."

"So why didn't you respond?" Two could play his game. Or

was I the only one playing? "That would have been the human thing to do."

"Yes. It would have been." With that, and clearly suffering, he forced himself upright. His big-knuckled fingers arched across his forehead. Oh, yes, I knew how it hurt: head-throbbing hangover beating at his temples. So was mine. He removed his garrison cap. So did I. He smoothed and prodded the rippling waves of his wheat-flecked golden hair. Enchanted, I watched. He watched me watching. Mirth scrunched the corners of his drunk-dried but lovely lips. "Actually, I thought you might just be the slightest bit crazy." His own eye glittered teasingly.

"Not yet. I'm just from New York. New Yorkers . . . dare more."

"I see." He smiled a golden smile. "But too much temerity, especially on the back steps of a barracks . . . that could get you into all kinds of compromising difficulty, doncha know."

"That a fact? Indeed . . . well, I thought the risk was worth it."

"Why's that?"

Playing with me, was he? He spun his garrison cap around the end of his finger, his smile about to break into open laughter. Exercising caution. Can't be too careful, his eyes clearly said. Wanted me to confess first, to say the magic word. *Cela n'a fait rien* to me, Manhattan tough that I was. "I was hoping you'd notice something we shared, something . . . different. At the very least I assumed we were gay together."

"Why I declare . . ." His cap stopped spinning, one shoulder dipping ingenuously. "At the very least . . . let us be properly introduced before you go ahead making assumptions. I am Samuel Tolan, late of Electra, Texas."

"*Enchanté,*" I took hold of his offered hand, "and I'm William Howards, lately from Brooklyn, New York." A firm, holding-fast handshake. Slowly he rose to his feet, rising above me by a head. " 'All of a sudden . . .' " he began.

" '—there's God so quickly,' " I completed: T. Williams connecting us. And then, grasping my shoulder, so did his hand. Ever so manfully he squeezed my bony shoulder. A palpable connection. The sensation darted deep, right down to my testes. They tingled. And, all of a sudden, my picked-upon scab of self-pity stopped oozing. Amfortas, healed by spears of affection. For the first time in two months the lock around my real feelings broke open. " 'I have always depended upon the kindness of strangers.' "

"As have I, William." His smile was positively beatific, beaming down on me, washing me in wave after wave of warmth. "You can't know yet just how you saved me from an uncertain fate. This weekend . . . but I'll get to that. You as hungry as I am? I surely hope you are. I know a place near to here we can go to for a decent Texas-type breakfast. . . ." Taking hold of my elbow with his free hand, from a finger of which a toilet-articles kit dangled insouciantly, he began leading me across the marble floor of this now-hallowed hall. "One thing I do know is Dallas. Spent a good part of my youth coming to it. And the better part of it leaving. Mercilessly cruel city, I can tell you. Cowboy cruel. This weekend, however, had nothing to do with a cowboy. A traveling salesman was supposed to meet me here. Sent a telegram to the fort telling me he'd get us a room at the Adolphus and then he doesn't show. If you hadn't appeared . . . and you a stranger—of course, you're not, William. You aren't a total stranger. As I said, I heard you call out to me . . . and I *did* bump you on that train. I did, purposely. I wish you could have seen the look in your eyes. I declare it was a sight for sore eyes— sorry about *sore eyes*. I hate talking clichés. Bet you do too. New Yorkers are always so original: creative and fast-talking, the ones I seem to meet up with leastways." We had arrived at the swinging doors to outside. He stopped us, adjusting his kit finger, raising it for emphasis, "I am overjoyed by our meeting. Truly I am, William. Moment before you happened by I was a razor's edge away from going into the men's room yonder and slitting my wrists. A moment of great despair . . . past now—

thanks to you." He bowed me before him out of the comfortably air-conditioned air into the lung-searing dry heat of a quiet Sunday morning. I gasped. Wasn't even high noon yet.

"Still getting to you, is it?" Sam tightened his grip on my elbow. "I promise not to go running off at the mouth again until we're safely inside someplace. Just my way of showing elation, talking."

The place he led me to was behind the Baker Hotel. Ever so soothingly air-conditioned, which made the thought of food once more appealing, especially coffee. We both needed that badly. It seemed to come with our booth, a pot of it, even as we sat down opposite each other. Sam poured.

No burnished throne, that booth. Tacky, cracked leatherette. No Nile out there beyond the awning-shaded plate-glass window. Deserted. Heat haze rising in waves off the soft asphalt. And Sam was not Cleopatra. Nor was I anything approaching a Mark Antony. I only imagined it that way. I offered him a Lucky Strike.

"My very brand. Gotta be kismet." He leaned forward to get a light from my Zippo. Blowing smoke, he relaxed, fell back against the padded leatherette. "Were you also a breach baby, William?"

"As a matter of fact . . . does it show?"

"You see, I'm carrying on this very unscientific experiment to explain our . . . condition. Choice doesn't come anywhere near the mark. About as far away as sin is. I surely don't see myself as a sinner. Not in my heart of hearts I'm not."

"Nor in mine am I." Smoking, I lazed back, settling in, warming to the way and play of his words. He wasn't just another beautiful body. Maybe it *was* kismet. Maybe this slow, murmurous restaurant was a floating barge. The wall paper, a faded shade of oil-streaked brown, might approximate antique wood— with my eyes squinted. But among the waitresses, nary a Nubian slave, in spite of how they had done up their breast-pocket handkerchiefs in the shape of a fan. *Très* Egyptian. Black uniforms trimmed in gold. Sam ordered us fried eggs, a steak and a stack of buttermilk pancakes.

He sipped.

I sipped.

He stared across, smiling, silent, his hand supporting the elbow of the arm with the cigarette, the cigarette cupped inside his palm, at the ready near his lips. "Now we mustn't try to study each other all at once, William." Carefully modulating his basso so the nearby patrons couldn't hear, Sam's mellow near-whisper caressed my ears: the sound of a breeze through tall grass. "We've got . . . 'world enough and time' . . . lots of time . . . before we get anywhere near knowing each other."

I nodded, acknowledging his allusion. Testing me, was he? Well, I didn't mind. It would make winning him—if I did—worth more.

"Why don't I just tell you what happened to me this weekend? A lot more revealing, but . . . friends . . . ought to know what they're getting in with. I was supposed to be getting in with a salesman this weekend. Given a choice, salesmen are not at all what I would select. In and out and usually married. This one was. Two children. Met him here in Dallas just before I was drafted. He's up from Houston. Met him at the Blue Bonnet bar of an evening . . . did you happen in there this weekend, William?"

I shook my head no, not wanting to talk. I preferred watching his every movement, hanging on them you might say, transfixed by them.

"Just as well. A madhouse last night, let me tell you. I stopped in there briefly . . . in a fit of pique. But, of course, you've probably had your fill of gay bars. Streets in New York City are lined with them, I hear tell. The bird circuit, it's called. The word has reached Dallas. We don't have anything near as extensive. In Dallas eventually everyone ends up in the Blue Bonnet, especially traveling salesmen. Mine sold leather goods. Gave me this reticule that first night we met. Genuine leather. Took it right out of his sample case, the case being up in his room at the Adolphus doncha know. . . . I surely didn't expect to be stood up by him. Not after that night. Of course, it could be one of his children developed the croup. I like to think that. But if he could send a telegram to me at the fort telling me to come up, why not one telling me the opposite? I do so loathe intentional cruelty in a human being, as I'm sure you do, William."

"Indeed I do, that, and all the lies we have to tell to get through each day."

"That is our cross all right . . . my cross, I mean, since you are, aren't you, Jewish? Meaning no offense, but I've never had a Jewish friend before. A friend of color I have had . . . a Christian . . ."

"I could convert."

"Never you mind. The way you are is just fine with me." Sighing, he stubbed out his cigarette. "I tell you, Blanche, honey, life's a tangled skein for most everyone. Much too much hating . . ."

At such a turn of thought, our food arrived, reviving Sam's smile. He poked holes in his sunnysides, poured a steady stream of maple syrup onto his pancakes, then, slicing his steak, released blood into the swirl of egg yolks and buttered syrup. "So goes my salesman. There'll be another one along sooner or later . . . but I do so need this food. Drank my whole bottle of Gordon's waiting in the lobby of the Adolphus last night, which accounts for the sorry state you found me in this morning." Heartily, he fell to. "Food heals, honey. Not even time does it better."

I started slowly, overwhelmed by so exotic a combination, used to a somewhat more fastidious arrangement of items. At least another plate for the steak. As I watched the bloody butter mix with the syrup, my gin-soaked stomach revolted. Waves of squeamish discomfort, rumblings from down deep, warned, "Thou dasn't"—but I did. No turning back now. I proceeded into the pancakes delicately. A bite of this, of that, of the other.

67

A gulp of coffee. I faltered, an alien, bereft, sailing off on an unknown sea of new sensations. Chew on, *mon vieux*. You are within sight of your . . . prize.

My prize, however, had arrived at the shore of his Lucky Strike: a legendary speed. Considerately cupping his cigarette, he settled back to stare at the waitresses padding by, breast-pocket fans flapping fast. The restaurant was filling up. Between gulps, I saw him next shift his far-seeing gaze to the Sunday scene outside the plate-glass windows. Things were picking up. Some slow-motion passersby passed by. Traffic was thickening. Sam seemed particularly attentive to that and to the red, amber, green rhythm of the changing traffic signals. Unduly attentive— and, so, not caught up with that at all, probably. Otherwise occupied, probably. Still thinking of his salesman, no doubt. Or his friend of color. Or . . . no telling how many others, but surely he wasn't thinking of . . . Blanche, his newly discovered Jewish sister, Blanche. What looked like forlorn seemed to be flickering on and off in his eyes. It came. It went. Came back again. Something melancholy had surfaced, dousing the green fire in his eyes, dimming the natural glow of his weathered skin. His expression stalled my knife and fork: melancholy seemed as much at home on the handsome features of his face as run-on, determined self-confidence had a few moments before. Whatever gave rise to it absorbed him completely. He didn't even know I was watching him. Embarrassed, as if caught spying, I looked down, studied the mess on my plate and decided to be done with it. If all I could arouse in Sam was instant disinterest, I was lost. I pushed my plate aside, startling him out of his melancholy musings. Forlorn fled in the blinking of an eye. *Augenblicklich*, Samuel Tolan seemed to be himself again.

"Didn't much like it, did you—but no matter. Like all things Texan, you learn to live with it. I'd give anything to be from someplace else. Not necessarily New York, mind you—no offense intended."

"None taken."

Sam leaned across to light my Lucky with his own Zippo. "We can save that topic for another day because I am sure we are going to spend many days together talking. So much to say and I want us to get started saying . . . important things. I want to show you things too. Here in Dallas. So I'm just going to pay up and we'll go." I reached for the check. He was faster. "My treat, my Dallas . . ." Leaping up then, electric with energy, commanding once again, he had us outside and walking back in the direction of the Adolphus, his hand cupping my elbow solicitously, once more leading me ahead.

He walked me past Neiman's and a restaurant across from it he would take me to the next time and he showed me some of his less conspicuous cruising spots a block up from Neiman's, near the movie houses—and did I like movies? He did. Seemed like he'd spent most of his growing-up life in Electra inside the Shadowland Movie Theater or if not there then he was inside the Electra Free Library with Miss Amanda Ogilvie, talking books and poetry: "You'll love Miss Amanda. One of these weekends soon I'll take you on up to Electra . . . and of course I'll have to introduce you to Oveta and Owen Murchison. They were my two closest friends growing up. . . ."

While we walked, Sam talked; melancholy was nowhere to be seen. Slow-blooded, he also seemed oblivious to the heat, easily outpacing me.

I wobbled, ready to swoon, for which, when he became aware of it, he said there was nothing to do but that we hightail it over to the Blue Bonnet "for a restorative beer, honey. Beer will have to do . . . unless you've got a pint hidden inside your reticule. . . ."

With show windows on either side of the entryway, the Blue Bonnet looked more like a shoe store than a gay bar. Nothing but a sun-faded placard announcing the joys of drinking Lone Star beer was on display. Not a shoe in sight. The bar too was long and wooden and plain stark. Austere. Seated on well-worn stools, we faced a wall mirror that ran the length of the entire bar. Ever so clever, that touch. All the better to see what went on behind one without having to turn to see. Midafternoon, we were no more than five.

Sam ordered us Lone Stars. Frigid, I nevertheless wolfed mine down. I was parched past the telling of it. So too was Sam. I ordered the next round. We sat silent for a while, sipping, settling in. At the rear was a black hole of darkness and a quiet jukebox. Facing us, reflected in the bar mirror, our faces. Mine, beneath the wilted edge of my garrison cap, a stranger's, even more than Sam's was. After only two months in the army I was a mere shadow of my former *angst*. Thinning fast. "Skin and bones," my mother would have said. I needed sleep. I needed surcease from my twenty-one years of life-protecting subterfuge, which the army had made more than ever necessary. Going to gaunt, I needed the familiar subway ride home to Brooklyn after a night's fruitless searching for Mr. Right. I needed that because, shifting my gaze to the face next to mine, the face preparing itself for speech, I saw the eager offer of . . . sorority, not the passion I longed for just then. Locked up behind those engaging green eyes the wanton I wanted lurked. Could I pick that lock? What wiles would work, Willy? Young as I was I'd flown the Bird Circuit many a night . . . the Blue Parrot, the Swan, the Flamingo . . . learned a few tricks all on my own. But Sam Tolan? He would take all my skill . . . and at a time when my energy level had sunk to near empty. Took an act of faith just to lift my beer bottle in a toast to that face turning in the mirror to face mine. "I am so happy to be here with you, Sam. Puts a skin around my immediate future in the army."

We clinked beer bottles, chugalugged. Sam ordered another round. The jukebox started up. Johnny Ray. Other faces were materializing in our mirror. Other traveling salesmen passing through. Getting on toward very late afternoon. Soon we would have to be thinking about . . . moseying on—but Sam was smiling again, smiling at me again. "That was Yeats, wasn't it, William? The skin allusion?"

Tears rose to my eyes. Through the shorthand of allusion we might . . . he might . . . see his way clear to wanting me. "Only my mother calls me William . . . when she's angry. Willy will do."

"Will-hee? Won't-hee?"

"If asked, he surely will. But if Willy won't do you can try V'lodya."

"What pray tell is a vah-lud-yah?"

"I'm one. Actually Vladimir, after my father's uncle. Uncle Vladimir had his stomach ripped open by a Cossack's saber during a pogrom in the city of Minsk, Russia, at the turn of the century."

"Don't know how mankind stands it," forlorn flickered in his eyes. He sighed. "If it isn't one thing it's another. Never seems to stop. Cossacks . . . the Klan . . . Nazis . . . the Holocaust. And here we are, no more than six years later, back in the army again, being trained to kill some more. In Korea this time— whatever that is. Makes me want to lay my head . . . 'on a lonesome railroad track'—but, then, there's absolutely no sense me talking us into the glooms, is there, Valudyah? Now how'd I say it that time? Better?"

"Magnifique."

"Enjoy talking tongues, doncha. Myself, I don't have much. A word or two of Spanish . . . learned from strangers." A flashing smile. White on white teeth. "In Electra, where I'm from, there's hardly much need for more. Electra's not too far from here . . . a hundred fifty miles. I should have gone on home this weekend, I suppose. . . ." With a suddenness that was becoming predictable, Sam's mood shifted gears. Constitutional melancholy. I recognized the symptoms. In situations of prolonged, involuntary repressions and/or guilt internal swelling threatens at times to close off the throat, to collapse the lungs, to stop the heart. "Sam," I said softly, so softly he didn't hear me, what with the jukebox going and the door to the bar opening with attention-getting frequency. Sam's gaze had glazed over: he looked, but he

71

wasn't seeing anything out there beyond the plate-glass windows. Dusk was beginning to sift down on downtown Dallas. "Sam . . . maybe we ought to think about a departure?"

"Not just yet, honey." He continued to stare past me.

"Another Star, Stella?"

"That would be ever so nice," he took hold of my hand, squeezing it, "and thank you for being so . . . understanding. I tend to get this way. Moody . . . from being alone too much, from having grown up . . . too far from a big city." Our next beer had come. We both took long swallows and then Sam apologized further: "And, of course, it's my salesman. Wasn't love, mind you. It was sex. Had my head filled with it these last few days. Natural enough—but here I go again talking. It's your turn, and I want to hear everything there is to tell about growing up gay in New York City."

"Well . . . when I was born . . . I was a breach baby . . ." The reward of Sam's rocking laughter penetrated the last guard on guard inside me. Or maybe it was just the string of Stars. Whatever: I felt free to feel foolish. His laughter was contagious. He stopped. I began. He started in all over again. The ranks of "talking eyes" behind our stools leaned closer, curious, warming me with comradeship. Just one big happy family. Anyway, further talk was out of the question, any serious talk, that is. Besides, I didn't have the strength left to compete with Kay Starr on the jukebox. It was enough that her "Wheel of Fortune," like mine, was beginning to spin up, up, up. Sam was even then suggesting that we had better get up and go, "not to Innisfree, unfortunately. Only to Fort Hood . . ."

Dark by the time we picked our delightfully drunk path back past the Greyhound terminal and beyond, into the tiny square where only the night before I had languished alone. Through that square we went, passed the *Dallas Herald* building done up in neon, passed by the darkened, almost deserted train depot; Sam led me by my elbow right up to the spot where the viaduct leading south rose up. "Now I know you aren't practiced in the art of hitchhiking, Valudyah, so mind what I tell you, child. Just point out, very Claudette Colbert like. Keep thinking high heels, not boots. . . ."

Short rides, our first few, and in each one the radio wang-a-wanging, the drivers chugalugging beer, flinging the bottles out into a black unknown nowhere, screaming "Sheeeeet" or "Mothafuckin' Yankees" or some such. Sam watched over me, always rushing in to take up the position next to the driver. "Know my way with them," he whispered the first time. After that I was glad to have a buffer zone established. Once, a war whoop went particularly shrill. The car zigzagged back and forth across the white dividing line. Sam ordered the driver to pull over to the side of the road, "and fast. Got to piss something fierce. You don't pull over, I'm gon' piss all over your car."

"The fuck you will."

"The fuck I will!" Sam began undoing the buttons on his fly, the great stone chin rising, ready, should the driver decide to force the issue to a fight. Sam's face said he was clearly willing to face a fight—and for my sake, to protect me. "O my dear, O my dear."

All it came to was a lot of "sonofabitchin'" each other and our being disgorged into a vast darkness, the car revving, crunching gravel, pulling away faster than the speed of sound.

And then there we were, alone together on the soft shoulder of the road, listening, at the center of an ear-filling silence.

I looked up. A star-dazzling, black velvet, big-sky Texas wonder of a night it was. I raced my gaze in circles through millions of miles. Dizzy. Drunk. Elated.

Sam put his arm through mine, steadying me, and then he talked about, "Lollygagging . . . even in the darkness. You can. Just slow things down in your head. Bring it all to a stop. . . ."

I had no sense of time passing or where we were. Sam said we were very near Waxahachie.

Our next ride got us as far as Waco.

From Waco to Temple. Temple right on down to Killeen.

From Killeen on into the official U.S. territory of Fort Hood. All that last part I slept through in the back of a Buick convertible. Sam was shaking me awake. The driver, a redheaded lieutenant, watched the scene with, I remember thinking, an undue amount of patience: "One of us" . . . and there we all were out in front of Eighty-first Recon Battalion Headquarters. "Thank you ever so much, sir," said Sam, smiling seductively, a mellow, haunting sound. "I feel certain we'll meet again." His words unnerved the lieutenant so, Sam barely had time to slam the door before the car drove off and out of a circle of lamplight. Sam did wave, and then he took hold of my elbow, guiding me across the battalion avenue and on up the cinder path behind the row of barracks. More like a stage set than a reality we would continue to inhabit day after day for at least the next eight weeks. Eerie, exotic, the silver moonlight on those cheerless buildings, on the clusters of guys milling around the back steps of each barracks. Hushed laughter. Susurrations, words escaping from the pack, "sweet pussy" . . . "meant for sucking" . . . "fucked something fierce . . ."

We found some space on a step behind Sam's B Company barracks . . . by scrunching close up, arm touching arm. A three-quarters moon, lacking only its crescent, whereas I, just then, lacked for nothing. The tics of tension in my circumcised flesh had all but dissolved, and there I sat, a gay Jewish lad in military Goyland, next to an inspiring presence. Why, tomorrow, I might even begin to shape up, so inspired was I. Make Heebler's head spin loose when he saw how fast I was going to shape up. Yes, sir, Sergeant Heebler . . .

Under cover of the silver-bathed darkness, all glowy and overflowing with spontaneous sensations and immortal longings, I slipped my hand beneath Sam's solid thigh. The clipped edges of my crew cut quivered.

He slid his hand in and on top of mine.

How long we sat so, innocently staring up at the almost-whole moon, I truly couldn't say. But finally the army intruded. From behind, inside, a commanding voice was calling one and all "to show it. Milk it down. You too, fucker. Milk it. Maybe your first short-arm inspection but it sure as shit ain't gonna be your last. . . ."

We stood, back-patting, hail-fellowing, asshole buddies, just what the army ordered us to become: Men at Arms, circa 1951. Sam waved me on my way. Elation kept me kicking cinders. I walked—I sprang up the path to Dog Company.

Short-arm inspection hadn't gotten that far. I stumbled through the darkness to my cot. No one near it was asleep anyway. Fuck stories filled the air.

At the bottom of my wall locker, I felt for my fatigues. I'd get them ready for reveille and just stuff my dress uniform back into the locker. First time I'd had any part of it off all weekend. It surely did stink. How nice a long hot shower would be about then . . . anywhere else. Shouts coming from the latrine, even with the door closed, made the possibility of any comfort in that quarter dubious indeed. The smoke would suffocate. All the shitters would be taken. And in the shower room? A chorus of drunken comrades. Probably throwing up . . .

So, Blanche honey, better to undo the pillow blanket of your cot, to fold it carefully, to slide in under the top sheet without too much disturbing the blanket above it, all the while musing on sweet-smelling roses. . . . And, in the morning, having saved time by not messing your cot too much through the night, you'll use those precious minutes in the shower. Futile. Heebler will flush me out, wherever I am. Heebler will force me to finish off my soldiering by the manual, just as he has, so far, dragged me along this far.

Malgré moi . . . I had learned to fire my M-1, to take it apart, to clean it, to put it back together again so that it would actually fire again another day.

And hadn't I shimmied and shook my ass under the barbed wire of the infiltration course with all those live bullets whizzing just inches above it. Indeed! And forced to, frazzled by fear as I was, hadn't I cowered in the front left gunner's seat of

75

Heebler's command tank? I had. And flung grenades, carried a bazooka on my shoulder, squeezed off rounds on a Browning automatic, directed fire from an 88-millimeter mortar? Yes. Done all that—and more, much more. To say nothing of too many, far too many, demeaning days on KP and on report and extra duty and extra rounds of standing guard at the motor pool through the night and out on bivouac. Done all that and cannot next get the crown? Cannot capture Samuel R. Tolan . . . of lovely Electra, Texas? Tut! "I'll pluck him down." . . .

Thinking thus in my narrow cot, I conjured up Sam's shape slooching the length of that sinuously curved wooden bench in the Greyhound bus terminal. And then the wind, whirring through the window screen behind my head, set off other scenes in other places. Back in Brooklyn my mother and father would be turning in their sleep. A creaking cot nearby roused that thought. A rhythmically creaking cot nearby . . . a comrade jerking off. The barracks sounds were settling toward sleep. Quiet would follow fast—and so would reveille and another day and then another and the ever-present fact that one day soon I might wake up and find myself in Korea, faced with the prospect of a premature death. That thought forced a shiver, then a stretch, and then I took hold of my prick, cupping it and my balls, cradling them. One cot stopped creaking; another began. Visions of Sam Tolan were stuck in my head. . . . A friend . . . I'd found a gay friend in the Greyhound bus terminal . . . of all places!

CHAPTER

2

A shuttlecock of young memories floats back and forth across the net of time. *Then. Now.* "Can you believe it, Sammy? Us? Together, here in your own home? After so many years?"

He stiffens at my side. "Not *so* many."

"Half a lifetime's worth."

He tugs at my belt loop, pulling me closer, redirecting my attention to the outside, to the sight of his gorgeous garden. Young, fresh, budding plants about to bloom . . . and I have plucked the strings of the wrong theme: time passing. "Far as I can see, you're about the same, V'lodya . . . except for the beard. Same sass you had that morning in Dallas. New York City sass. Took to you right off. No woebegone naïf. Not you. Knew your way around. You surely did—except around me."

I nodded, smiling, acknowledging by my silence the truth of his memory of me, remembering how, after our Dallas meeting, we became inseparable. Asshole buddies . . .

Infatuation rendered me insensible to every new sling and arrow of outrageous fortune, the most outrageous being my advanced basic assignment: front left gunner in the captain's company command tank. Heebler would have me believe it to be a seat of honor. "Ah even recommended ya, How-itz. You's

77

skinny eenuf to snake on down there and when ya get into com-
bat you'll be glad I did. Doncha worry none. All dat steel be
proteckin' ya. And durin' trainin' you be direckly unner me.
Captain's too busy ta show you fuckers this here simple shit.
Happy, aincha, How-itz?" He surely was. Gleeful. I? I thought of
Sam. That thought sustained me through each of those loath-
some summer days.

Sam's new assignment was bazooka launcher. Those broad,
big-boy shoulders could easily accommodate the weight.

Daily, right after morning chow, Heebler marched my squad
up to the motor pool, where our war-tested tank awaited us. As
was his custom, Heebler demonstrated each procedure using me
as his test case. And it was true, being slim helped some when I
was forced to shimmy down into my steamy, cramped cubicle.
V-chested Private Stewart Parsons had a harder time of it over
there on the other side of the tank's cannon shaft. I could hear
him squealing above the clang and grind of the tracks hitting
concrete as Heebler, racing gears up there in the open turret,
whooped us out of the motor pool and on into the field for our
day's training. I steadied my steel-helmeted head on the butt of
the machine gun pressing perilously close to my chest. No comfort there. No comfort anywhere nearby. No comfort until the
afternoons when Heebler marched us over to the starting place
for forced four-milers.

Soon, I would spy Sam's bare back, muscles flexing, twitching
while he idled, waiting for me to catch up. And when I did, his
hand would grab hold of my shoulder, slip down to my waist,
keep me moving right along, keep me quick-walking, side-by-
side, Sam leaning in closer, revving my spirits for the long pull
ahead of us. Nothing unseemly in that leaning. Just good ole
asshole buddies. By the manual. SOP. Watchful warriors. Just
like the Greeks did it. Not even Heebler saw anything amiss in
my linking up with a buddy from B Company. "Best thing fer ya,
How-itz. Texan, ain't he? Ah can tell the type. Big-assed. Big
shoulders. He'll toughen you up all right. . . ." What could

Heebler know about assholes and the longing therein! Not a speck, I suspicioned, nor did I care to find out. As long as he laid no claim on me for extra duty, afternoons, after our forced four-milers; as long as he dismissed me into Sam's care, then Sam and I were free to head away from the barracks, go on over to the Queen Bee for a root beer float should we so desire. Those summer afternoons it got to be one hundred in the shade, a root beer float at the Queen Bee was ever so comforting. What could the army know about the comfort for such as we in that name? The Queen: a secret oasis of sanity in the vast military desert stretching all around us.

There were three Queen Bee concessions conveniently located within Fort Hood's boundary. Ours was a five-minute walk away. We went there to lollygag over a float or a soda or cones. We went there drawn by the honeyed balm of sitting among our secret band of sisters. A simple solace, reality retreating for an hour or two. Secret sensors in the bloodstream lured us there. The thrum and hum of the soft ice cream machines gave us a peace that passeth understanding. Some afternoons, Sam and I would sit on our wooden bench in the farthest corner of the Queen's concrete slab and watch the dusk darken into night, watch our sisters come and go, nodding at some, not each and every—as much difference within our difference as the Romans in Gaul. And all the while, just beyond the slab, MPs in their jeeps drove slowly by, on patrol. Up and down the division avenue they went, watching, on the lookout for disorder. Some afternoons Sam and I would sit there until well after sunset, talking. So much to tell, to catch up on from *before*, before that troop train morning. So much difference between how each of us had grown up to be different, he in Electra, Texas, I in Brooklyn, New York. "Why, Willy, I even grew up on a street only halfway paved, paved up until where the Johnsons used to live. Wanderer Street . . . imagine growing up on a street with that name. Imagine my growing up with Deron Johnson as my best friend, a colored best friend in west Texas. . . . Wanderer ends at the

79

river. Dried out of course. Dried-out riverbottom. Bone dry since the Depression. The dust bowl, Willy, was right there in Electra, right there on the way up into the Panhandle. . . . Anyway, once a week, maybe twice, I'd go over to the Electra Free Library and get me a supply of books to tote down to the riverbottom. Loved to read there, alone. Sometimes Deron would come with me. I'd read to him from those books from the Electra Free Library . . . Miss Amanda Ogilvie, librarian. She let me check out adults' too, not just children's. Right off she did. Love Miss Amanda. . . . Some weekend soon I'm going to take you on up to Electra. You'll meet Miss Amanda . . . and you'll meet Oveta Murchison and her brother Owen. Oh what a pair they are! . . ."

Our words never wore us out. Some nights we would talk our way right through lights-out time back in the barracks and the Queen Bee shut off its soft ice cream machines and the neon lights stopped buzzing. Some nights we would sit there in the darkness talking right up until taps. "Reading, Willy . . . reading down in the riverbottom, alone, that was a particular kind of joy. Never felt lonely down there."

"I did a major part of my reading on the subways. Back and forth from Brooklyn up to City College, but before that, too, going to work. I was never alone in the subway. I even met some good friends down there, one in particular—but I'll save that story for another time. We're talking about reading now. I got my first job in a bookshop. It was Times Square and I started working there the summer after I was fourteen. I learned a lot that summer. I could even buy books wholesale so I decided to read my way right through the Modern Library series, the small ones and the giants. Between the trolley and the subway it used to take me an hour to get into Manhattan . . . now there's something I can give you, Sammy, Manhattan. After the army . . ."

That would stop me, that phrase. That would give me pause. Like a wall might. I would retreat. Go back to *before*. So would Sam when he happened onto *that phrase* after.

He talked. I listened.

80

I talked. He listened.

Once we got going there was no stopping us; those nights, when Heebler had laid no extra duty on me, not even taps stopped us.

Days, we humdrummed our way through advanced basic training. Nights, it seemed like we could just pick up our talk from wherever we had left off.

Some evenings we'd meet after chow and head over to the Fort Hood Library and scour the poetry stack—a thin selection to be sure—looking for those poems that had made a difference in each of our lives. We enjoyed reading them to each other, enjoyed the giving and the taking, the exchange, the sharing, the tightening of the connection between us. I liked going to the library most of all—until the night Sam went to the men's room and discovered a glory hole cut out of the wooden wall between the two commodes. I knew he'd been gone an unconscionably long time for a piss, but I never imagined that. Certainly not a glory hole in the middle of *Four Quartets*.

"A blessing, V'lodya, let me tell you. Did me the world of good. Will you, too."

I resisted. Not out of prudishness. What I felt all filled up with just then was love, not lust. "It's so . . . unromantic."

"Never you mind. This is the army, mister. Just go on in there."

I gave in to Sammy's command.

So, we even shared that anonymous mouth.

After that, we didn't go to the library as much, only when Sammy thought he could do with a quickie. There always seemed to be a welcoming finger beckoning. Maybe, I mused, I might manage to slip into the other stall before Sammy went into his. But, of course, he would have recognized my finger. . . .

The time of the month just before payday when our combined money supply limited our movements on or off base most often we would spend a quarter each for a movie at the Fort Hood Theater. The next to the last week in July they showed *A Place in the Sun.* We rationed cigarette money so we could go see it every night that week—except Friday: pre-inspection night. That night Heebler had me doing windows all over our barracks. Sammy came calling, however. Got me out back for a quick scene. He loved doing Liz Taylor in her scene out on the dance floor when she was all breathless and in love, "They're all watching," he whispered, clutching me to him in the darkness, ever so briefly. "You know, V'lodya, you do feature Monty Clift some. Same gaunt, haunted look. So very attractive, doncha think?"

Other budget nights Sam liked to go the PX to watch the other men at arms at play. We'd sit for an hour or so nursing a 3.2 beer, listen to the jukebox, follow the passing parade of troops to and fro, from the pinball machines to the beer counter to the jukebox and back again. Coming and going, pairs of them paired off. Asshole buddies, same as us, except they felt free to grab ass, grope and laugh. Just fooling around. Just feeling for some skin until pussy time. Idling. Chugalugging. Ever so touching, those scenes, Sam thought, melancholy washing white all over his glowy, wind-etched, Texas-tough skin as he watched those loose-limbed, free and easy bodies ambling by, gyrating their asses at the end of a pinball machine. Those nights I didn't much like. Those nights I felt left out, lost. Inside his head Sam had gone off on his own to those places I might never get to share with him. I had places like that too—but I was more than willing to open them up to Sam's view. Night after night I felt more and more willing. . . .

Those nights when we had not so much as a *centime* between us, not enough for one pack of cigarettes or one beer, those nights we went to the service club. I particularly loathed going there for a fistful of reasons, the most compelling of which being the service club director herself, a Mercedes Muldoon. We became enemies the first time we ever laid eyes on each other back in June when Sam took me there to meet her. "Merry hails from Willbarger, William, which is just across the border from

Electra. We used to meet up with each other in Dallas . . . at the Blue Bonnet—if you catch my drift, William. As you are a friend of Dorothy's, Merry is a friend of Duke's." Sam watched us draw away from each other, watched in astonishment as Merry turned her back on me. "William is a special friend of mine, Merry. He's far from home, from New York. I'd especially like it if you'd make him feel comfortable. . . ."

But Merry was not about to make me feel merry that night or any subsequent night we happened into the service club, her being a friend of Duke's notwithstanding. I knew why on the spot. Sam couldn't fathom it, charitable Christian that he was. I saw it in the lift of her piggy nose, in the set of her bloodless thin lips, in the way she turned her back on me to talk to Sam. I knew all the signs. My Jewish nose could smell them out. My Jewish heart heaved a Holocaust sigh. When, O Lord? When will it stop? Probably never. And certainly not in the service club of Fort Hood, Texas, not with Mercedes Merry Muldoon as its directress. Not even her being a closet dyke friend of Duke's had helped her any. So, it took the deepest level of desperation for Sam to lure me back into her proximity: we had no cigarettes and no money and over to the service club Madame Muldoon was holding her monthly Name That Composer contest, the first prize for winning said contest being three cartons of cigarettes.

We arrived in time to hear Merry, behind her lectern, announcing the rules for entrants.

The great hall was filled to overflowing—a captive audience of penniless soldiers before payday—but Merry's hate-filled, glittering eyes seemed to single out my appearance: "Anyone, just anyone, can come right up here and enter his name and serial number on the official entry lists. There'll be preliminaries and then the jackpot. Take your pick or do both. . . ." Standing there daring me, the bitch! Sam was taken aback. "Well I declare, Miss Flare!" His hand went to the small of my back. "Why you just go on up there, Willy. You show her."

With all deliberate slowness, I walked down the aisle on my way toward the lectern, my eyes never once straying from hers. I heard others falling in behind me, but I saw only Mercedes Merry Muldoon. Her half-size hulk began trembling with a rage that strained the buttons of her USO jacket. Bending over the table next to the lectern, I decided on arrogance. I would enter only the jackpot contest. She saw. She saw it all. "Hurry it along, Pri-*vat*" (*vat*, without the *e*, to make it more Yiddish), "New York Ci-teeee," spitting each of those *e*s at me as if they were sharp-edged projectiles, "you are hogging the list. Others are waiting after you, ya know. Of course, perhaps, your sort don't know about hogging. . . ." she was saying all that into the microphone. On my way back to where Sam was now seated, I saw him smoothing the seat next to him. "For you, Willy. You deserve it. That no-account bitch. I'll get her." The red of his face matched the red in his lovely plaid shirt. We had decided to dress up in civvies for this special occasion. Sam had on a pair of crisply starched jeans and his best high-heeled boots and he smelled alluringly of Old Spice. He pulled me closer in a kind of bear hug. "She's acting a veritable Nazi. I do apologize, Willy. I truly do."

I fairly swooned inside his brief embrace, imagining myself beloved, pitied, and protected all at once. But then reality returned. Sam did a backslap routine, undraped his arm. Embarrassed, I smoothed the fronts of my Hershey-brown baggy corduroys, pulled at, straightened the collar of my Oxford-blue button-down, which had somehow gotten bent beneath the edge of my beige V-neck pullover. I even leaned over to retie the laces of my friendly, down-at-the-heel City College sneakers. What love can do to one, especially to one surrounded by a swarm of restless soldiers.

"Let us now get on to the preliminary rounds," Merry bellowed propitiously. The troops applauded. Sam squeezed my shoulder. "Now get yourself set, Willy. We need those smokes."

"Only one package if you win one of those. I entered the jackpot. All or nothing." You or no one, I wanted to say, but didn't, of course.

The opening rounds were Cole Porter, some Rodgers and Hart and then Hammerstein, a little Irving Berlin and a lot of "God Bless America," which Mercedes Muldoon whipped up into a community sing. Inspiring. The troops loved it. Biding my time, I scanned the crowd, nodded at a few of our Queen Bee sisters standing at the back, on the prowl. The service club latrines had a host of glory holes, I had heard, but never would verify, not with Muldoon loose in the area.

Finally, it was jackpot time. Muldoon reviewed the rules, fixing her eyes on me once again, "First hand up gets to go first. You must name the composer . . . the piece . . . the name of the section I play. In that order. That's important, so remember: composer . . . piece . . . section. . . . Is everybody ready?" A hush. The Duke lifted the tone arm—"Here we go"— and settled it at the edge of an already spinning record.

Barely had the first phrase of music swept out into the vast, acoustically dead great hall of our home-away-from-home service center, when up went my hand. Not for naught those years of my raw youth spent in and around the cultural nexus of New York City.

In a state of livid shock, the Duke sputters into the microphone, "I don't believe it." She is enraged, hands-moving-to-broad-hips enraged, Redwood-tree-legs-spread-apart enraged. "What is your answer, Pri-vat New York Citeeee?" The record continued to spin.

Oy vay, do I know the type. From my earliest years I know the type. From out of the mouths of my Polish Catholic classmates in the quaint town in New Jersey where I was born I know the type. "Sheeny-Kike, Sheeny-Kike," they would call after me affectionately.

"I'm waiting, Pri-*vat*." Sammy rubbed himself along my side, rousing me.

Anapests pounded in my bloodstream—but I would turn the other cheek: nothing was too much to bear in order to present those three cartons of Luckies to my would-be lover. "Dimitri Shostakovich. *The Age of Gold Ballet Suite.* The polka from it." Out of the corner of my eye—only that, for most of my attention must be directed to my bloodstream enemy: *semper paratus*—I see that Sam is beaming. Saved! We are saved.

Meanwhile, Merry Muldoon sputters some more: "How in the world? . . . You must have cheated. When you came up here before, you cheated. You looked through the pile of records."

That did it. I sprang to my feet, began a deliberately slow approach up the aisle to the lectern to claim my prize. The cartons were piled on top of the table next to it. The Duke's hand slapped the top of them. She wanted the cigarettes for herself, was sure she'd never have to give them up. Why else play Shostakovich in the contest at the service club of Fort Hood, Texas, July 1951? Who could guess the answer? No one, she had greedily, hatefully assumed, no one but an uppity, commie, gay Jewish bastard only partially—but effectively—educated at City College Uptown, said school located in the Jew capital of the known world, New York Citeeee. Fuck her! I slid the cartons from beneath her pig's knuckles, held them aloft for Sammy to see: the Grail.

I executed a perfect about-face—Heebler would have been proud of me—and strode off smartly to the continuing strains of the *Age of Gold* polka.

I never reclaimed my seat. I didn't have to. Sam met me mid-aisle, followed me from the great hall. The troops applauded.

For the rest of that week before payday at least we had cigarettes—but not much else. We went to the library for the solace of a consoling read-out, eschewed the glory hole, planned our escape to Dallas that upcoming weekend. All I had to do was pass inspection. Payday was Saturday . . . after inspection. And Saturday night—but those plans I did not share with Sam that night in the library. I suppose I should have. I suppose I should have blurted it out, should have said, "Listen here, Sam Tolan, as soon we get to Dallas, I'm getting us a hotel room and we are going to get into its bed together and I am going to tell you I love you and you are going to say you love me"—but just thinking those words gave me pause. What if he was just leading me on, playing with me, teasing me, for want of something better to do? Maybe pushing too fast, too soon would spoil all the simple, near-perfect good times we might share for all the months to come before we were . . . shipped out, parted? What if there was no Sam to sit next to in front of the window fan at the Fort Hood Library? No Sam to read to me from Eudora Welty? (He was doing that just then: "Why I Lived at the P.O.") Would I—should I?—trade that for a bed of peace at the Adolphus? While he read I sought to piece things out. I thought of my tank, my Heebler, my certain fate. I thought of the army-time limbo every day had become: suspended time between before and whatever there might be of an after. Maybe there wouldn't *be* any after. If so . . . at least there would have been a before . . . with Sam . . . with some few others before Sam, back in New York. Yes. So . . . better wait. Better ask a question about before instead of risking the loss of never being able to ask anything at all. That night I asked him, "Sam? Did you ever think of not letting yourself be drafted?"

"And let them mark me 4F for life? Never, V'lodya. Besides, there's not a thing wrong with me or you. I wasn't about to let them foreclose on my future."

"What if it gets foreclosed in Korea?"

"Had to risk it. Had to get out of Electra somehow, especially after Daddy let me know there'd be no money for any kind of college. Didn't have it. Wished he did, but wishes, Blanche, honey, you know what they're like, I expect. So the army seemed sense enough. I just couldn't face an entire lifetime cashiering at Woolworth's or the A and P. Let myself be drafted. Just as you did. Your reasons may have been different, but that doesn't much matter. We ended up at the same place anyway. And about that I am more than ever grateful, V'lodya."

"As am I."

"Well, then, there we are. I got out of Electra. You took stock. Not once, Willy, honey. Twice. Second time's what got you into this mess. Un-American to take too much stock of things. I learned that lesson early on. They'll spring the trap on anyone looks like he's sitting still too long. Me, I'm different. I laze around all right, but I got my eyes wide open every second. No one's going to take advantage of me. Always ready to jump up and go. You, on the other hand, you think too much. Thinking's just fine, Willy, except you show whatever it is you're thinking. It's right there in your eyes. What you're thinking . . . what you want. Frightens most people to see such wanting. World's not set up for that . . . to say nothing about being set up for our sort of wanting." He sighed.

I sighed, stared ahead at the spinning, whirring window fan. But nothing just then could cool my young, hot sorrow. He'd seen right down to my "heartes roote" and what he had seen there he had found . . . wanting. That had to be it.

Walking back to our barracks we were unusually silent. The darkness, the vast starry sky, Sam's grazing, brushing touch at my side stilled my wanting will. Even if I passed Saturday's inspection and we got to go up to Dallas, Sam wasn't going to want . . . me.

When I left him at his barracks, he did, however, squeeze my shoulder with a fair amount of feeling. All need not be lost. Where there's a will, Howards . . .

But the army doesn't know from wills and wanting. It's in business to break your will to want, to disrupt the best-laid plans, to frustrate your secret belief you're a free man.

The next morning, long before reveille, there was Heebler flicking the lights on and off. "Up an' at 'em. On the double. Up an' at 'em. Goin' out inta da field. Got ten minutes to get yo gear together. Battalion maneuvers. Battlefield equipment. Every piece a shit you got. Be out dere more'n a week. . . ."

At that morning's pre-chow platoon formation, held in almost

88

total darkness, Heebler elaborated, "Suppose ta be a surprise attack. Got ta be ready fer anything . . ."

"What about payday?" The voice came from somewhere back. "What about a weekend pass?" Another voice. Too dark for Heebler to tell whose. Wasn't mine. I was right up front. He kept me there, always watching me.

"Gonna disregard dat shit. We got too much ta do, 'cept ah'll reassure ya you all gon' get paid. Out there on Rattlesnake Hill come Saturday mornin'. We gon' be guardin' dat perimeter. So, now, go get yo chow. Be ready in ten minutes to roll. Dismissed!"

A daze helps. Helped me that morning. Not until our tank began rolling out of the motor pool and I was stuffed down into my very own private cramped cubicle did real reality break through the daze. The tank's rolling tracks shook me up some. I peered through the slit above my machine-gun housing by removing my steel helmet and helmet liner. At least I was riding. On either side of the tank two lines of marching soldiers stretched beyond the limits of my vision. I saw backpacks, weapons, foxhole shovels. I saw mortar squads, bazooka squads. I saw jeeps whiz by and half-tracks loaded with troops maneuver around us. I didn't see Sam. The sun blazed pale in a cloudless sky. I could just manage to make out Heebler and the captain riding the rim of the open turret, conferring, and then Heebler called down to me, "Get yo helmet the fuck back on, How-itz. Dis chere battlefield conditions. Suppose ta be lookin' out." Above the clang and bang of the revolving tracks I heard him all right, but I responded over the intercom, "What am I looking for, Sergeant?"

"The fuckin' enemy," he shouted back down, disdaining the radio, leaning down, squatting, making sure he saw me put my helmet back on. "Dat's it, How-itz. Now you is a soldier again."

Morning came and went and I saw no enemy.

At noon we stopped in a thicket of mesquite for K-rations. Heebler let us out of the tank. The captain called for a

89

jeep to take him back to the officers' mess hall for lunch. I didn't eat much. Heebler warned us snakes were everywhere.

Late that afternoon we engaged the enemy without firing a shot: a Charley Company tank raced across our trajectory. That's when we found out every other company in the battalion was an enemy.

By nightfall we arrived at the base of Rattlesnake Hill. K-rations again.

As he usually did on overnight bivouacs, Heebler paired me up with Arnie Weintraub, a sixth sense he had about *landsmen*. Arnie and I were grateful. "Betta getcha tent up proper before dark. Weintraub, start diggin'. How-itz, stand guard. Two hours on. Two hours off. Be lookin' out fer dem Chink-Russkies." Black curls creeping out from under the edge of his helmet liner, Heebler paced off our territory. "Ahm gon' be over yonder, watchin all night. Gon' string me up a hammock. Dint come through the Yalu River Koreeea ta get dem rattler fangs up ma ass. . . ."

On bivouac, nights were a nightmare. Arnie and I never wanted to sleep. We had never yet seen a live rattlesnake and never wanted to. We sat guard together in front of our ramshackle pup tent whispering spells made up of Grandma's Yiddish to keep them at bay. It seemed to work. We slept in ten-minute snatches, happy for the first sight of the dawn's earliest light, happy when Heebler came calling. He always came calling for me first out on bivouac. I was his steady KP. " 'Mersion heaters need lightin', How-itz. Troops gotta eat. . . ." Heebler had touching faith in my ability to get things started properly up at the mess tent. A gas-filled container attached to the inside rim of a water-filled galvanized iron garbage can had to be lit to start the water boiling, otherwise there would be no sanitary washing of mess gear for the troops. I preferred KP to my tank. I loved serving up those blocks of congealed scrambled eggs, those slices of burned soiled toast. Inspiring to watch the grateful soldiers pass through the chow line out there on Rattlesnake Hill. Every morning of that week I had the opportunity to be so inspired. After breakfast Heebler would call me back inside the tank.

Day after day of that endless week I lit immersion heaters every morning, rode the tank every afternoon, even getting to squeeze off hundreds of rounds of ammunition filled with red dust, to mark off direct enemy hits. Heebler counted up five of mine for the entire week. Every night Arnie and I shook each other awake. Fatigue kept me afloat.

Only once did Dog Company encounter Baker, but I never saw any sight of Sam—not until the Friday night the battalion arrived back in the motor pool. Sam found me among the milling throng. We only had a minute before re-forming. "You must do all in your power to pass tomorrow's inspection, Willy. We have got to get to Dallas."

And then it was back to the barracks to unpack and clean our gear, to clean the latrines and the windows, to straighten our wall lockers and footlockers, to empty butt cans, to sweep down, wash down the aisle and under our cots, not once, but twice, and then a third time because Heebler found dust under Parsons's wall locker. By midnight we were free to start working on our personal equipment.

I paid Private Calvin Barbee from Fort Smith, Arkansas, five dollars to clean my M-1.

But I shined my own boots, polished my own brass, tidied my own lockers, making triply sure my books were carefully hidden in the furthest corner of the foot locker. I rolled and re-rolled my khaki socks, stuffing them as a barricade in front of the books, folded my khaki underwear into knife-blade edges in front of the socks. And all the while I conjured up visions of Sam and me hightailing it on up to Dallas. We would stop first to purchase our supply of Gordon's. And then I'd make a grand New York gesture, the kind my used-to-be suitors had sometimes made for me, I'd rent us a hotel room—not the Adolphus. Someplace with no painful associations for Sam; a neutral, new place. Maybe the Southland, just across from the Blue Bonnet. We could make an early entrance there, at dusk, the sun low, aslant, reflecting fire on the surface of the glass door, the entrance of the gods to Valhalla. . . . "O my dear, O my dear." Such conjurations caused a thrum of blood to course through my balls . . . we'd go up to the room then, hearts eased, bathe and gambol. He'd give in. He'd come . . . around.

By three A.M., delirious and dazed by the events of a wearisome week, but exhilarated and tickled by feathers of hope, I made it to the shower room. I was not alone.

I did pass inspection, even earning a compliment from Captain Quarles: "Finally got your ass in gear, Howards. Keep up the good work. You got the fighting spirit now. . . . Sergeant? Dismiss the barracks."

Heebler beamed, blessed me on my way. "Now ah can get me up to my sweet tender pussy in Waco. Gon' fuck the linin' outta her. . . ." So far, so good . . . but then Arnie Weintraub, feeling as if our week together at Rattlesnake Hill had brought us to the threshold of buddyhood, asked if he could join Sam and me out on the road. By then, reticule at the ready, Sam had come calling for me. Didn't see any reason why Arnie shouldn't come along with us. He understood my dilemma. He had also expressed admiration for Arnie's rugged, off-balance virile features, especially his curly dark hair. "Three's a crowded car, but we'll manage handsomely."

We did. First ride took us from Killeen to downtown Dallas just at dusk. We never even had to waste time at a non-gay bar with Arnie. He had his target for the night waiting for him up at Neiman's: "a Jewish model. I met her at the temple the last time I was up here." We arranged to meet him the next night at seven at the foot of the viaduct. It was then that I proceeded with step number one: the hotel room.

Yes, Sam thought that to be a splendid idea. He liked the Southland, knew it from a past encounter or two.

Our room was big, a big double bed dominating it. "Now

wouldn't a soothing bath feel good, Sammy? A soothing bath and I'll fix you a tumblerful of gin with lots of chipped ice in it?" I had even gone so far as starting the water, "uumm"-ing over its soothing warmth.

Sam, however, declined a bath, accepted the gin, gulped it, then suggested I go on with the bath. He'd keep a stool for me over at the Bonnet. He'd also leave the Gordon's with me, buy another. "We'll surely need it tonight, because tonight's the night for my Mr. Right. I feel it deep down. . . ." He left me at the tub's edge. Oh, well, the night was young . . . and a bath would do me some good. Might as well plunge in, sip some gin, ponder my outcast state, call up a familiar Saturday-evening scene, a comforting scene. Back up there in Brooklyn my mother would be setting the table. Smoked fish platter. A salad. Bagels and cream cheese . . . when I got out of the tub I'd telephone home.

More than a little high—and low, brought very low; no one had been home up there in Brooklyn—I too began gulping gin, and by the time I pushed through into the crowd at the Blue Bonnet bar looking for Sam it was nine-thirty. A clutch of camerados surrounded my every step. The smoke haze stung and blinded and Johnny Ray's wail added to my woebegone. With me it was not, nor would it come to, good—even though I did spy Sam's flashing eyes flashing out at me from the mirror behind the bar. He had even managed to save me a stool, had gin and ginger ale chaser at the ready, embraced me warmly, then raised his glass—but it was then, precisely then, that I realized he was directing my attention to another sight, to a certain someone behind me, was tipping his glass in the direction he would have me look.

All my currents went awry. Fate spins its own top, Will-I, Won't-I. And what's a Private William Howards in the Grand Scheme of Things? Nothing fucking much. Just another little life of noisy desperation—for what should my wondering eyes

93

come to rest upon through a Pyramus-and-Thisbe chink in the clutch of busy camerados but a familiar face, a very handsome familiar face, one attached to a long, strong neck and shirt-straining broad shoulders. He was seated at a booth, but that was how I knew him: from his waist up. Every time I had been called up to battalion headquarters he had been sitting behind a desk. Never even looked up at me on those occasions. He'd ask a question. I'd answer. He'd wave me away. Yes, I nodded, confirming Sam's recognition. It was he.

Sam lowered his glass. Slow-motion-like. He was in love. In an instant. The chink filled in. Camerados swayed before my dazed eyes. A drift of thick smoke circles descended between Sam and myself. I chugalugged. Sam struggled for another vision of that familiar face, searching out another opening in the press of bodies.

I struggled for my immediate survival, summoned up some New York nonchalance, some dignity in the death of the spirit. Let Sam crane to see. I would steadfastly stare dead ahead, into the bar mirror . . . and maybe by the time Sam caught sight of that booth again the face would have fled.

It hadn't. Fate would have it otherwise. Fate opened up another channel. Fate had that face look up suddenly, had it direct all its attention to the bar, to Sam's unwavering gaze. It was all there in my mirror. Never mind the smoke, never mind the crush of bodies, never mind the screaming, the laughing, the loud music on the jukebox: that clear channel between those two pairs of eyes remained unobstructed; Fate willed it so.

And then I saw the lieutenant—for that's what we both knew he was, a first lieutenant—slide out from the booth, stand up, say something to his companions, his fine, fair face breaking into an embarrassed grin. He was all done up in civvies, as were we, but his were elegant, all tan worsted and silky beige. He smoothed the crease of his pants. A perfect fit, those pants. Bulging thighs. A decided fullness at the crotch—slung right. Surprising. Sam stared. The lieutenant stared back—but he did not

94

come over. He pushed through the crowd, moving with an athlete's ease, broken-field pushing, but politely. He was on his way to the men's room. I saw him lower his cleft chin ever so slightly, meaning for Sam to follow him.

Sam didn't. He had his reasons.

On his return, the lieutenant did not resume his booth seat. He and Sam had begun the next phase: confirmation. No denial in either pair of eyes. Both of them were taller than most. Both of them had crowns of glowing blond hair. Both of them were standouts in any crowd anywhere. No gainsaying those facts. And then they entered the final stage: the movement toward each other.

I saw it all.

I saw my bridal chamber at the Southland go up in the desperate puff of smoke I blew mirrorward from my Lucky.

But Sam, noble Sam, ever unpredictable, had prepared himself for an unpredictable sacrifice. Even as the lieutenant offered his hand, I heard Sam saying, "I think it's only fair to tell you that my friend and I . . . my friend . . ." he was pulling at my sleeve, urgently trying to get me to face front, to face reality, not its reflection. I didn't want to. He was otherwise connected. The lieutenant was not my cruise, not my concern. All I wanted was more gin. Sam squeezed my elbow harder, his fingers pleading the case: Help me, please. Help me do this. It's the right thing to do. He needed me. Even at the edge of drunk I perceived that much. So, I turned my other cheek. "My friend and I, we . . ."

"I thought you were . . . alone." The lieutenant's fair face flushed. He was embarrassed.

"I am—but that's not the issue, sir. My friend and I are from the Eighty-first Recon Battalion."

"Oh." Confusion caused his gaze to quickly scan the area for conspirators. Had anyone heard?

It appeared not. Not a camerado's raised eyebrow anywhere in my sightline. Only laughing faces and pressing bodies. Sam had whispered his considerate, compassionate words of caution. So noble, Sam's nature. The lieutenant would have nothing to fear. But instead of adventure, he chose safety. He nodded. He was grateful, his expression clearly indicated. Thanks, but no thanks. He executed a humble about-face, retreating, with all deliberate speed, toward the exit.

Sam's following stare overflowed with martyred self-denial. His eyelids flickered, closed, stayed closed until the fair-haired lieutenant disappeared into the night. "Do be a dear, V'lodya, and pour me a thimbleful of gin, neat."

I did as bid; it was the last of his fifth.

He sipped. He shuddered, sipped again. "Well, honey, affairs between officers and enlisted men can only come to grief."

"True love knows no limits, Stella for star."

As he drained his glass, I saw the white of melancholia creep across the heat of his former feeling. The quick was gone from his eyes. "Meaning no offense, V'lodya, but I do believe a walk-out just now might be bracing. Can we split some of your gin? And would you mind if I did?" Cautiously, testing, he slid off his bar stool. Steady enough.

Of course I would mind, not splitting the gin, but his going. Saying so just then would have served no purpose, however. I would only have driven him further away from my own feelings. I offered up my brown paper bag. "I won't be wanting any more of this. I'm going to get some food. . . ." I paused, hoping he might decide to join me. Nothing doing. "Think I'll make an early night of it. I'm feeling a touch homesick."

He chucked me under the chin, clutched the bag, smiled wanly, turned and left.

I waited until he was out of sight before I pushed my way through the thickening throng.

Sam never did return to the bridal chamber that night.

Nor the next morning. In my heart of hearts I knew he wouldn't.

I searched that Sunday morning for a shop that served what passed for a bagel and cream cheese. That helped me some.

I wandered alone, went out to the fair grounds, imagined "It Might As Well Be Spring," stopped for a frank and a beer.

Later on, I stopped in at the Blue Bonnet for a string of beers, which led me inevitably to the time of meeting Arnie at the viaduct. Sam did appear there. His expression? Inscrutable.

We were silent during the first series of hitches, but that was the habit of a Sunday's return: silence followed by a what-the-fuck resignation. Not so that night. Only Arnie volunteered eventually as how his model was having her period. Only his bitter laughter ensued. Neither Sam nor I offered any explanations for our separate solemnity. Arnie didn't care.

And when we arrived back behind the Baker Company barracks, Sam hardly paused to say good night. Kept right on. Said he was too tired for a sit-out.

My Monday morning broke hot and sultry, and, choicelessly, I had no recourse but to follow Heebler and the other hearties of my squad up to the motor pool for a day's runaround in our lovely tank.

Monday afternoon Heebler excused me from FFMM so that I might be free to tidy the tank for inspection. "Colonel's comin' first thin' tomorrow mornin', How-itz. You got the honors. Better clean the shit outta this here asshole. . . ." By evening chow time I was still cleaning. Heebler came up to tell me he'd ordered the mess hall to keep a hot tray for me, "until seven, so ya better just hustle yo ass." I told him I never wanted to eat again.

"Not even pussy?" Ha-ha, and away he went.

Back at the barracks, no Sam. I showered and went to sleep.

On Tuesday it was the company commander's turn. "Because Heebler tells me you did such a good job on your tank, I'm gon' excuse you from the four-miler again so you can clean out the orderly room. . . ." The captain insisted I had to break for chow, even leading me himself to the mess hall. Franks and beans and a deadness of despair such as Moses himself might have moaned over.

That night, relief came in the form of an empty latrine and an empty shower room. And then Sam did suddenly appear, insisting on our speedy departure for the Queen Bee, "before it's too late, V'lodya. And don't ask me a thing until we get there." He positively glowed with good humor. He had on freshly starched jeans, too. I caved in, in a swoon of affection and fatigue . . . and without so much as a whimper.

Once out of my barracks, out there in the darkness, Sam took hold of my elbow, to hurry me along. He was electric with energy, a stream of seltzer, all abounce. I labored to breathe, just as I labored to love—unrequited now, for sure, that love. The lieutenant held the field. I'd stack my tank on it.

Sam insisted on buying the first round of floats.

He carried them to the furthest table, away from the buzz and hum and murmur. There were others quietly sipping. He needed privacy—"because, what I have to reveal is more than major news and meant only for your ears, V'lodya. A slip of the lip and we all go down. So, have a care. Lean closer."

I did as bid. I looked into his flashing green eyes, but they were on the move, shifting from side to side, checking to make sure no one was near enough to hear. Oh, how I had missed him these past few days! Would he see that when his gaze returned? Would he care? Others had looked into my hazel eyes, had touched my skin—and bones—and felt lust. Why not you, Sam? Was I condemned to sisterhood and nothing more?

Without looking across at me, he broke into speech, "Today, Willy, this very morning," a quick sip from his float, drawing up, up, up, "this morning when you and your squad went marching by . . . oh, yes, I saw you. I always look for you on your way up to the motor pool. I saw you lower your rifle just as soon as Heebler turned his back. Naughty, Willy—but never mind that because this morning, no sooner had you passed by when there comes a summons for me to go on up to battalion. I was to report to a Lieutenant Rodney Harper in charge of personnel assignments. And can you guess who Lieutenant Rodney Harper just happens to be?"

I could. Oh my prophetic soul! But I didn't say. He didn't want me to. I held fire, as if hanging on his every word.

"Well, honey, Lieutenant Rodney Harper and my Blue Bonnet lieutenant from Saturday night are one and the same. Imagine that!"

I could. "You're toying with me, Sammy. Deny it if you can, but didn't you meet your Rodney again after you left me?"

"I would never lie to you, V'lodya. I did meet him. But by chance. Pure chance was what it was."

We sipped. Behind the tip of Sam's lustrous pompadour evening-blue light had deepened to starry darkness. The Queen's neon flickered a cooler shade, an Alice blue. Oh, how my "heartes roote" ached. Too much love was hidden there.

"Cross my heart, Willy, honey. You believe me, don't you?"

I nodded, not trusting my voice. It would betray me. I would scream out the clauses of my own suit.

"Good, because what happened is that when I left the Blue Bonnet, I crossed over to the Adolphus side of the street and who do you think was on his way inside? He was. He spied me. We exchanged a word or two. He had a room . . . all to himself. Now, I will swear it on a stack of Bibles, that whole night through and all the next day I never did say one word about any special ability—professional ability, that is—I might possess. Never. But he, first thing Monday morning, all on his own, researched my Form 20 and found listed thereon a simple enough fact. I could type. I can. Astonishingly well, I can, William. I see doubt in your eyes. I know those eyes of yours. Always questioning. Always skeptical. Penetrating. Honest eyes, yes—but so am I being honest. I did, in point of fact, win a typing medal when I was graduated from Electra High School. Right there it was, listed on my Form 20. The clever lieutenant questioned it too. Just as you are. He truly did. Wanted to know was it truth or a fiction? 'But fiction, Lieutenant, what is it save a reshaping of the truth?' I actually said those very words. I screwed my nerve to a sticking place which was, at that moment, the tantalizing cleft in his lovely, strong chin. Mesmerizing, his chin. And all the while I'm standing there saying such things, there are all those officers whizzing by my behind. I smiled my bewitchingly best smile, but I also blushed, because he was doing a whole lot of coded winks and throat clearings . . . he is quite massively manly, doncha think? And trying to do camp he looks even more appealing."

"Did he pursue your definition of fiction?"

"Oh Will-hee? Won't-hee? Am I telling this story or are you? Timing, honey . . . timing is everything. What he pursued was the truth . . . about my typing, that is. Could I or couldn't I? Because he had an opening for a skilled typist but he wasn't going to risk embarrassment by taking on someone who couldn't measure up. I told him, whispering it, 'You know I measure up, sir.' Which had him reaching for his tumbler of water, so I decided right then and there to tell him how I won my typing medal at Electra High. He, by the way, is from Annapolis, Maryland. His father's navy. A commander of something big. Anyway, you don't know my typing story either so I can feel free to tell it just as I told it to him. Originally, Willy, I never expected to take typing for more than a year, typing offering no great challenge, doncha know. I didn't see myself becoming a secretary. Too big for desks, even in high school. But my teacher thought I had a gift. A *he*, that teacher. He just went ahead and entered me in the annual type-off. The competition was open to contestants from within a hundred-mile radius, which, therefore, included cities as big as Wichita Falls, and that, honey, is a city considerably more populous than Electra's 3,304. Well, as you surely have surmised by now, nothing in Texas gets done small. The type-off was held out on the high-gloss gymnasium floor, a line of typewriters stretching from under one basketball hoop clear across to under the other. The grandstands were filled to overflowing with spectators from all the other schools and towns. *Quelle* . . . what would you say, Willy? Expectation? Well, whatever. It was that and more. All

100

those hovering fingers poised waiting for the gong to go off so they could turn the page placed, face down, alongside each machine. Telling it to Lieutenant Rod this morning I felt the excitement all over again. He hung on my every word, even to the point when I turned the page and realized it was Dickens. One of my most favorite moments. The description of Miss Havisham. Well, honey, I set to with great abandon. So did the others. All that tip-tapping ricocheting every which way all over those lacquered surfaces and, lo and behold, I did win: a truth none can deny. Not a bit of reshaping necessary. Truth and fiction . . . the very same. My Lieutenant Rod sat convinced, although I offered to produce my graduating yearbook from Electra High to corroborate my story. And it was then that he said, 'No, I don't think that will be necessary, *Corporal* Tolan. Corporal. In the wink of an eye—and I am to be transferred to Headquarters Company as well, promotion and transfer to be accomplished after reveille tomorrow morning. I am to be typing directly for the colonel. Can you imagine it, V'lodya?''

I could and I did imagine it. I imagined all of it. And in my imaginings I saw my own hopes for happiness being dashed against the rocks of despair. I also could and did feel sisterly elation, spontaneous elation I am happy to add, for Sam's good fortune. My fate, my kismet, only mine, had been derailed. Forlorn I was, selfless in Gaza, the dregs of my float a faded foam, my straw torn to shreds. *Wohin?* My destination in the grand scheme of things? Sam's talent . . . talent in all things . . . had been discovered and rewarded. But what of me? In a few more weeks, advanced basic would draw to its inevitable conclusion and whither would I go? To Korea? As a front gunner in a tank? *Quelle horreur!* Bemused and nonplussed, I drooped lower over my empty glass, feeling so alone, of a sudden, sighing loudly.

"Why William! Such a sigh! Do I detect suspirations of despair, my lady?'' Since it was dark enough to do so safely, he reached across the table, touched, patted, my trembling fingers. I checked my wrist watch. Fifteen minutes shy of lights out. We

101

were alone by then, there at the far corner of the Queen Bee's concrete slab, at the edge of the abyss, it might as well have been. "Just you have a listen to me, Willy, honey, because if you are feeling the slightest bit put out by Lieutenant Rod's attention to me . . . you are, aren't you? I can see it. Well, never you mind. He's just another pretty face. Not a touch of tenderness in his body. Boring is what he is." He lifted my chin. "Up, honey. Lift up those hooded deep dark eyes of yours. Come on. This is no time for us to fail each other. If you're in desperate straits, why, then so am I."

He didn't let go of my chin. By holding on, he got me all the way up. He came around, wrapping his arm behind my waist, all very man-to-man like.

He started me walking, whispering sweet things into my ear, but mostly he was telling me how nothing about Lieutenant Rod had anything to do with the two of us, "but he means well enough and he can help us. He can keep you with me. . . ." We stopped for a warm sisterly embrace, under cover of the darkness. No MPs in sight. No shell-shocked troops sleepwalking, lost under the stars. No one. Just us. "Mark my words, V'lodya, as God is my witness, we'll make it back to Moscow . . . together."

"Asses and elbows . . . asses and elbows. Thas all I wanna see. You hearin' me, How-itz? Gonna be yo ass don't pick up them butts. You steppin on 'em 'stead a pickin' 'em up."

Even on company cleanup, Heebler pursued me, positioning himself behind my behind each morning, bending me lower and lower. My Gethsemane was everywhere, especially after that night at the Queen Bee, especially since time was literally running out for me. The longer I trained inside my tank, the more certain I was I would be led to a lonely death on a corpse-littered hillside in Korea. Either that or, perhaps, permanent company cleanup, permanent latrine duty, permanent KP; bending, I pondered those possibilities; field-stripping a discovered butt, I rubbed it as if it were Aladdin's magic lamp. Freedom. Give me freedom, not death, not a sere scrap of cellophane from an old pack of Luckies.

"Thas it, How-itz. Now you got it. After all these months you finely got it. 'Cause those fingers a yours is jes made for field-strippin'. Long and thin lak 'sparagass. Betcha yo' dick's long and thin. Ain't it? 'Ceptin' yo' lost some in the cuttin', dincha?" *Ha! Ha! Ha!* The fucker almost tripled up with laughter, he was that tall. Why me? When there were fuck-ups to the right of me, fuck-ups to the left of me, as we moved and bent, moved and bent our way around the Dog Company perimeter each morning of those days leading me inevitably closer, ever closer to my doom: after advanced basic, where to, V'lodya?

"Pla-toon . . . dismissed! You too, How-itz."

Which meant we had five minutes to idle through, to waste in any wild way of our devising, before next formation. Usually I hastened to the latrine. If not then, my day in the tank was made even more miserable. Every time we maneuvered the rise of some bramble-bush hillock, Heebler would shout for us to, "Keep a tight asshole." An agony, those mornings I couldn't find a free commode. But another agony even when I did. Sitting, shitting, I worried out the string of my fate, straining to avoid five other pairs of eyes similarly straining to avoid notice. Oh, how we all wanted to be alone to sit and shit and worry out the string of a private's fate. The smell of mutual fear rose in the still, hell-hot air of those Texas mornings, late summer 1951, when I made it to the latrine and found a free commode.

August melted into September.

Daily, new levies came down from division headquarters to the Eighty-first. All of them were for Korea, not a one for European replacements. Sam's job it was to keep the count.

By October our ranks had thinned quite noticeably. Of a morning, riding out in my tank for another day's forced fine-tuning of my killing skill, intimations of mortality froze my boiling brain. At noon, scrunched up next to the tank, mess kit filled to overflowing with an inedible, unnameable mess, I imagined the moment of my death, alone, trapped beneath the barrel of my machine gun on top of a numbered hill in Korea. . . .

Evenings, Sam struggled to revive the drooping flag of my too-young-to-die spirit. But the facts turned me toward despair: I had eighteen months left to serve. Guys like me, superfluous guys, nothing essential, nothing special like Sam, we were expendable.

"But aren't they this very minute negotiating for peace?"

"They've been at it for four months already and you know it better than anyone else, Sammy, they're still sending guys there who are still dying."

"Now you stop all this brown study and gloom, V'lodya. Stop it immediately. I command you to—and I'm your superior officer so better listen. Better let me tell you about what I have planned for us this forthcoming weekend. A long one, remember. Columbus Day on Monday. We are going to hightail it all the way down to Monterrey, Mexico, and see us a bullfight. As long as you pass your Saturday inspection I'll see to the rest. I'll see to it Lieutenant Rod adds Monday to our passes. Miss Ida Flare will work her magic. Therefore it is incumbent upon you to cuddle up to Heebler just this once more, V'lodya, honey. . . ."

Since having been reassigned to Headquarters Company, Sam never had to stand inspections.

I always did, and there never was a way to predict what part of me and/or my possessions Sergeant Heebler might lay siege to—"But surely, Stella, you know I shall try."

That Friday night, with Sam supervising my efforts cotside, I polished my brass three times . . . the Holy number. Three times I polished my boots. Three times I arranged and rearranged the sequence of hangings inside my standing locker. I paid six dollars this time to have my weapon cleaned and properly oiled. I even re-washed the window next to mine, the window belonging to lazy Larry Lavagetto who had done it so slovenly the streaks were sure to show up when the sun shone through it the next morning. The sunbeam would point to my cot. By then I knew all the angles. And, by then, and again, desire stiffened my all but blunted will: Columbus Day weekend would become the weekend Sam finally discovered what he felt for me. Time was running out—even as he riffled through my Wallace Stevens, his green eyes widening exquisitely, filling with tears of pleasure—for words—his slippery, wheat-blond hair falling free. Fine feelings of longing tickled my testicles. "Tomorrow and tomorrow and tomorrow . . ."

Even if I have to tell you so myself (Who else can tell you? And how much? And when?), standing at attention the next morning, having taken the prescribed step away from the foot of my cot, my right, bright boot toe pointing to the edge of my opened foot locker, its upper tray angled, just so, I fairly gleamed, brighter than my shiny boot toe, brighter than the spear of sunlight in which I stood. Proud—and, yes, pride does goeth before the fall.

Sergeant Heebler, at Captain Quarles's side, rolled his eyeballs, astonished—and pleased. If I passed inspection, so did the sergeant's honor. He too would be free for an entire weekend. He'd get his ass in gear and on up to Waco and his sweet sixteen-year-old pussy he kept locked up there. Rolling his eyes, he had begun to taste it—freedom, that is.

Captain Quarles bent low over my footlocker.

Too low! And, digging into a far, bottom-level corner of it, he pulled out one book after another: *Four Quartets*; Conrad Aiken; Pound; *Ulysses*; Wallace Stevens—in that order. He left Yeats alone. "Private Howards, you ben toll before to take your fuckin' books outta your fuckin' footlocker. Why the fuck they back in there?"

"I don't know where else to keep them, sir."

"Why keep 'em at all?"

"In order to read them, sir." Wrong. Wrong. Wrong.

Straightening with the speed of light, he blurred before my eyes, his mouth ending up an inch or so from mine. But he did not intend to kiss me. He screamed, "Don't you smartass me!" In an instant he ripped off the pillow blanket on my cot as if it were a flour sack. "Too loose. Demerit, Heebler." He rubbed his finger along Lavagetto's window sill. "Dirt. Demerit, Heebler." He returned to face me, man-to-man, using his fingertips to touch my chin. "Shave not close enough." (It was. It was. I had cut my Adam's apple.) "That'll do it, Heebler. Confined to company area . . . the whole weekend. Jus' Howards . . . and you, Heebler. You are responsible. Dismiss the barracks." Quarles stood there, waiting for me to salute. And if I hadn't I suppose he would have shoved my own sun-glinting bayonet right on up my ass. I saluted.

Captain Quarles moved off smartly.

"Bar-racks . . . dis-missed!" Heebler screamed that right into my ear. Sweet nothings! "Fuckin' New York . . . smartass." I read *Jew* in his eyes. But he must have read my message too: if he had said *Jew* just then, I think I would have choked him with my bare hands. "Get yo ass up to the orderly room *now!*"

I collapsed back onto my cot. Lavagetto from Jersey City came to squeeze my shoulder consolingly. Youngfelt from Minneapolis came next. So did Crumb from Burlington, Vermont, and Lundberg from Grosse Pointe. No one from below the Mason-Dixon line. Fear of horns and the evil eye. (Remember, I'm telling you about America, October 1951, at the doorjamb of the Eisenhower-Nixon Dynasty; in a few years the witches would return to Washington.) No need for me to rush over to the orderly room. What greater horror could be piled on top of the horror of having failed!

Sam would be waiting for me up at battalion. Alas! By the time I could get there, he would know my fate. Probably he would be the very one to type up the order from Captain Quarles.

I stayed where I had fallen, in a heap, watching the barracks

106

empty. I heaved myself to a sitting position, blinking back tears—yes—tears, knowing I had no recourse, no appeal. *Nulla. Rien.*

I locked Eliot and Aiken, Joyce and Stevens back into my footlocker on top of Yeats.

Wearily, woefully, I made my way out of the barracks into the heat, scuffing up dust as I proceeded on to the orderly room and Heebler's wrath. Calm. I must be calm. Not surly. I must erase surliness from every crease of my furrowed forehead. Young Sad Sack must not seem to be in vulnerable, susceptible perplexity.

And, miracle of miracles, Heebler seemed to sympathize. "You oure did try, How-itz." He didn't put me on KP or on any extra duty. "Jes come 'round hee-yah every few hours. If I ain't 'round, look for me, 'cause I'm not gonna be skippin' anywheres. My ole lady's gone over to kin in Lubbock." He didn't *have* to tell me any of that. It did help, that human touch.

Sam, of course, was disconsolate. Which was one of his most bewitching moods. And didn't he look handsome that morning! All done up in a freshly starched uniform of transfixing fit. Sammy for star! Iron-jawed. Far-seeing wide-open eyes of unsurpassed green—but they were, indeed, shaded by dark thoughts, when we met in the middle of the paved street that separated battalion headquarters from the long line of barracks. His soft cap set at a rakish angle, low down on his forehead, he looked the very model of the ideal soldier: a Randolph Scott—but a deep-thinking model. Not angry. Not joyous. Pensive . . . about . . . what? Other than my obvious failure?

By my elbow, he guided me to the side of battalion HQ, "To talk, Willy. We have to talk about . . . something. Something I just did for you. I just took it into my hands to do it, right then and there . . . while you were failing inspection. Only other one who knows is Heebler. I phoned Dog Company to tell your orderly room."

"What, Sammy? What did you tell him? Had to be something pleasing because Heebler acted like a human being."

"I told him about your destiny, V'lodya. This very morning, we received a levy from Camp Gordon, Georgia. They want five bodies for a radio repair school. Six months, Willy . . . for six months. You go to Georgia and you study . . . electricity."

"Electricity? Me?"

"Yes, honey. You. You'll be saved." He drew me semi-close. We were, after all, semi-visible, standing there just off the main artery of a United States army base. Soldiers don't just have at each other. No. Only our thoughts could grab hold passionately, unrestrainedly. "Seemed like the only sane thing for me to do, V'lodya, to . . . blow out your candles. I'll be the loser, but you'll be saved."

As I suggested a while back, Fate spins its own top, will-we, nill-we. Slowly, ever so slowly, that fact spread into the dark corners of my numbed brain, and with it came the electroshocker, a simple enough jolt: Sam would remain in Texas; I would be going off to Georgia. We would be separated, maybe for the duration.

Sam, at my elbow, roused me, began leading me away from battalion headquarters, back across the street to the barracks. Out of the corner of my dazed eye I saw Lieutenant Rod step out from behind a screen door. He paused, studying us. Aha! So he knew too. The Final Solution: diaspora! He wanted me out of the picture.

But that couldn't be true of Sam. Nothing but affection was in that hand cupping my elbow, guiding me this way and that way up behind the long row of battalion barracks to the back porch of my Dog Company home. He sat me down, nuzzling closer as he did.

Behind us, from inside, nothing. Deserted. Stillness. All the *Soldaten* gone, to Dallas, to Austen and Houston and San Antonio. A big weekend—but no sunny side for us down in Old Monterrey. A shambles, our plans. *Alles. Alles* . . . chaos—but why should Sammy have to suffer for my failure? "You should take off somewhere, Sammy. I'll get by. I'll . . . read."

"I won't hear of leaving you. Not after what *I* did this morning with your future. But you don't blame me, V'lodya, now do you? Because I took what I thought to be the lesser of the risks to come. Lieutenant Rod had just finished warning me there was going to be the biggest levy yet for Korea. It'll be coming this very week so I just . . . acted . . . on your behalf, thinking, well, six months isn't forever. Korea could be—you know what Korea could be . . . and if you are in Georgia I'll get you back, Scarlett, honey. As God is my witness, I'll get you back. . . ."

I nodded, allowing myself to be convinced that he cared, even if he didn't care in the way I had hoped he might. That kind of caring, for now, Lieutenant Rod had cornered. And anyway, the hazy heat of high noon was melting any fugitive trace of resistance. Why worry out the beads of an already sealed future! Georgia it was to be. *Finito!* I lapsed into a far-off, staring silence. Beyond Sam's profile stretched the last of the row of yellow, green-trimmed barracks leading right up to the motor pool fence. There was my tank, one among many. Good-bye to that, happily. Good-bye to the jeeps and half-tracks, all of them lined up, at rest, mute, empty of any human purpose. But, even when in use, what life-enhancing enterprise charged through them? None. Not a one I could bring myself to care about. All I cared about, just then, was Sam's closeness.

He was studying the sky. I did too. Billowy clouds. Hanging there, still. For a moment, no breeze. Vastness . . . and the sun, the central sun, nourishing each and every one and thing, indifferent to what we do with our lives, what we care for, what we come to in the end. . . . So, might as well tell Sammy plain, before it got to be too late, before the sun went behind a cloud.

But Sammy, as was his wont, sixth-sensed something. He stood, rousing me from my reverie. "What we'll do first of all is go on over to the Queen. Heebler won't even know we have . . . and then we can sort things out from there. Kinda prepare our future plans. . . ."

We lingered long over our floats, lazying straws round and

109

round the rims of our glasses. Once, I went back to Dog Company orderly room to check in with Heebler and he excused me for the rest of the afternoon. He told me he trusted me. Imagine. Even put his side-of-beef hand on my shoulder, squeezing it with something akin to affection.

When I told all that to Sam, he wondered out loud about the "mysteries lurking in the hearts of men. I mean, V'lodya, we simply never do know what to expect next, do we? Which is why we sisters must always be prepared, must always be ready to protect each other."

"You don't need any protection."

"I most assuredly do. Much more than you. I grew up surrounded by Heeblers. You . . . you rode subways." He dragged deeply on his latest Lucky. The insides of his cheeks seemed to touch. Very Bette Davis. "You know the hard part, about life after sex."

"I also get repeated hard-ons."

"We can go on over to the library if you'd like."

That was not it at all . . . and he knew it. I said nothing, scanned the sky instead for some sign. Even the billowy clouds were breaking up. *Schwester! Geliebte!* My Sam, casting me to the winds of a separate fate. Rejecting me. Others had . . . loved me—and not for my golden hair. On the streets of Manhattan the color of reality, like my hair, is brown.

But Sam specialized in subtler feelings. I knew that. I knew that when he reached across the splintery wooden space between the empty glasses of our floats, covering my busy fingers with his big hand, he meant to touch me with the purest of affectionate feelings. "You know what I'll do, Willy, honey? I'll just go into Killeen and get us some of that lovely chili from that place that gives you unlimited chopped onions. You know the place I mean. Would you like that?"

It worked: his touch, his tone, his tough tenderness. "Why yes, Miss Ida. That would be pleasant." They had sustained and saved me up until now. But now what? "Lots of chopped onions, mind you . . ."

*   *   *

I slept a troubled sleep, belching and farting and dreaming tangled dreams, waking to the realization that I was pinned to my cot. Sergeant Heebler had me so wrapped up beneath my blanket, leaning over me as he was from his perch along the edge of my cot. "Sleep any longer, How-itz, you miss Sunday-morning cooked eggs, to order, some mighty good bacon too. You eat bacon, doncha?" Ha-ha! He was leaning low over me, gripping the far side of my cot, his face dangerously close to mine, and smiling, which made it seem all the more dangerous. Had I forgotten to do something for which the only punishment could be a firing squad? No. No KP or extra duty . . . "Ah know you gon' be leavin' us, How-itz. You frien' from battalion calt to tell us. . . ." A pause. Which lengthened into a silence; which lengthened into my realization that there didn't seem to be any one else in the barracks, it being a Sunday morning of a holiday weekend.

"Did I fuck up, Sergeant? Was I supposed to report in this morning? And I overslept? I'm sorry, but . . ."

He kept shaking his head no, his dark curly hair bouncing because he had begun to laugh and to move his forearm back and forth over what he had to know was my piss-filled dick, playing with it—and me. Jes a li'l ole boy's game, meaning nothing at all by it, acting as if he didn't even know what he was doing. Jes a smiling down at me and tellin' me he jes came over ta get me down to chow before the mess hall closed, "thas all, How-itz, friend-to-friend like. Spite a you bein' a fuck-up, I like yo." And all the while rubbing and smiling ingenuously, unaware of doing anything unusual at all.

Now what the fuck did he want from li'l ole me!

Ugh! The mere thought of his closeness like to suffocated me. And there he sat, rubbing and smiling as if he had been seized by some Korean memory. What if someone had come into the barracks, just then? Court-martial for sure. Mine, not his. They would blame me—the cunning queer—instead of a bemedaled, battle-scarred, muscle-bulging veteran. So, better rouse him

111

somehow, without having to touch him. Although I had heard tales of hate breeding longings of lust, that was not in me. That was-is-never what I meant at all. "Sergeant, if you would just let me go piss and shower I'll promise to race my ass over to the mess hall. . . ." I stopped short of batting my eyelashes. Since I wasn't supposed to know that he knew what he was up to, any sign of response other than my usual big-city grudging compliance would have been suspect.

He did decide to stand up—moving quickly aside, but an unhidable hard-on gave his game away.

I turned the other cheek. All these months Heebler had been courting me. Imagine! The twists and turns of human nature, of hetero and homo alike . . . deep down feelings—with a will all their own—leap fences.

After that morning, right up until I left for Georgia, Sergeant Heebler never so much as whispered "How-itz."

The weekend before I was to leave for Georgia, Sam asked me up to Electra. He telephoned ahead to his folks and then to Oveta and Owen Murchison, "my sister and brother friends. My queerest and dearest. Oveta insists on a party for us. She dotes on parties. She'd give one in honor of a hat pin, let alone a hat. This one's to be for Halloween . . . since I won't be home for the real Halloween. I told her I was bringing my New York friend home—which excited Owen no end. Owen's . . . unusual—but you shall see all that yourself soon enough, Will. . . ."

The closer our rides dropped us to Electra, the less often I heard "V'lodya" or "Will-hee?" or "Honey" or "Sister" and the more his South rose in an unrestrained rush, overtaking camp and quotes and studied poses: just another loving son coming home to Mama, doncha know. . . .

And Mama was the first one to greet us. We had stopped under the chinaberry tree out in front of the Tolans' white, red-shingled bungalow. The house had a broad front porch with a glider on it. I loved gliders from my Catskill Mountains days. I loved standing under a real honest-to-goodness chinaberry tree too. I also loved moving toward a house located on a street named Wanderer, a street that ended at a dried-up river bottom. Sam had described it all for me and how his mother would look when she stepped from the porch to greet us: in a butter-yellow wrap house dress, the butter yellow matching her coiled braided bun. A long face; a handsome woman. Sam's face was in hers, all right. His mother's son.

And before the screen door could slam shut, out came Poppa, but stopping on the porch until Mrs. had had her fill of Sam.

Mr. Tolan towered taller than most men one chanced to meet, and, as with most tall men, his was an accommodating nature: he bent to shake hands, meaning no harm to anyone. Couldn't help being tall. Couldn't help being string-bean lean and bent low, his skin tanned and weathered, etched and eaten into creases by the dust-dry Texas wind. Mr. Tolan's grunt of greeting for Sam didn't disguise the overflow of his affection. Embarrassed, he stood before Sam nodding, stooping, shuffling. He stopped short of a kiss, covering up that weakness by offering me a huge, rough-hewn manly hand and a mumbled "How do . . ."

Meanwhile, Mrs. Tolan circled me, searching, no doubt, for horns. Finding none, she re-found the flow of her natural decency. Her eyes welcomed me warmly. "If you are here with Sam, you are family, William." Real down-home hospitality.

But her "William" cut through me to the softest center of an indefinable longing, to that place where nostalgia is always on the lookout for a way out. Standing there, "among the alien corn," I imagined another mother in another home saying *William, wash up, dinner's soon. . . .*

"Dinner's soon," Mrs. Tolan did, in fact, say, "so let's just step inside now, Sam, and you can show William where he can wash up."

Where I washed up was a basin in Sam's room, a small room with twin beds in it, one for Sam, one for me. "It's an add-on.

My father built it for my brother Ray and me when my sister Susanna was born. It's got one of those corrugated tin roofs. When the wind blows up a real storm the rain beats down on it something fierce. I loved listening to it. And when birds skittered across . . . soon as my brother moved out I loved listening even more. Mostly, these days, Ray lives with his girlfriend. Mom asked him home for dinner tonight, unfortunately. . . ."

Sam led me next outside, right outside his room, to a sheltered corner behind the bungalow. The whirring wind didn't reach there. Neither did the dun-colored dust.

Ray had arrived. Sister Susanna held him by the muscle of his upper arm, a formidably developed arm and muscle. Wouldn't want to mess with it, or with any of the rest of him. Chunky, sharp-featured, mean and menacing he was. Leering was his best thing. His beer belly was about five months into term—and only nineteen. Clearly, brother Ray was the family's cross to bear.

Sister Susanna, on the other hand, cowered. Hollow-cheeked, her face was oval, her forehead furrowed, her hair a pale, sad, center-parted version of Mrs. Tolan's butter-yellow braided bun. Only her chin said something: it had the dot of a dimple in it. Most like Sam's, I thought, but, at fourteen, there was no sign in it that she would ever set her course on any kind of defiance. Her watery eyes implied she had not set herself to anything. Holding on was about all she could foresee. Before she let go of Ray's arm, she took hold of Sam's. First kissing him, next burying her face inside the curve of his shoulder, shyness overtook her. I expect I frightened her. So un-Texas-like my hazel-eyed, unflinching stare. Or was it my full, ruby ripe lips? Or my big New York Jew nose stretching down my face like an exclamation mark? Is that why she turned away for a clearer view of the fields, turned Sam to see them with her? "Mama's beans are doin' real well this year. . . ."

And, in point of fact, there came Mrs. Tolan, slipping in between Sam and me, relaxing herself by holding us at our waists while Sam pointed out the pintos, the black-eyes, the navys and

114

limas. "Mama grows 'em, tends 'em, uses every which one of them. We'll be having some of them for dinner, won't we, Mama?"

"Sure will, son. And dinner'll be about ready. Don't want to rush things, but I know you'll be going out tonight. Oveta's been callin' over here all day lookin' for you. And I was so hoping you'd be visiting more with us this weekend."

"Mama, don't let's start in about that now. I wanted Willy to meet them and Oveta was giving one of her parties so it just worked out. It's Willy's going to be leaving after this weekend. I want him to have as good a time as we can provide him."

"You are one-hundred-percent right." She squeezed at my waist, relaxing me a mite; not more than that because Susanna was staring at me queerly and I could hear Ray's breath coming bull-like from somewhere behind me. "And Daddy should be about done washing up. So we can all go in now. . . ."

Mr. Tolan was already seated and waiting at the head of the table, hands clasped, head bowed, ready to say grace.

The dining table was in the kitchen. The kitchen was the biggest room of the house. Bright linoleum floor, waxed to reflection. Eyelet curtains on the eye-level window above the sink. The hot water heater behind Mr. Tolan's bowed head. It gurgled.

"For what we are about to receive, we thank thee, O Lord."

Mumbled *amen*s included mine. What did that cost on the open market of my experience? Not a cent. (Hypocrisy in the service of civility tasted like mother's milk to an undercover homosexual in those unlamented long-ago days.) Besides, for the food that followed I would have said a mass.

Of beans, there were buttery black-eyes and a lima-bean casserole, a sweet-and-sour concoction. Put me in mind of a dish my own mother made some Sabbath nights.

There was a beef stew of tender bits and homemade buttermilk biscuits to sop up petals of onions and turnip pulp and crunchy fresh peas and carrots. Fresh flavors, beautifully blended. But no garlic. My mother put garlic in her stew. My

115

mother would have given us thick slices of challah for mopping up. So long since I'd sat at table with a real family, even one so unlike mine, this family of grace and tamped-down feelings. As I ate, Brooklyn broke back into life behind my eyes. I sighed.

Sam heard it. He smiled a comforting smile. Oh how well he had come to know the way of my head in so short a time. I had never had a friend like that. I would more than miss him. I looked up into his knowing eyes. He nodded, rubbed his knee against mine, ever so gently—and then he nudged my elbow, calling me back, directing my attention to the sight of his brother Ray, opposite, splishing and splashing a chunk of biscuit through tomato-brown gravy. Next to him Susanna trailed knife tracks across the hills of her mashed potatoes. Exasperated, Mrs. Tolan took hold of her daughter's hand, "Stop your moonin'. Winds going to blow you clean away you don't start eatin'."

Mr. Tolan never looked up until he had biscuit-wiped his plate spotless.

And all the while Mrs. Tolan kept watch, passing and refilling and urging me to have more. She wanted to say more, too. But what? Nervously she returned to her braided bun, patting it, pushing at bobby pins, her eyes in perpetual motion. I offered praise for her food. So did Sam. No one else did. And then there was Mr. Tolan, scraping his chair back from the table, standing up. "When it's dessert, Edna, call me. Be readin' the paper out on the porch." His departure meant Ray could go too. "Don't enjoy eatin' with . . ." had I actually heard him snarl, sotto voce, ". . . kikes"? Probably. Probably belonged to the Klan. Blood drained from Sam's lips. They locked looks. Ray turned away first. And instantly, Susanna was offering to collect. "You sit, Mama." Susanna scraped and cleared; Mrs. Tolan's eyes filled up, her head swinging slowly back and forth: a silent apology. No and no and no. A sad scene.

Stills of my mother filled my head. Her little-girl face. Her tiny frame—just under five feet tall. Her brown hair done in a fleecy feather cut the last time I'd seen her. She'd be wearing

116

one of her favorite Bemberg silk print shirtdresses, it being Friday night. She'd be up and down and around the table, serving out the food she had so proudly prepared—but always self-effacing when complimented. Which Sam would surely do, compliment her, thank her graciously. And then my father, finishing, would turn to Sam, ask him about Texas, would listen attentively, expecting equal attentiveness when it became his turn to tell Sam about the time he and his wife drove through most of Texas on their first car trip down to Mexico City. And as he talked he liked to place his open palm on the tablecloth, pressing down firmly for emphasis, propping up his elbow, pointing it one way and the other, or at my mother, his signal that she could serve out the next course. He was finished talking. He was ready for more food.

Clearly the Tolans were from a different tribe. Mrs. Tolan remained pained and confused. "Don't know what gets into us. Take Ray, for example. Nothing like Sam is. No one on my side of the family's anything near to being mean as Ray can be. And on my husband's side, well, there's never been much talk about them. Not much to know he always says. That man won't talk much about anything. Breaks my heart how quiet your father gets, Samuel. All these years I have tried and tried to get him talking. Just no use." She smoothed her bun, looking off toward the window. Dusk out there.

"Mama?" Sam whispered. "What's dessert? Because we are going to have to leave for Oveta's pretty soon."

She sprang to her feet. "Why I'm more than sorry, son. And you too, William," she smiled down at me, her long, lean face rounding warmly. "It's Sammy does it to me. I do so miss having him around here to talk to. Only one I can. Only one who ever listened to me. Sammy, honey, how I do miss you." She held out her arms and he moved to her. Embracing her, he smoothed the back of her butter-yellow wraparound house dress.

Dessert was a light-as-air cinnamon apple pie: another madeleine evoking the taste of my mother's.

117

*　*　*

Mr. Tolan drove us out to Murchison Manor.

"The Tara of Electra, Texas," Sammy called it when it came into view.

We were losing evening light fast. Mr. Tolan geared down, idling only long enough for us to hop out of the pickup. He couldn't wait to rev and race away. Can't say as how I blamed him. The sight of the festooned facade of the manor all done up in orange and red silk ribbons and bows bulged my wondering eyes. The Christmas show at the Radio City Music Hall came to mind. Three floors. Three verandas. Thousands of nile-green shuttered windows. Corinthian columns wrapped in swaths of red ribbon from the roof line down to where their pedestals rested in beds of purple, yellow, pink azaleas. A long sloping lawn, a peninsula of open lawn, bordered by lines of disheveled willows and the tallest honey locusts I had ever seen, stretched before us. "Oveta's gone all out." Sam stepped ahead excitedly. I? I hung back some, my mind filled with dreams of a white Rosh Hashanah, of sitting on the porch of our two-family house one green evening in Brooklyn reading "Peter Quince at the Clavier" out loud to my mother and father. Why just then? Those thoughts? Why so "alien corn" a mood? A sudden breeze rippled, snapped the ribbons and bows, whipped through the bordering trees. This was no place for white and green thoughts of a safer, saner time in my life. Those were not the Rockettes skipping and kicking down the lawn on their way to welcome us. They were a whiplash line of motley costumed shapes led by two gorillas. "Those apes will be Oveta and Owen. They'll swoop down on us, so prepare yourself, Willy."

One lunged for me, the other for Sam.

I fell to the grass to the sound of laughter. On my back, I looked up into a black fake-fur face with yellow button eyes. I was pinned. The darkening sky filled with out-of-focus, whirling forms. Columbines and harlequins. Footballers, helmeted, padded, gladiatorial, huddled above me, broke away, made way for

118

baton twirlers, the suede fringes on their vests beating the air above me I so badly needed. My gorilla was heavy, its laughter hollow, eerie, unstoppable. And so were the costumed bodies bending over me. Skeletons and Frankensteins. Count Draculas and a bevy of bats. Cowgirls and cowboys, chaps flapping, as they circled and danced away. I pushed up against my gorilla, pushed and tugged and squirmed, trying to roll out from under. My gorilla pressed me more firmly down to earth, its distorted, funhouse laughter becoming distinguishable as words, "H-h-happy H-h-hallo-w-w-ween."

Sam's head appeared above, and then his hand grabbed hold of the gorilla's ear. The whole head came off. "Unhand him, Owen. Unhand him this instant."

Obediently, head now in hand, Owen Murchison rolled onto his side, offered me black fake-fur, silvery-clawed fingers to shake. "I l-l-l-like you."

I sat up, striving for a semblance of New York City insouciance. "Why we've only just met."

"B-b-b-but I know you. Sam wr-wr-wrote me."

Another headless gorilla leaned lower in greeting, this one as blond and pert and rose-red as mine was ebony-haired, gauntly ivory-skinned, conspicuously androgynous: a painful case, mine—but fun-loving. "I'm Oveta. Sorry about Owen. He tends to overdo when he takes a liking to someone." She and Sam extended their hands to help me to my feet.

"I'd prefer sitting here, thank you. Owen and I can get to know one another better."

"Why, of course, you just go ahead and do whatever pleases you." Miss Petite Oveta lifted her hairy arm, waved it through the air. The motley crew surrounding her broke into motion once again. "Have all the fun you can find." She took hold of Sam commandingly. They joined the others now snaking their way back up the lawn, all of them singing and dancing to a country music beat the breeze blew downwind. I struggled to stand up.

119

With much more grace than I had been able to muster, Owen rose, lighter than air it seemed, his gaze never wavering from my face. Bewitched! By me. Imagine that! But his hands were active, were happy to help me brush the back of my uniform. Sam had insisted on our wearing uniforms as costumes. Mine looked like one: the pants too long, the shirt sacklike, the garrison cap, issued before my wavy brown locks had been reduced to a crewcut stubble, sliding low down onto my ears. Sam's fit him to breathtaking perfection; mine flapped everywhere and Owen's ape claws pawing me made me painfully aware of the contrast. "I appreciate your help, Owen, but your nails are a bit sharp."

He dropped his arms, shook them until the gorilla gloves fell to the grass alongside his head. "S-s . . . s-s . . . sorry." He looked up from under, batting his thick eyelashes.

"Perhaps we better go join the others."

Only too happy to obey, he bowed low, a plié from the fifth position, the true perfection of which was marred by the hairy legs of his gorilla suit. Painful cases, both of us: he in his illjudged, inappropriate costume; me in my all misfitting army issue. Nothing about me soldierly; nothing about him apelike. But, I suppose, our incongruities connected us. We were exiles together. His anxious, thick-lipped smile touched me. He even waited for me to make the first step so he could follow my lead. I stepped out cautiously, wishing more than ever I might instead turn around, go back to where I had come from. Not back to Wanderer or Fort Hood, but all the way back to Brooklyn. This darkening lawn, this beribboned manse now staring down at me menacingly, this stuttering, ivory-skinned admirer now slavishly retrieving my fallen garrison cap, these were not *it*. This was no country for a gay Jewish lad from New York. Love had led me adrift, had left me bereft in Goyland, and now what I needed was a stiff gin. Unheedingly, I stumbled up the lawn to where the lights were . . . pursued by an undone gorilla. . . .

Gallumph-galloo. Gallumph-galloo. Heavy breathing. Over my shoulder I spied the struggle of Owen Lawrence Murchison. None of my making.

I made it in under the portico, pushed headlong through the giant doors and on into the entranceway.

Down either side, either corridor beckoned. I promenaded left. Apelike, Owen followed me to the nearest bar. There were several, each placed alongside the doorway of each sitting room, each sitting room done up in a different style. Rattans, wicker and chintzes in one. A thick jungle of plants and trees and sod, printed pillows piled high in corners in another. I stopped at each bar, peeked into each sitting room. In a pastel, furry, silky French-boudoir room I saw the daffodil head of Oveta going wild in the center of a circle of admiring football helmets. Nearby, Sam was the center of his own admiring circle and shaking his own wheat-gold pompadour winsomely, Rita Hayworth-like, sweeping imagined tresses off his broad shoulders just as I'd seen him do it a hundred times at the Blue Bonnet or the Queen or sitting before our whirrring fan at the Fort Hood Library. Shameless hussy! And there came Oveta, sidling into Sam's circle. She had slipped free of her gorilla getup, changed into something more comfortable, a red silk bikini. Ripely petite, Miss Oveta, with pudgy poky fingers just then grabbing the ass of the footballer closest to hand. Drunk, the whole lot of them—but, soon so would I be, so there you are.

Passing on down the corridor, I came, at length, to the final sitting room, my gin glass freshly refilled. A room of sensible sofas and club chairs, of Oriental rugs and a marble-framed fireplace, it welcomed me, promising some measure of safety, a place to pass out in alone.

But I was not alone. Owen had not faltered in pursuit, had matched me gin for gin, sitting room for sitting room, and was now gently taking hold of my thin shoulder, was shaking it gently, was stuttering sweet nothings into my bemused, only slightly focusing eyes. "I wa-wa-want to ta-ta-talk to you. I l-l-l-like you."

"Why?"

"You're Je-Je-Jewish, aren't you?"

"You could tell?" That hurt him. On his knees in front of the leather club chair I had sunken into, he lowered his alabaster, ebony-topped head. "Sorry." I was, too. All he wanted to do was talk to me. Little enough to grant. His was the only friendly face I had so far faced; his the only hand that had touched my crushed spirit with affection. He cared, and caring had transformed the features of his confusing face. Such a face! The bright spotlight under which he knelt before me told a truth which the semidarkness of the lawn earlier had somewhat muted, softened. White on white on white his skin. No eyebrows. No hint of any beard. Dark brown wide-open hurt eyes. A long, broad nose. Thick red lips. Sunken hollows where cheeks should puff and billow. But above it all that ebony hair, lustrous, wavy, thick hair. I gaped. I looked away, to the bookshelves, to the planters, to the paintings of landscapes hanging on distant walls. I thought green thoughts before my gaze returned to his.

He wanted to tell me about his mother and father and how they had died when he was twelve and Oveta was thirteen. He wanted to tell me how Oscar, his father, and Ouida, his mother, had taken Oveta and himself out for a ride in their newly purchased, gold-trimmed, ivory-painted Packard. So caught up was he in his telling he never stammered once, not until the very end of his story. "My daddy loved that Packard, loved me too. Had the car painted the color of my skin. Could hardly wait to take us all out for that ride, a fateful ride indeed it turned out to be because as it so often happens up here near the Panhandle, thunder and hailstorms will blow up of a sudden. Out of nowhere. When they did there I was, skipping along with Oveta, both of us following along after Mama and Daddy. Hailstones bigger than grapefruits, let me tell you. Oveta dragged me back to the car in time. Mama and Daddy didn't make it. A matter of minutes is all it took for them to be pummeled to death. That is truly what happened. We saw it with our own eyes. I loved Daddy so . . . and he loved me. Only one who ever has. He wanted me to be a great pianist. I'm going to be too. Someday soon. Daddy left us trillions. Oil . . . I l-l-l-love you too."

"Oh, yes. I'm sure you do." Haughty How-itz. Naughty How-itz. Drunk and bereft. "Why don't you remove that silly costume?" *Mea culpa*—but it was Sam for whom I longed. For Owen, the androgyne, I felt . . . pity.

Nevertheless, he proceeded to obey my imperious command with unruffled sweetness. Standing, he unzipped. Fake fur fell away. He was done up in white ballet tights, white T-shirt, white ballet slippers. Such thin ankles—he stepped free of the fur pile. All of him thin, thinner even than I. And defenseless. His sloping shoulders fell forward, so far forward I thought they might fold in two. Embarrassed by my staring, he cupped his hands beneath his privates, lifting them toward me: an offering. A sizable protuberance, indeed.

"Is this some kind of joke, Owen? Did Sam put you up to it or are you just a little bit crazy? Which?" How terrible of me. Aware of the two deaths he had witnessed, I surely should have shown some compassion—but I was the one who was nowhere I wanted to be, wanting only to be left alone to stew in my own juices, to await my fate in Georgia and beyond.

"Oveta tells me I'm tetched. But if I am I never ever hurt anyone." He struck a pose, *en arabesque*. Lovely extension, his hands shaping a cup beneath his crotch once again. I was to take note of that. That was to be the way to my heart.

Instead, I leaped up—unsteadily—rushed to a set of French doors. Locked, of course.

I leaned against them, peered out longingly at the swaying honey locusts, the live oaks lining the perimeter of the vast lawn. No stars out. No moon. Total eclipse. "Listen, Owen, I'm drunk. Good . . . for nothing."

"I'll take you to a place outside. You need some fresh air is all." As if by magic, his stutter has stopped. Determination has stiffened his tongue. He reaches up to a hidden key hanging along the molding of the French doors. He opens them, replaces the key, takes hold of my arm, leading me out into the darkness.

And why not? Why not Owen? His has been the only human

123

response all evening. He took pity on an alien in an alien world. God's will be done—by Owen, if it is so fated.

Clear across the lawn, to its farthest corner, Owen leads me to an old oak, settles me upright against it, Murchison Manor at my back. On the breeze, phrases of music sound, fade as the breeze dies down. I close my eyes, feel Owen sliding to his knees before me. I make no effort to stop him. It's what he wants. What I want is . . . Sam. Or, just now, someone familiar, like Harry. Harry Harlan Royce . . . "A touch of Harry in the night" would be nice. But Owen's fingers at my fly are gentle. I press back against the rough bark, trying to slow the spinning in my head. The gin has done me in. I lift my arm for some handhold. There is none. Only an imagined one. It fills my head . . . and there is Harry. I'm swaying. I grab hold. A subway strap. Saturday night . . . on my way home from work. The car is almost empty. The train accelerates, rocks from side to side. The sensation soothes—but I am tired. Under my other arm . . . *War and Peace* . . . Modern Library Giant edition. Brooklyn and home are an hour away. Sitting, I begin to read. . . .

The subway enters the tunnel on its long run under the East River from Wall Street to Clark Street in Brooklyn. The lights flicker. Annoyed, I look up, absorbed by the sentence I have just read: "What she drew from the guitar would have had no meaning for other listeners, but in her imagination a whole series of reminiscences arose from those sounds." A face opposite displaces Natasha's in my thoughts. A man's face, looming large. A broad forehead. Shocks of tweedy brown hair. Sanguine, mottled skin. Commanding features. And yet a winsome, candid smile. For me?

Once more the lights flicker. This time they go out.

When they come on again, the train rumbles and roars into the Clark Street stop. The man has risen, is walking toward the cab of the car and the exit door, beckoning with his strong chinny-chin-chin for me to follow him. He even holds the door open, waiting for me to decide, unconcerned whether the other passengers see what he is up to or if they care that he is holding up the subway's departure. Flattered by all that attention, my debate is a moment's work.

Side by side we watch the train pull out. A big man. What Lawrence would call "strapping," lion-loined. Following was not at all, in point of fact, my habit—but this doesn't feel wrong. Nothing threatening in his gesture for me to follow, wherever he might lead me.

A few steps, to a bench. I feel exhilarated. No matter I have worked a Saturday four-to-midnight shift at my weekend holiday bookshop job. At seventeen, fatigue is not a consideration in any decision I choose to make—or have made *for* me by having been chosen. I have reserves of energy. I have entered another story. I will play a part in someone else's script. A thrilling thought—or, when the next train comes into the Clark Street station I can get on it and continue on my way home.

But I know I won't.

"You saw me staring at you. You looked up suddenly and you caught me at it. What were you thinking about?"

"Nothing." Brilliant.

"Nothing?" He laughed . . . but not *at* me. Not derisively. Affectionately, I decide. "You're not afraid of me, are you?"

I needed a minute to catch my breath—but, no, I wasn't afraid. Nervous, yes. Embarrassed by the situation. He wasn't. He was playing with me. Indulging a whim, big strapping man that he was. Confident. Probably more than twice my age, and looming larger the longer I forced myself to stare back directly into his dark, slow-moving, deep-set eyes. Nothing of a threat in them. Inviting me to trust him. So, I did. "No. Not at all."

"How old are you?"

"Almost eighteen."

"You look more like twelve."

"You look more like forty."

He laughed again. A hearty laugh. "Thirty-five." A fact that

125

ended his laughter, turning him suddenly contemplative. He took hold of my chin, lifting it. There was no one else on the platform just then.

And just then I realized that he had been drinking. Leaning closer, I could smell it on his breath. Now the debate began in *his* head. His square face settled into a trace of jaw jowl: a ridge that ran from a dimple in one cheek, under his chin and on up to the dimple in his other cheek. He had taken a chance. He might not have taken it if totally sober. He let go of my chin. "Where're you coming-g from so late?" A slight slur.

"Work."

"You're pulling my leg."

"The truth. A bookshop. In Times Square." I made ready to stand up. I heard a train approaching. He had changed his mind. Didn't want me. It roared in. Screeched to a stop. It was going in the wrong direction, anyway. Silently, we watched it depart. The few people who had gotten off walked quickly to the end of the platform where the escalator was.

And then, once more, he studied me. "If you come home with me, can you spend the night? You'll have to. Can you?"

"I think so."

"Yes or no. No thinking about it. Can you?"

"Yes."

"You're sure? Not going to create any problems at home? Your mother going to be worried?"

"I'm . . . old enough. It won't be the first time I haven't gone home after work. And, of course it causes a problem. But I'm learning to handle them. I get better at it the older I get."

He seemed to like that answer. So did I. I had gone from being a child to a young man. I saw that reflected in his eyes. I felt it inside me too.

He stood up. He buttoned his corduroy jacket. Chunky broad fingers. He lumbered as he walked. Bad arches. Heavy cordovan shoes, but he moved fast, like a graceless skier.

Should I run back, away, before it was too late?

Too late for what? He wasn't looking back. He had made up his mind. He assumed I had too. He brought us to the elevator instead of the escalator. Clark Street had both, because up above it was the Hotel St. George into which the elevator emptied. We stepped out onto Henry Street. Brooklyn Heights. Dark. No stars. No moon. October chill.

His pace quickened. He was a step ahead of me. If someone, one of his neighbors, perhaps, had seen us, it would not be certain we were together. I maintained the distance he seemed to favor.

We came to an unlit brownstone at the end of Montague Street. Four floors of brownstone. And a long flight of slate steps to climb to reach the front entrance. Before unlocking the door, he took hold of my shoulder, whispering, "Probably we won't, but if we should meet anyone, don't be alarmed. They'll be family. Mine. We live on all the floors. Nothing to worry about. Got it?"

"Got it." But I surely was alarmed. A first for me, such a possibility. I clutched my heavy *War and Peace* too tightly. Had I heard its spine crack?

Inside, a nightlight, dim and comforting, and a long rise of carpeted staircase.

Up, up, all the way up to the top floor. His own floor. A suite. His bedroom had windows to the west. I went to stand in front of them. To see what I could see: the rushing current of the East River . . . the Brooklyn Bridge . . . Manahattan . . . "Flood-tide below me! I see you face to face. . . ."

He did not put on the light. No need. There was glow enough from outside. From across the river nervous sparkles of light, lighting up whatever needed to be seen. I felt suffocated by the sudden flush of rushing sensations. He touched the sleeve of my windbreaker. His arms wrapped around me, his body pressing against my back. I felt . . . secure. All the nonsense thoughts I had ever thought about what I was . . . whatever *that* was . . . made sense suddenly—and I didn't even know the man's name.

I didn't ask. I didn't care. . . .

I didn't find out until afterward. Sometime during the night, warmed by a down quilt and the touch of our bodies, he told me his name, "Harry, Harry Royce. Harlan, actually, but call me Harry. Got it?"

"Got it." I reached down between us, to take hold of it, to yank it. I told him my name. He yanked mine. "How do you do, William."

Soon, I slept again. Dreamlessly. Deeply. Peacefully. I supposed that was because of what I thought I was sure I was feeling.

Had to be something with the force of love because, when a rapid knocking at the door began and I realized it was morning, and then a woman's voice called, "Harry? Harry? Are you up? Nine-thirty, Harry? We should leave within the hour. Harry?" "Yes, Mother. Thank you. I'm up . . ." if what I felt wasn't as strong as love is made out to be or as strong as infatuation—whichever is the strongest feeling one can feel for another human being—then I am absolutely certain I would have trembled myself into shock. Harry held me still. "I told you last night. Nothing to worry about. Just do as I tell you and there will be no problem whatsoever. You're a big boy now. A man of the underworld. Right?"

I didn't trust my speech. I nodded, waiting for instructions. Whatever he told me to do I would do. I didn't want him to be disappointed with anything about me.

"My mother and aunt and sister live downstairs. I'm driving them all to the airport where we will meet my fiancée. Then we go on from there to the North Shore. To Glen Cove where my fiancée's parents live. She's arriving home from Europe today." He paused, securing me tighter inside his arms, and then he went on to tell me to make sure I called my mother, so she wouldn't worry about where I had been and to make sure I left my telephone number on his desk so he could contact me as soon as he was able to. He wanted to contact me. Did I want

128

him to? Now that I knew his situation? If I had had a change of heart, he would understand, but he would also be unhappy about that because he liked me—not that he would try to make up my mind for me: "You'll know what you want to do. You decide. But, for now, you just stay put here in bed until we leave. I'll be the last one out of the house and I'll call up to you that the coast is clear. Make sure you call your mother. Do you work today too?"

"Yes." This couldn't be happening. I didn't believe it. "Do I wake or sleep?" . . .

"In that case leave your work number. If I can call you later I will." He threw back the blankets to untangle himself, but he didn't leap away. He kissed me . . . then again. He meant business. He meant to do *it* again, but fast. A quickie, "for the road." He didn't stop to ask me by your leave; he got down to it. I didn't shilly-shally. My feelings at seventeen overwhelmed me, fast. He dissolved every bit of fear I know I felt. I could hear people scurrying around below, up and down the stairs.

When I came, he went, but not before he piled the quilt back over me, framing me with it. "Better now, Willy?"

"Better."

I watched him stretch up, reach down for his toes, grunting.

"Got to go on a diet." Strapping. Big. Overweight, yes. A happy bear of a man. Life-loving. The feeling was infectious. Sometime during the night, while I slept, I had caught it.

A stretch up. A reach down. Grunting. Three. Four. Five. Six. "Good enough." He switched on his bedside radio, WQXR. "*O terra addio, addio terra, addio . . .*" He tousled my hair. "Don't be afraid. None of this hurts, does it?"

"No. Only when I think about it. . . ."

"The gin . . ." I mumble, but I am about to begin my approach to the distinguished moment. I thrust . . . parry. Thrust . . . to the point of no return.

It goes off.

More than it comes, it goes.

I begin to slide down the trunk of the live oak. Owen, kindness itself, helps me land lightly. He assumes the lotus position before me, leaning closer, ever closer until I feel his face burrowing into the voluminous folds of my ill-fitting khaki shirt. We sit that way, allowing a silence to grow, to connect us for those moments. Something in each of us has been comforted, eased, for the moment.

And then, coming from what seems a great, great distance, we hear voices calling. We separate. "Ow-wen . . ."

"That will be Oveta," he whispers.

And, then, "Will-hee?" Sam. I rise cautiously, smoothing myself into what I hope will be some semblance of order.

Owen says for me to go. He will stay put. I should just mosey on out of the darkness and back up to where they are.

They are on the second-floor veranda. I see them before they see me, Oveta and Sam, clinging close together, her yellow hair aglow all over Sam's shoulder. They call again, "Ow-wen?" "Will-hee?"

I approach, poking a precarious path among bodies I discover underfoot, pairs of bodies mostly, joined, but spent. The fun was over. The drifting music had become Johnny Ray, crying again. Oveta has hold of something, something she pulled at vigorously, something which seems to pin Sam to his place. Sobering, such a sight.

I dash for cover under the veranda, posing against the side of one of those fake Corinthian columns that make up the facade of the manor.

The moon breaks through a scud of clouds. A luminous moon. The moon became Electra.

I saw a streak of white dancing, a spirit, Ariel, dancing out there at the furthest corner of the lawn—but then the scudding clouds covered the moon. If the dancing continued, there was no one who could see it.

And then, anyway, Judy Garland began singing inside, "You

130

Made Me Love You." Nostalgia froze the flow of blood to my brain. I remembered more and more. I wanted to remember.

With Bernice Rosenbaum, dancing to "You Made Me Love You" had to be done in the darkness of the living room in her house. Didn't matter if her mother and father were drinking tea out in the kitchen. As soon as she put the Dick Haymes recording on her fancy new phonograph, out went the lights, and on went our dancing shoes.

And when we danced I was supposed to enjoy her singing in my ear. I was supposed to find her heavy breathing in my ear sexy and romantic. I didn't. Because when the record came to its end and she turned on the lights again, she would always tell me, "It's the truth, Willy, I didn't want to do it. You made me. You won me over. You weren't my type. Too quiet. I like to laugh more—but you made me love you. You really did."

Once I asked her why she thought it was necessary to tell me that all the time?

"Because I think it will make you feel happy to hear it." She meant that. She was hurt that I would ask. Bernice didn't have a mean bone in her body, her very petite body onto which were attached oversized breasts. Her breasts were her most striking feature, those and her flowy, thick wavy hair. Piles of hair that tended to cover too much of her narrow, long oval face. Bernice, in her best moments, looked a little like Loretta Young. Just a little, because her expression, her almost constant expression, tended to be simple, even, at times, simpleminded. But guileless. Yes. Definitely guileless. She didn't know from irony when she told me how I had made her love me, she didn't want to do it. She didn't know what ironic was all about. I didn't explain it. I never asked her that question again.

I asked myself. I also asked myself some other relevant questions, the most relevant one being why had Bernice Rosenbaum become my steady girlfriend? Or, put the other way, why, once she knew she didn't want to do "it," had she allowed me to

131

make her love me? The least complex answer shamed me to the quick: every sixteen-year-old had a steady girlfriend/boyfriend. I had both. So why, after a few dates during which I could tell she was never going to do "it," why did I persist?

Because I wasn't sure. I wanted to be one-hundred-percent sure. The scientific method: try both, then decide. I thought I believed that. I was a senior then at Samuel J. Tilden High School. So was Bernice. We had started to date when we were juniors. I had even taken her to the junior prom. At the Bal Tabarin in Manhattan (long since gone, the Bal Tabarin, and with it junior proms), we drank gin rickeys and ate all manner of unkosher food. I used up a month of my bookshop salary trying to get her to want to do "it" that night. I even took her on one of those hansom cab rides through Central Park at sunrise, trying. No, Willy. Don't, Willy. No. We arrived back at her house on Linden Boulevard in time to have morning coffee with her mother and father and older brother, Melvin.

After the prom night, habit held me close to Bernice, kept me dancing. The furthest I ever got was to stroke and gently squeeze her oversized breasts. She liked that. And she loved Dick Haymes. She loved singing into my ear how she didn't want to do "it."

I should have insisted, been more aggressive.

When we danced and she semi-accidentally kneed me to make sure I was hard—which I was—I should have undone my fly and taken her passionately right there in the dark of the Rosenbaum living room with her parents sipping tea out in the kitchen. I didn't.

I just kept on dancing, pressing hard against her breasts, and going out on double dates with my best friend Jerry Saperstein and his steady girlfriend from Tilden, Rhoda Yellin. And, most of the time, after I left Bernice, and Jerry left Rhoda at her house on Church Avenue and Fifty-fifth Street, Jerry and I would meet and walk home together. Jerry lived two blocks away from where I lived. Jerry and I jerked off together. We had, actually, done a lot more than that. Actually, Jerry thought we should give up spending our money on Bernice and Rhoda and spend it on ourselves. He thought we should go into Manhattan, to a hotel where we could really have a good time together. Jerry felt we should be more than best friends.

When I asked him what he thought we should be, he didn't know any word to explain it. Neither did I—and not until I had sex with a woman was I going to seek any. It was one thing for Jerry and me to do what we did together. Every guy did that. True. Jerry didn't argue that case. He had a stronger one. Not every guy, Jerry suggested as we walked the dark, familiar streets of our neighborhood at one A.M. or two or three, most guys hadn't worked in a bookshop in Times Square from the time they were fourteen and a half, summers, weekends, holidays; most guys hadn't had the freedom to just call home from work to say they were going to a show at Radio City or the Roxy or the Paramount or to a Broadway Theater or to stand in line for a ticket to the Metropolitan Opera. Most guys didn't do those things, "and most guys we know don't do some of the things you did when you *didn't* go to those shows but only said you did. You know they don't, Willy. You said so yourself. You've even told me what you did. And all I'm asking is for you to do it with me."

I never said anything like *love* to Jerry Saperstein. I never lied to him. I liked him too much to lie to him. And I *had* told him those things that had happened to me, things that, I had to admit it, didn't happen to most guys we knew, played ball with, went to Chinese restaurants with. I told him about the first man I "went to bed" with. The man had spoken to me after the performance of *Salome* at the Metropolitan. A legendary performance; a legendary night in my life: Ljuba Welitsch, and then a man who lived down in the Village, on Grove Street. He was about thirty. I was fifteen and a half. I was frightened but I enjoyed what he did to me and what I did to him. I didn't feel guilty or dirty or desperate. I felt, after that first time, free and

133

relieved, relieved to know that what I felt, others felt . . . and did. That winter before my sixteenth birthday I fell in love with my life, not with anyone in particular. On paydays I loved buying books at cost, Gide and Chekhov's plays, Sartre and Camus, *War and Peace* in a deluxe edition. I loved treating myself to oyster stew at Toffenetti's, which was just down the street from the bookshop. I loved the night I saw *The Glass Menagerie* with Laurette Taylor. I had gone alone, but I wasn't lonely, not in New York City, not in 1945 and 1946, when World War II ended.

And not in Brooklyn either. Weeknights, Jerry Saperstein and I would meet, no matter the weather, and take long walks on the deserted streets of our neighborhood, our talk turning to those unknown distances we would travel to in the future, those exotic experiences our so-far-limited lives kept us from. We believed, oh how we believed, that all we wanted to happen to us would happen eventually, perhaps sooner than our imaginations could perceive or know. When it got too cold or if it snowed or rained and his family was home and my family was home, we would sit in the lobby of his apartment house mapping out our strategies. First of all, Bernice and Rhoda, as good as they were, as sweet and decent as they were, had to go. Instead of all the elaborate double and triple and quadruple dating we did, instead of stickball and kick-the-can and Johhny-on-the-pony, instead of those lousy Chinese restaurants on Church Avenue with the gang, instead of those boring parties where everyone ended up with blue balls, we should, we could, be doing things we wanted to do, not the things we thought we had to do to be one of the guys. Fuck that! That should be over with. We weren't kids anymore. We knew who we were and what we wanted. Jerry wanted me to want him. But that *I* didn't want to do. I didn't want to do it.

I?

I just wanted to wait . . . for some sign, from, "out there," I would tell Jerry, waving my arm through the darkness to point it at a direction, at a place . . . unknown, because, "What the fuck am I now? Nothing yet. Nothing . . ." And no matter how much Jerry would try to convince me otherwise, I knew I had miles to go before I could even begin to approach being what I dreamed of being. And, even then, what could I hope to do when I got there? "I'm not exactly heroic-looking." "Neither is Frank Sinatra, but he's got . . . something." Jerry thought I looked like Frank Sinatra. I wore my hair in a pompadour. I was thin. I had, "his eyes. They bring out deep feelings in . . . people, your eyes," is how Jerry put it. What I saw when I looked at myself in the mirror was that my eyes seemed to bring out pimples—but I *could* sing. I had a nice voice—Bernice had told me that, so it had to be true.

And then winter was spring and then summer and autumn and I had the opportunity to graduate from Tilden a semester earlier by doubling up on junior and senior English, which I loved doing. I took the entrance exam for City College Uptown and passed it and it was February 1947, I was seventeen, and every Monday, Wednesday, and Friday at eight A.M. I had Ancient History to read for instead of spending evenings walking with Jerry or dancing with Bernice. I had Latin to study and Physics and a survey of Calc and Trig to loathe. Gym and Public Speaking and Freshman Comp were the only classes I deigned to like. The rest was . . . silence. I wanted to be filled up with the Romantic poets, the Metaphysicals, with Joyce and Yeats and Eliot, with "dappled things" "unleaving," and with Auden, with *The Age of Anxiety*. I rode the subway from Brooklyn up to City College and back to Brooklyn, reading, reading, reading. Dreaming too of breaking it with Bernice and Jerry and leaving Ancient History and Latin, Physics and Calculus, of making enough money at the bookshop to get out on my own, to get out from under, to fly away from pictures of the atomic bomb aftermath, pictures of the Holocaust, from proof of man's continued inhumanity to man. I would go to . . . to . . . Tierra del Fuego.

But when I got home, my mother told me that Jerry had called and so had Bernice and dinner would be soon, as soon as my father got home from the office. My brother was in our shared room doing his homework, NYU homework, his sophomore year of homework. I sat at my desk and tried to concentrate on the Fertile Crescent—but that was decidedly not it at all. I wanted for it to be Friday so I could be at the bookshop until midnight. I wanted to be in Times Square and, after work, to go searching. . . .

A shuttlecock through time, my mind. "Siftings on siftings" of stored-up sensations in free fall. Inside each of us, like rings inside a tree trunk, all the selves we ever were, stored . . . until our ending . . .

Leaning against a fake Corinthian column in Electra, Texas, I wait for my name to be called out again. It will mean it is time for Sam to seek me out, to take me back to Wanderer Street.

And there he is. Coming up behind me, I feel him before I see him and into my eager ear he whispers, "One of the helmeted revelers has graciously offered to drive us home."

Not so subtly, I inch back, my senses having left me in desperate need of present warmth. Perhaps he will take pity and wrap his strong, capable arms around me.

"Why, V'lodya! I would have thought you had had a sufficiency this evening." And, instead of taking *me*, he took hold of my elbow, as usual.

O life! Rejected by some; accepted by others, never by Mr. Right. Is that my fate? Will there never be peace and harmony in the valley, Huck, honey? . . . Well, at least I wasn't *pulled* off. The mere thought!

Sam hands me into a pickup. A fresh breeze, driving. Dark scudding clouds—dark on dark—break open. Moonlight silvers the blacktop.

We are back on Wanderer. Sam tells Mr. Helmet how ever-so-thankful he is, how ever-so-drunk his friend is . . . we watch the pickup pull away. And, since we have moonlight, Sam directs us down the street.

The blacktop ends a short distance beyond the Tolan house, out in front of a house that appears to be empty. Rotting front steps. Tangled growth. Sam follows my glance, stops us. "Used to be the Johnsons lived there. Deron Johnson . . . my best friend growing up. Before Oveta and Owen and Miss Amanda Ogilvie, the librarian. Johnsons were colored. . . ." We resumed our walking, Sam hunching closer, snaking his arm down my back, holding me to him. "When I was very young, Daddy'd walk me down here and once-upon-a-time me, telling me about the bridge and how it caved in and how the water just dried out to a trickle and then there was none. Dust-bowl days that was. Snakes came to sun in it then. Daddy told me how to take care if a rattler was there and I was alone. A forked limb would hold a rattler's neck. Got so I couldn't have cared less about rattlers or anything else. I'd just come on down here after school with my books from the library and read in the sun until Mama had to come find me. Wasn't anything I didn't try to read. Miss Ogilvie'd let me check out just about anything I had a mind to. I'd make myself understand it. Lots of poems I'd memorize once I liked them enough. I'd say them for Deron. . . ." His voice trails off. We have arrived at the stony hard crust of what was once the shore's edge. Now, what a falling away was there. A path, bare in the moonlight, crosshatches its way right down to where the rocks are. "See those steps, Willy? Deron and I kind a made them happen. Deron and I'd go down to a spot . . . but that's for another time's telling. Tonight it's sisters' night at the riverbottom. Blanche and Stella's night out." He stares directly into what must be pearls the moonlight makes of my eyes.

"Is that what you think the Fates decree? Sisterhood?"

"It's what we're best off being. Lasts a lot longer than sex." Standing there by my side, looking down, he draws me up close. The moonlight stings my eyes. Tears spring into them. I'm drunk enough not to care, drunk enough to say, "I don't want to go away . . . from you." I lean in closer, up against him, so he can feel what I'm feeling: a deep-down, let-loose, drunken longing.

137

He pats my back. "Now, now. It'll be all right in the morning. You'll see, honey. Your going away will be for the best. . . ."

In the morning it was not for the best, not inside my head it wasn't. A fire alarm in there. Sam brought me some coffee. "They've gone to church. I told Mama I had to watch out for you so I got pardoned. You up to some breakfast?"

"Never want to eat again."

"Good. Get dressed and I'll take you walking. Some things I want you to see before we have to leave. No telling if you'll ever come back up here, is there? Besides, the air'll do you good."

The air did help some. The big open view of sky helped even more. Perspective returned. Autumn fields. A freshening breeze. Not cold. Not hot. Right enough to ease all sorts of pain, to quiet longings of the flesh—if not the mind. Melancholy rose up, rushed along the edges of the scudding clouds. So did bits and pieces of the night before. "O my dear, O my dear . . ."

Sam took me first to meet Miss Amanda Ogilvie. It being Sunday, the Electra Free Library was closed but Sam knew she'd be there and that she would be more than happy to see Sam. Ecstatic is what she was; responding to Sam's knocking, seeing who was there, she flung the door open, took hold of his shoulders, pulled him up close. "Made my day, you have. You come right on inside here. You too," meaning me. Dazed by the sun and hangover-hurt, my movements were slow motion and Miss Amanda's were speeded up. We collided. She laughed a trill of tee-hees, her reed-thin fingers rushing up to cover her buck teeth. She blushed, and then, her laughter subsiding, her hand flew to the back of her head, to the neatly braided silver-gray bun back there. She flattened it, squeezed it, palmed it, let go of it only long enough to move us closer to her desk where she seemed to see a speck of something alien on its dark wood surface. "Just been polishing it, Sam. A Sunday chore, you remember. You always did enjoy visiting with me here on Sundays. Helped me straighten the stacks—but please excuse me, young man, your name is?"

By then my eyes had grown used to the dim light. I introduced myself. She took hold of my offered hand, shook it warmly, sat me down in a rush-bottomed chair on one side of her desk, pointed for Sam to take the sister chair on the other side of it. Miss Amanda retired to her rocker, bending her enormous height with ever so much grace to fit its delicate proportions. With her hen-high breasts and a gull face, Miss Amanda was mesmerizing. Her pale gray eyes brimmed with a liquid joy as she studied Sam's smiling face. "I had a letter just the other day from one of your admirers, Samuel. Miss Mercedes Muldoon. I always suspected she was a sapphist—not that one thing has anything whatsoever to do with the other. She would stay here some afternoons clear into the nighttime, bothering me so she did. Remember how I used to tell her she should tackle Henry James?" Her laughter broke freely. Again her hand went through its fugue of tics, this time ending on the lace collar of her mauve crepe shirtwaist dress. It needed no straightening. Neither did its mother-of-pearl buttons need fingering. "I mean no malice, but that image of Mercedes tackling Mr. Henry James . . . why Samuel you know I mean no malice." He nodded, his green eyes dancing with devilish delight. They were like young lovers, the way they stared so deep into each other's eyes. I envied that connection, needed a touch of something like that to soothe the stabbing thoughts of those faces so far away that might have comforted me through this, my morning of melancholy. "Do you know, William, that Samuel here holds the record for the most books checked out since the library was opened in 1928? I know because I have always been librarian. Old man Murchison gave the money for it then . . . for my salary too—but you don't know the Murchisons, do you, young man?"

"I know Owen . . . and Oveta."

"They're all that's left. I expect Samuel took you out to meet them. Good friends they all were growing up. But you, Sam . . . you came most every day, faithfully. Libraries are made for people like you. Why I remember I let you check out adult books long before I should have. 'Cept you were mature at ten. So tall then too. So loyal . . . always helping me . . ." She reached across her desk to take hold of Sam's hand.

Embarrassed by their intimacy—not really, but indulging my alien, self-pitying state—I looked away, gazed down behind Miss Amanda at the stacks: row upon row. Books: This is your life, Miss Amanda Ogilvie . . . better than most lives, I'll warrant . . .

"Don't know what it is about you, Samuel, but you could always wind me around your little finger. I do so hate using clichés, yet when they apply—and isn't that another wild image? Me? Wrapped around your little finger, Samuel? Good thing I'm old and ugly because I would surely have made a fool of myself over you." By then she had hold of Sam's chin, her reed-like fingers fluttering all over the cleft in it. "There's not a soul comes to say poetry with me anymore, Samuel. No one. And no one reads aloud anymore either. I do so miss those reading evenings we had." Forgetting me, forgetting herself, she began to recite:

> " O love is the crooked thing
> There is nobody wise enough
> To find out all that is in it . . ."

And, without the slightest pause, Sam continued,

> "For he would be thinking of love
> Till the stars had run away
> And the shadows eaten the moon."

I was surely unnecessary. I stood. No one stopped me. I backed up cautiously, found the door, stepped outside and into the glare of high noon.

Idling, I waited, shielding my eyes to stare off into a blur of nothing much, a far-off stand of what looked to be live oaks, a sudden flash of sumac burning burgundy across a farm field of indecipherable distance. Behind me, inside, Miss Amanda of the

140

stacks held Sam in thrall, the celibate Miss Amanda who probably felt more for others and . . . things . . . than most bodies ever get to feel . . . Miss Amanda, who started Sam thinking those thoughts I loved to hear him say . . .

When he came out he said nothing, just headed us down Main Street in a direction leading away from Wanderer.

I matched my steps to his rhythm, stopping when he did to point out those places he had so far only described: Electra High School, "where, you will remember, I won that infamous type-off which has led to this incipient juncture in our lives, V'lodya"; and then there was McFarlan's Pharmacy, "lots of lemon Cokes I had there, let me tell you. Lots of lemon Cokes with lots of chipped ice. And next to it is Thayer's Hardware. Deron Johnson's brother used to work there. Even more perfect than Deron . . . until my brother Ray and his redneck friends beat up on him. For no reason. Just playing with him. Followed him home from work one night. Jumped him. Broke his arm so bad he couldn't use it afterward. And they all got away with it. I hate my brother Ray. Can hardly bear to look at him. It's what makes Mama go on so. She can't believe her own flesh and blood could've done so mean a thing. . . . The Johnsons moved away after that . . . and I lost Deron . . . my first love. My black beauty . . ."

By then we had walked as far as the Shadowland Theater. *A Place in the Sun* was playing there, matinee at two; evenings at seven. In silence we studied the stills and then passed on by.

Beyond the Shadowland the blacktop ended. Sam kept me walking, beneath a canopy of drooping willows and tall honey locusts. Cool on that path, we walked past Murchison Manor, past the very oak I had leaned against the night before while Owen had his way with me—but then Sam turned me into a brambly thicket, took the lead and found a clearing for us to pass through unscathed and unscratched.

The path ended at the edge of a small pond. All around the pond, except where we stood, swamp maples leaned low, shading the water, cutting off any other way to it. "Oveta and Owen took me here . . . took me skinny-dipping here after school. She was close to twelve then—going on twenty-two. Miss Betty Grable, I used to call her. She had that upswept honey-lemon hair. Frizzed and foamy up front. Pert, doncha know. She'd wear the tightest white shorts and middy blouse. Even then her titties were big and Owen'ud be about hanging out of his underwear. Overdeveloped the both of them. Anyway, no sooner do they lead me in here than they're undressing and sliding into the pond and screaming for me to do the same. . . . Oh what a time they gave me, V'lodya. Such splashings and carryings-on. Owen'ud take hold of Oveta and they'd float side by side, her tits flopping every which way and his prick rising higher and higher, getting as hard as a cucumber. And with his sister, no less. Well . . . I got so hot I just had to join them. We were surely hidden enough; as you can see, the sun can hardly get in here. Flickerings, dit-dottings of it, just as it is now. So beautiful and cool. I remember dropping my Big Smiths . . . always wore Big Smiths then—with a T-shirt and boxer shorts and my scuffy sneakers and white wool socks . . . but what is the point of recalling such details, V'lodya? Just accumulates dust in my head. Serves no purpose whatsoever I can discern, except to show it to you, to tell you all about how when I dropped my Big Smiths, Miss Pert Betty Grable laughs out, 'Why Samuel R. Tolan, what a pretty prick you have. We need you in this water this very minute so you just better get your ass in here.' . . . Oh the oozy cool underfoot. And the two of them so brazen. They owned the world. Owned me. They took hold of me, got me to float between them rushing their hands every which way all over me. Can't ever lose feelings like that. End up measuring all feelings against that. Spoils you for life. . . . First time I ever fucked was with Oveta. In this very pond . . ." He hunkered down, staring into the water as if what he said were recorded there. "Fucked with Owen, too. Lots and lots of times with both of them. I even brought Deron here. Best times we ever had were out here . . . 'I

142

from white and he from black cloud free' . . . I used to say to him. . . . Gone. All that . . ." He stood up suddenly, stretching up, grabbing hold of me, playfully, as if he might just throw me into the water. "I wanted you to see some of my things, Willy. There's more, but there isn't time. Mama will be doing lunch soon. I just wanted another person's memory to take hold of mine. If something were to happen to me, I'd be sure someone would know about this. . . ."

All the way back to Wanderer we said close to nothing. I had so much that was new to memorize. How I would have liked to whisk Sam up to see my Manhattan . . . afterward maybe—if we lived that long . . . then he and I could share the memories of each other's growing up, all very quietly, in time, all unrushed. And, quietly, he would grow into loving . . . me. . . .

Mrs. Tolan was on the porch searching for us. We were late, according to Mr. Tolan's railroad wristwatch, and Brother Ray was using that as a reason for his not staying for the meal. He just rushed by us without so much as a grunt. Mrs. Tolan's sighs were heart-stabbing, cross-to-bear kind of sighs.

But the meal she served out showed no signs of suffering. Some time between coming home from church and then, when we took our seats, she had baked corn muffins and puff biscuits so we would have something to soak up the gravy from the roast beef. And there were fresh green beans and a tangled kind of squash I had never set eyes on before. We all fell to, Mr. Tolan finishing first because "I got some business out back. Septic tank's acting up again, Sam. Y'all excuse me. . . ."

"Need any help, Daddy?"

"No, son. Help your mother clear. You take William out onto the porch, Susanna."

Susanna blushed. Being so blond, so febrile, so shy, the rush of feelings were reflected one by one on the fair skin of her fine-featured face. A Laura-like face, with skin as smooth as glass and about as susceptible to breaking, I thought, standing, offering her my arm. That about undid her. I imagined myself a Gen-

143

tleman Caller, but she hadn't the least idea what I was up to; Sam did. He calmed her, handed her to me, smiling his most winning, green-eyed smile.

We went out to the porch glider. After four o'clock by then. All signs of my hangover had vanished. My melancholy had settled into resignation, what with the walking tour Sam had taken me on, and now the creaking glider, the sun westering so that its rays slanted long columns of rose-red tinted light through the waving fronds of the chinaberry. A lovely breeze, not too busy, not busy enough to raise any dust down Wanderer where the blacktop ended. A weary, bluesy West Texas breeze, A "trouble in mind" kind of breeze. Unfortunately, I had no chewing gum to offer Susanna—which, as a proper Gentleman Caller, I should have had. Nor did I have any properly inspiring words about my future to offer up. She blushed. We glided. We listened to the breeze rush through the chinaberry fronds. We heard Sam and Mrs. Tolan talking, dishes clicking, being stacked, the silverware planging . . . a mournful sound.

Back in Brooklyn my mother and father would be doing . . . what? Reading the Sunday *Times*? Or maybe my sister and brother-in-law and my nephews would be visiting, or my brother and sister-in-law and, soon, my mother would be going out to the kitchen to fix a pickup kind of meal, it being Sunday and nothing much in the house except Friday-night leftovers. Maybe some gefilte fish, a little chicken soup, pieces of pot roast, and she could always improvise with potatoes, pancakes probably, and then tea and homemade cake and pie; always some of that. I could have been telling Susanna all that—but the language would have sounded foreign and, anyway, there wasn't to be enough time because there came Mrs. Tolan and Sam to tell us dessert was on and there was coffee, "if you take that. We're tea drinkers here. My English heritage."

"We are in our house too. My father's from Russia. They drink tea in Russia."

But she didn't seem to care one way or another. She wanted us back to table because Mr. Tolan was already seated there and waiting.

There was a fresh lemon meringue pie, some leftover apple, and a latticework crust on a peach. I had lemon. The Alp-high peaks of toasty meringue seduced me. Nor was I disappointed. Even better than my mother's—but I thought it would have been a betrayal to say so. I asked for a second slice.

Mrs. Tolan beamed.

Sam said, "I'm afraid we're going to have to get ready, Mama. Willy's leaving for Georgia first thing tomorrow and we'd better get back to camp earlier than later."

Mr. Tolan drove us back to the highway. Sam and I rode the back of the pickup; Mr. and Mrs. and Susanna scrunched together up front.

No production number good-byes. Waves and a "Pleased to meet ya." Not much more. Mr. Tolan revved and away they went, driving into a fiery sun.

Next morning, early, there we were: on the shore of our first meeting; Sam inside, me outside the screen door up at battalion.

I was a member of an assemblage of six. A Corporal Busbee would be in charge all the way to Camp Gordon. Orders! It was all happening too fast. I never even saw Sam's shadow disappear from behind the screen door.

Corporal Busbee, late of Able Company and before that Korea, took my measure: ordered to lift my duffle bag and to step out smartly, my ankle folded under me, doncha know. . . . And where was Sergeant Heebler? "They flee from me that sometime did me seek. . . ."

CHAPTER
3

Pacing up and down the crumbling concrete platform of the Temple, Texas, train station, Corporal Busbee rendered unto us his version of our travel orders. He kept us behind duffel bags, at parade rest—"an' we git ta N'yah-leeeens, you fuckers fuck wit' me, ahma gon' bust you balls ta pellets. Hee-yah?" The whole wide world could "hee-yah." "Ah bin to Ko-ree-ya an' ah got me one mo' monf ta discharge. Ah aim to git da fuck back up to good ole Birmingham alive. So you fuckers better not fuck wit' me. Which one you are, Soldier?"

"Howards." I suppose my eyes had been wandering.

He reapplied his concentration to the printed pages, looking for me on them, I surmised. As big as a side of beef before dressing. And with beady eyes. Reading required a mustering of magic, an incantation: "Fuckin' shit . . . shit, piss, crap . . ."

And while he prayed, my peripheral vision leaped from the platform, raced the thirty-odd miles back down to the fort, spied Sam . . . doing his typing proper by then for sure. . . . "Eyes front, Soldier. You supposta be at parade rest!" The eternal return: reality. But, hold on there, my neighbor to the right is smiling *with* me. A friend? Not of Dorothy's—but a friend? Perhaps. Dark hair . . . curly, ever-so, and in some perplexity . . .

"Says hee-yah you from New York, How-itz."

"And so I am, Corporal. Is that illegal?" Why not sass him? What worse fate can await me than the fate I'm facing?

146

"Doncha fuck wit' me, How-itz."

"Never, Corporal. A promise . . . can we smoke?"

"You can fuckin' A do what ah tell ya ta do. You fuckin' smartass city fuckers ain't tellin' me nothin'. Ah known me some New York Cittee pricks ova ta Ko-ree-ya . . . flat-ass dead. Dumb sonofabitch bastid ki—"

He stopped himself. Must have spied my boot sliding back, making ready to kick him in the balls. Better the stockade in Fort Hood than a lonely cot in a lonely barracks somewhere in the loneliest corner of lonely Georgia. Fuck Busbee. Fuck the army. Fuck every Christian hypocrite I came near from now on. Busbee was looking into my eyes. He saw my aim in them. He actually backed down, the racist, cocksucking . . . no cocksucking was too good to waste on the likes of him. . . . "Stand at ease," he went on to say, "smoke if ya got 'em."

First, Bob Youngfelt introduced himself: ". . . from nowhere, Minnesota." Big blond. Babyish and aw shucks. And there was Peter Stein from Grand Bluff, Nebraska: "Yes, my father's the Merchant Stein." Next came George Cartwright, a lanky lout, distant kin to Busbee's clan, who grunted. Didn't really care about meeting me. And last, there was he-who-had-smiled! "Anthony di Carlo . . . Troy, New York . . ." Smooth, the skin of his palm. A pale olive all his skin. Brown eyes. Serious. Tightly coiled black curls close to his scalp. A classic Roman, the nose, very, but with something off-center, a bump, midway down: the only flaw in an otherwise simple, awe-inspiring perfection. For whatever reason, he lingered over our handshake . . . and just when I was in mourning.

He also lingered beside me on the train down to New Orleans where we had a four-hour layover and where Busbee made us check our duffel bags over to the K-T train station, from where, he went on to say, he would march us over to a cafeteria at the foot of Canal Street after which he would march us back to the station to wait for the train that would take us to Camp Gordon. Well, I never. "Meaning no offense, Corporal, but I know a restaurant in the Quarter a friend told me about. I plan to eat there.

I plan to get my money's worth—which according to the orders I received included sufficiency for a decent meal."

"You go off on yo own, How-itz, you ass gon' be in a sling time we get to Gordon."

"Ah, well, Corporal, life always costs us something. Besides, by then, I will have New Orleans to remember for a lifetime." If I had had a mantle blue, I would have twitched it. In any case, I sashayed away, all very macho-like, of course, but playing Blanche Dubois in my head as she dissolved in the steam near the train.

I walked my way over to Jackson Square Park, passed up the cathedral in favor of a stroll beneath the wrought-iron balconies of the Montaldo Apartments and across the French Market with its view of the barely rippling Great Brown River. Yes, alone—but only Sam would have been right to share it with.

I retraced my steps, headed for the Quarter and the Court of Two Sisters, where Sam had said to go for the shrimp Creole and where who should be waiting for me but Youngfelt, Stein, di Carlo, and, much to my surprise, Cartwright. I had told di Carlo where I would be going, because he had asked; only for that reason. I hadn't brazenly volunteered the information. I meant only to encourage his display of a very human emotion. I thought of it as camaraderie. That was all. And I hadn't asked di Carlo to come looking for me. It was he who had managed to lose Busbee in a bar on Bourbon Street.

It was he who followed me—leading the others—to our lovely table: al fresco, beneath a massive willow.

We began with a sour, but switched the next round to bourbon straight up, just one rock. "For purity's sake," I suggested, in a celebratory mood, but uncertain what there was to celebrate other than the existence of Tennessee Williams because only Sammy's presence could have made the moment purer. A melancholy pleasure, those limbo hours: an in-between, the sun dappling the slate underfoot with polka dots, swaying polka dots when the slight, warm breeze blew through the tree's heavy limbs, clicking their leaves. Aye me! Bourbon blessed us all, I mused, silent, content to be among this company until Peter Stein, merely being civil, began to ask civil questions concerning who was who and what we had been before we were soldiers, Peter taking the lead by saying that he was his father's son: he would take over the Grand Bluff Dry Goods; he planned to marry soon, on his first furlough, which he hoped would be at the completion of radio repair school.

And then Bob Youngfelt from nowhere, Minnesota, felt as how the one thing he knew he wouldn't be doing soon was settling down—"too horny for that. I was hoping they'd ship me to Europe. Maybe just stay on there. Got too many brothers and sisters home for anyone to miss me much. . . ."

Cartwright meowed about pussy here, pussy there—"but best of all's my pussy back home in Columbus, Georgia."

Which brought all eyes to rest next on the flushed face of Anthony di Carlo. What of him? "Far on the ringing plains of windy Troy," what? He had a *premonition*. The word popped out—for my ears alone—because he leaned toward me then, and then just as quickly away, to say how he expected he'd go on back to Troy because he'd been promised by his mother to marry the daughter of the woman in the next bed to his mother's, "when I was born. Isobel and I, we grew up together. My mother wants it. Her mother wants it. So we'll just get married. Might as well. And what about you, Willy? Who you got?"

Before that morning di Carlo's path and mine had never crossed. He was in Charlie Company. Said he'd never much gone down to the PX, never up to Dallas. Wrote letters home is what he did. "So who you got, Willy? You dint say yet?"

I still *dint* say. Instead, I ripped the tail off a tomato-bloodied shrimp. "I used to have a Bernice Rosenbaum." And a Jerome Saperstein. A Harlan Royce. "Now I write to an Amelia del Viso." Which was a lie. Amelia and I had stopped seeing each other just before I was drafted . . . and then I had met Sam Tolan. . . .

"You drunk, Willy?" Anthony had a way of leaning toward me, as if to make it perfectly clear he really wanted to talk to me, that he had things to say to me he knew I would understand. I thought that—or perhaps I was really drunk. And if so, I wanted to be drunker. Years of knot-in-the-throat repression rose up and out onto this table for all to see. Fuck the consequences. Once and for all I, too, want to sit on honest ground! I looked into his serious brown eyes. So intense his gaze. "I have a . . . premonition, Anthony. I have a premonition I'm going . . . to get drunker." My flash of self-possession guttered.

"If you do, I'll watch out for you."

I had learned never to depend on the kindness of strangers. But perhaps just this once more.

After lunch I led them to a dark bar called Jean Lafitte's in Exile. On Sam's list. Empty and sad. From there to Pat O'Brien's where one could sit on the sill of a window opened to the street. We ordered pousse café. I thought we were of good cheer, but then, for no ostensible reason, Cartwright took out after me. My guard was down. The army had dissolved. Slow-motion time inside. Drowsy afternoon. Sweltering and sticky and drunk I surely was. So, too, was Cartwright, which seemed to raise visions of his "pussy up in Columbus." "Don't," is all I said at first, hovering there, as it were, on the windowsill, staring out at nothing very much. Too hot for any passing parade. "Don't," I seemed to repeat it, not wanting his images of pussy and tits to intrude on the still-point scene beyond the windowsill. But, having said *don't*, I found myself saying more: "Doesn't she have a face and hair? And eyes and lips?" And then I saw di Carlo's broken-nose profile move between me and a . . . blur: Cartwright had left his bar stool. "What the fuck's eatin' at you?" My Trojan warrior blocked the view of Cartwright, which encouraged me to say more, "Is your *pussy* a sump to fall into or is she human?" Why try reason in an unreasoning world! Cartwright's hand shot out over di Carlo's head, took hold of my khaki tie, pulling it tighter. Cartwright was lanky; di Carlo was

150

quicker, nimble, a fighter. Two heads shorter, he had nevertheless assumed the boxer's stance. At the ready! My defender! My
knight errant . . .

And then there was Youngfelt taking hold of Cartwright's
right arm, Stein his left, and then the bartender barked out a
command to "Beat it, boys. Too hot for trouble . . ."

I remember Cartwright cursing all the basic kike curses all the
way over to the K-T station. I remember feeling as if I were
floating freely before him, steady as we went, keel breaking the
waves cleanly, evenly, Cartwright following in our wake.

And then Busbee, close to falling-down drunk himself, asked
di Carlo to assume leadership. Which he magnificently did. I
remember his struggling with two duffel bags. I remember the
steaming train and the window seat he sat me down in. I remember his saying, "Try and close your eyes and sleep."

I did as he bid, my heart overflowing with gratefulness, my
head spinning, spinning, spinning.

When I awoke, I awoke to darkness, and, at my ear, *clickety-
clack, clickety-clack.* I felt more than a mite queasy and cold. I
seemed to be burrowing into some sort of curved surface over
me. I could not account for any detail in the sequence of events
that had led me to wherever in hell I had gotten to.

On a train . . . in an upper berth . . . where else?

And what else is *clickety-clack . . . clickety-clack . . .* echoing
back . . . and a forlorn whistle . . . but the loneliness of the long-
distance train? Ah, yes, I recall it all . . . even to the moment
when I would or wouldn't throw up.

Would I now? Would I not? Will-hee? Won't-hee?

A clanging out there . . . fierce . . . near to my ear. Going by
. . . *awang—awhoosh* . . . away . . .

And in my breast, *"ein messer,"* slicing clear to the soft center
of my most recent shameful dissimulation: at lunch, in the case
of Bernice Rosenbaum. . . . I want to tell the truth. I want to tell
the truth, the whole truth, and nothing but the truth, all the
time, to everyone, about myself, about how I have had to live by

151

hiding the truth, by having to, because, when I did tell the truth, that once, to Amelia del Viso, the truth did not set me free . . . not exactly. . . .

 " 'I ran . . . all did . . . all ran and gathered about the terrible thing at the edge of the lake. . . .' "Jessica Tandy, as Blanche Dubois, says those words. Amelia del Viso mixes her fingers with mine on the armrest between our seats at the Barrymore Theater.

I think: Amelia must know, and she understands . . . about me. She is not disgusted, as Blanche is saying she is disgusted, disgusted by what she has seen her husband doing. . . .

Afterward, I tell Amelia, taking the initiative, I have to talk to her. I have to tell her something important. Will she go to the Childs Restaurant beneath the Paramount Theater?

Yes . . . but, as soon as we are seated, I lose my nerve. I stare off at nothing at all, feeling done in before I start out, because where do I begin? And how should I suppose?

Amelia smokes, never really inhaling, letting the smoke ooze out of the side of her mouth. The smoke rises, veiling her almond eyes . . . green eyes. Peering across. Intensely peering. Waiting, patting the uneven edge of her sandy-beige bangs into imagined straightness. She holds her Pall Mall between the middle fingers of her left hand so that if her mother checks for nicotine stains, she will always check the wrong fingers of the wrong hand. Amelia is right-handed. I'm the one who is a lefty.

"Where are you, Willy?"

" 'Somewhere I've never traveled . . .' "

"Where?"

"New Orleans."

"Why are you there? What are you doing there?" Amelia fingers the edges of her many-colored silk scarf, of greens and yellows and reds on a field of heather. It has been funneled under the collar of a maroon silk blouse. The nails of her fingers have been bitten down to the quick.

152

"I'm drinking coffee . . . somewhere . . . I don't know where it is. Someone is with me . . . laughing . . . *at* me."

"Is it a woman laughing, or a man laughing?"

She knows which it is. Of course she does—and all I have to do is confirm what she already suspects: You and I, Amelia, we're one way, one side of . . . things . . . we're a couple . . . a City College couple . . . in classes . . . in the sun in Lewisohn Stadium . . . on dates—but I'm also part of another . . . coupling . . . or is it tripling? . . . with a man who is soon to be married but who still wants to . . . see me. And who I want to go on seeing. That's the truth, Amelia—and I want to say that. I want to tell her . . . all. "I shall tell her all"—but I don't. I don't say anything.

Which exasperates her. She stubs out her cigarette. "A woman or a man, Willy?" Her almond eyes concentrate on me; they pierce so. They punch holes in whatever is left of my resolve. I don't want to hurt her. Petite, yes, but potent, Amelia confronts, she doesn't settle for cozy compromises. The fact that she is in school at all came because she fought her father. "I will not be your dutiful Italian daughter. I will not go to church, get married, have children—not until I am good and ready." She told all that to her father and she won. She has force. She has style. She is a handsome young woman. Instead of spending his money to send her to Barnard, her father gave her money to buy good clothes. She is wearing a nile green corduroy jacket, nipped in snugly, smartly. Her skirt is tweed, tweed on a field of heather. "I repeat, Willy. I expect an answer."

"A man. An older man. A man old enough to be my father— but he isn't my father."

"I didn't think so. Is he someone you like . . . inordinately?" One of our Henry James words. She is using it to make it more than possible for me to speak with ease. "And he is laughing *at* you, you say. Why would he be doing that? Tell me why?" She is, she has always been, responsive to elaborate circumlocution—but she will not hang fire for too much longer. She circles closer, closer, and closer to the central issue. Her eyes blink fast, opening, closing; her mind is made up: she will not wait any longer. "Rouse your almost blunted will, Willy."

"He is laughing at me because he is someone . . . I like. I might even love him"— There! —"and he wants to discourage me. He thinks love is beside the point."

Calmly, she lights another Pall Mall. "I see. But you? Will you be discouraged from love? From loving him?"

"I don't know. I've never been to New Orleans."

She is not amused. She strikes. "Don't be evasive. Answer the question as I asked it."

"I can't. Honestly. I can't. It's all imaginary. The restaurant. The city. The hypothetical man . . ."

"Hypothetical? Bullshit!" Oozing smoke, she folds her arms across her blouse, crushing maroon silk, leaning back, from the table, from me. "I hate bullshit, Willy. Usually, you do too."

"I do, but the hypothetical man has just told me he is going to be married. How does one . . . how do I . . . make the measurements your question implies? I'm . . . confused. There are no precedents for me to apply. No rules. No laws. I feel alone."

"But you're not. Nor have you been. For months now we've been dancing around each other. Tonight we are going to stop. No more listening to *Songs of a Wayfarer* up in the music library of City College. It's the real thing now. One or another. I'm willing to put my body where my mouth is. Are you?"

"I thought I was."

"And now you think not? You would rather have sex with, not necessarily love from, your hypothetical man? Is that it? And you prefer discouraging me . . . from wanting sex . . . from loving you?"

"I don't know that as the truth. Not really."

"But you're not really acting the way I've known you to act, either. Suddenly, you're being too easy on yourself, too selfish. Anyhow, listen carefully to what I am about to say . . . you do not disgust me. Did you hear me, Willy?"

154

She had reason to wonder. My head had lowered precipitously, much too close to my coffee cup. I felt confounded, bloodied, bowed. I felt disgusted with myself—even if she didn't. Lust is what I should have been feeling, not lost. At eighteen, if lust isn't part of the process of love, then that love has no future. Amelia knew that. I knew that. One sun-drenched afternoon we had sat out in Lewisohn Stadium reading *A Painful Case* to each other. During one of Amelia's turns, we arrived at the famous sentence: "Love between man and man is impossible because there must be sexual intercourse." Then, she had stopped to light a cigarette. We had nodded, then, and she had gone on reading. Now she wanted us to say whatever needed to be said. It was now—or it was never. Friendship would not work. "I repeat, Willy, you do not disgust me. Therefore, I am willing to keep on trying. I want sex *and* love. Do you? Answer that question. Take all the time you want, but answer it honestly. Our lives will be altered by how you answer it."

I didn't have to take my time. I also found the courage to stare up and across at her as I spoke. "I can't say for certain what I want, except I don't want to hurt you or act selfishly. So, I have to say no, no I won't try." In the saucer of her coffee cup she punched out her Pall Mall. And then she gathered up her purse, her suede gloves, buttoned her nile green corduroy jacket. "I want to go home—but I don't want you to take me. You have to be at work early tomorrow morning. I'll see you in school Monday morning. I'll continue to sit next to you in class. We'll be polite. Civilized. We may even go up to the music library to listen together. That will be all, except to say I'll never forget the night I saw *A Streetcar Named Desire* with you. Of that, you can be sure."

I wanted to help her into her coat. She waved me back down. More than capable, Amelia. More capable than I. I felt I might be the one to cry. She even leaned down to kiss me. I remember the feel of the tip of her tongue touching mine, ever so briefly. And when I opened my eyes she was gone.

155

I remember paying the check, ascending the stairs back up to and out into a still-busy Times Square, the band of bulbs around the *Times* Building still flashing instant news reports for up-turned eyes to process into facts. Close to one A.M. I watched the blinking bulbs, thinking. I saw that Frank Sinatra would be coming soon to the Paramount Theater. The life-sized poster next to me announced that fact. I wondered, as my mind wandered, what next? After the truth is told? Where to? Loneliness struck. The absence of Amelia would scatter the pieces of that "other way" for me, forever. Over with, that illusion about my being a husband and a father. Because, surely, and however weakly, I had managed to segue to the truth. Amelia would go her own way. So would I. More than a year of drawing closer and closer comes to its . . . proper . . . conclusion. Right, with might on its side, wins another round. No, Ma, I will not be marrying an Italian girl. Now everyone will be made happy. Even my battered sense of morality feels salvaged: Amelia will not be *hurt* by what I do or don't or can't do. I will be hurt by me, which, I suppose, is how it has to be. And it will not be easy on myself, Amelia. No. Consequences are always far more complicated than simpleminded rules of right and wrong allow for.

Frankly, I remember feeling relieved. No lying. No more dis-simulation. And, in that spirit of truthfulness, I had to admit that what I wanted more than anything else, just then, was a touch of Harry in the night.

I decided to telephone him. If he gets angry, he gets angry. A pox on me. And besides, it isn't likely he's home. Friday night . . . Glen Cove . . . I screw up my courage to an available place: a telephone booth at the corner of Forty-second Street and Seventh Avenue.

I use the number which will only ring in his bedroom. Since he has given it to me for "emergencies" and since I feel this night's events represent such an emergency, I feel free to proceed. I will awake no one else; nor can I possibly hurt anyone else but myself.

156

He is home. He is not angry. He is welcoming. He has worked late, has sent his mother and sister and Aunt out to Glen Cove on the Long Island Railroad. He will be leaving for there in the morning, and, yes, he would like for me to spend the night with him.

Two by the time I arrive at the Clark Street station.

Two-thirty by the time I am safely and warmly in bed. I want to tell Harry about "what happened," but he stops me, it's too late for that, too late for anything other than some sleep, "and not much of that. You have to be at work early, don't you?"

"By ten." We are facing each other, me inside his arms. He is too big for me to hold him so, so I enjoy his pleasure in holding me. It pleases me too, to feel . . . guarded, protected from . . . what? Reality? Too much reality? And from my confusions, great and small? We lie in the dark of his bedroom, listening to the sounds from outside, the rush of what I imagine must be the river's current, the distant *blang* and *blong* of trafic, of tugs forlornly moaning . . . listening to his heartbeat in my ear, to his calm, easy breathing, deepening, moving toward sex—or sleep? Hard to say, unless I have the temerity to reach down between us to find out. I don't, just then.

Just then, I say, quietly, a word, disconnected from any context of sense—but Harry will understand: "A dilemma."

"Nonsense. No need for a dilemma. Be patient. Everything gets solved."

"Maybe in your life . . ."

"Yours too. You'll see Amelia again—or you won't. You'll meet someone else. Life gets solved. Even for you. It will." But he held me tighter, showing me he felt much more than there was any sense in saying. "Stop thinking so much," he laughed, into my ear, which was another way of showing the same thing. He had said that so many other times when he meant those words seriously, on those once-a-week nights we met and would go to dinner, to a restaurant "friends" had told him about, *friends* being the code word for "don't ask me any questions,"

157

enjoy what we enjoy; the food he ordered, the wines he described, teaching me about them, telling me about a kind of living that might even prove pleasurable for me, "some time . . . soon enough . . . when you're your own man and can afford to pay your own way. . . ." And from whatever restaurant in Manhattan, it was always home to Clark Street where I went first to the western window of his bedroom to peer into the darkness, nervous, until he called me to come to bed, to "stop thinking so much." "Easy enough to say that, isn't it, Harry?" "No it's not. It's not easy for me either. But I work at it, all the time. Nothing's easy for anyone. No one ever told you it would be. So stop thinking so much about what you can't change. Come to bed." I always did. That night I never stopped at the window, but I was thinking, thinking, thinking. Harry felt it, and so, when he laughed into my ear, "Stop thinking so much," more than I ever expected to, more than I could have known I needed to, I loved him. I hadn't lied to Amelia. "Can't you see me more than once a week, Harry?"

His arm-hold went slack. "Why ask now, Willy?"

"Sorry."

"Don't be sorry—but I'll always say no. You're still in school, for Christ's sake. You've got your friends. I've got mine. I work. I'm about to be married. My future is happening to me now. Yours will be coming along soon enough. Better plan it. Better prepare yourself for it . . . or you'll have to take what you get. I've told you that a hundred times. Tonight's no different. Tonight's even worse because you're making it harder on yourself. You've had a tough time. Why not enjoy what you've got right here, now?"

"I'm trying to."

"Don't try. Do it."

"Doesn't seem to work that way for me." Inside the slackness of his arms, however, I didn't have to try. Skin-to-skin every problem inside my eighteen-year-old head seemed solvable, at least temporarily.

158

Once more I felt his breathing in my ear. "Persuade yourself, Willy. Best way. Don't think about anything else for now."

And, for the rest of the night, I didn't.

The next morning, by nine, he was ready to go, out to Glen Cove, to his fiancée's, his mind at peace, presumably. He sat at the edge of the bed, all done up in wide-wale beige corduroy, freshly showered and shaved, ruddy and round, smiling. "Call home before you leave for work."

"You'll make a good father."

"I hope so. I look forward to being one." He took hold of my chin, shaking his head at what he had to see was my confusion. "Don't worry so much. . . ." He let go. "I'll call you. I'll tell you where we'll meet." Heavily, he stood up, lumbered off, waving back, smiling . . . *at* me.

I listened for the front door to slam, burrowing my head into his pillow, smelling his Old Spice, smoothing a circle of dried semen on the sheet.

The telephone was on a shelf next to Harry's pillow.

"Where are . . . are you at work yet?" My mother's careful questioning cut deep. Touching, how she always trusted my version of the truth.

"Not yet, Ma. I'm at my friend's, Harry's. . . ."

"Oh. But didn't you go out with Amelia?"

She knew only names. Amelia was from school; Harry was more of a mystery; from the store: "—guy who comes in to talk books. We've become friends. . . ." She let it go at that. "I did, Ma. Harry was at the play too . . . a coincidence. We all had coffee afterward. It got too late to call you. I took Amelia home and then I went back to Harry's because it's closer to work . . . which I have to leave for . . ."

"You'll be coming home tonight?"

"Yes. Probably by eight. So, if you and Dad are going someplace, go. I'll take my own meal."

"We'll be here. I'll have your dinner ready. Maybe we can talk. Something's on my mind I want to talk to you about."

159

On mine too. And oh, how I wanted to talk about it with her. Lying to her hurt most of all. The longer I did it, the more it hurt. "Fine, Ma. I'd like that too. I'd like it if Dad joined in." "He will. I already asked him."

All that day after my *Streetcar* night, even while I wrapped books and replenished the greeting-card racks and matched Statue of Liberty salt-and-pepper sets for anxious tourists, I rehearsed my speech: *Dearest Mother and Father—you are dearest. I love you—but there is something I have to tell you . . .* I dawdled. I dreamed, and Mr. Braunstein wanted to know, maybe, I was out all night doing monkey business? I should be careful I don't get into trouble. I shouldn't *knock up* some little girl. Mr. Braunstein knew my father, which is how I had gotten the job in the first place, and so when Mr. Braunstein talked to me, I listened, imagining my father speaking—but I could never imagine my father saying *knocked up*. *Shiksa*, he might say—but without caring whether I did or did not marry one. That was my mother's concern. That was what she would be talking to me about when I got home. Certainly nothing about Harry.

Indeed. The subject was *shiksa*.

Very few preliminaries. Barely had the plate of beautiful braised pot roast slices with roasted, browned potatoes and tsimmis been placed before me when there came my father from the living room, trailing his *World Telegram*, reluctantly leaving his easy chair next to the Philco. Reluctance was all over his face. "It's your mother wants this conference . . . but I'm glad you're allowed to eat first." Nervous laughter. "Everybody . . . everyone was here last night for dinner. Friday night, Willy. Only you were missing." Neatly, my father folded his newspaper, took his seat opposite me. My mother, her hand cupped beneath her chin, sat in her usual seat, waiting for my father to proceed. They had rehearsed their strategy.

"I realize, Dad. I know I was missing, but Ma knew I would be. After work, I went to the theater."

"With who, may I ask? That's the question I want answered."

160

Tougher. He had to toughen up because, clearly, his heart wasn't in this interrogation. He wanted his easy chair.

"Why didn't you tell him, Ma? You knew."

"Yes. *I* knew." That's all. Not even looking at me. Rolling challah crumbs back and forth across the stiffly starched white linen tablecloth. Silent. So silent I could hear the scratching of the crumbs.

"Okay, Dad. Let me have it. What did I do?" The direct approach. He would appreciate that. Save time. His. Mine. I was tired. Amelia and Harry and now this, with more dissimulation on its way . . . inevitably. Oh how I deep down wished I had the courage to lay it all out on the table before us . . . among the challah crumbs and horseradish stains. "Tell me, Dad. What is it?"

"What it is . . . it's your mother, not me. I'm satisfied you'll do . . . what you'll do. I won't care with who. You don't do wrong. That I know. If you did wrong, I wouldn't stand for that. Never . . ."

"Sol. Please. We're not talking about wrong."

"Don't *please me,* please. You asked me to talk. Let me handle this my way. . . . Your mother is concerned about your . . . friends."

"Friends? All of them? Or just one, Ma? Just Amelia?"

"Yes. Just Amelia . . . and just because you never talk about her. I'm interested . . . to know about her. I'm interested to talk to you about her. A mother . . . a father . . . should . . . at least talk. Shouldn't they?"

"Yes." Chastened by a few well-chosen words from my indomitably decent mother and supported for the moment—no small achievement—by my always commanding father, I would listen. I would be as reasonable as they were trying to be—and they didn't have all the facts either. Because if my father was angered, he could easily talk me, shout me, reduce me, to sputtering silence. We were trying reason and love; no fights. "Ask me anything you want to know. I'll answer. I promise."

161

"How serious are you with Amelia?—who I don't even know. I've asked you to bring her home for a dinner . . . so we could meet her at least. Why haven't you? Are we monsters, your father and I?" My mother took charge. After all, this meeting had been her idea. My father merely nodded, satisfied with what my mother had gone on to say: "If you are serious . . . then you are. It wouldn't be the first time people of different faiths—"

"I'm not getting married, Ma. Not now. Probably not ever . . . and not just because Amelia and I decided to . . . end . . . things between us. Last night we did."

The hand that had been rolling the challah crumbs came to rest on mine, patting it, making it better, all better. "I'm sorry to hear that, Willy." She actually was, sorry for me—but relieved too. Her small hands, her small features, everything about her small, except her feelings, she wanted me to know she sympathized with how I felt. Her tapping fingers told me how much she did—and now that that was over with, should she make some tea? She had baked a new batch of pinwheel cookies and brownies. She asked nothing else. Nothing about Harry.

My father pushed back from the table, rose slowly, retrieved his newspaper, slowly; everything he did seemed slowed up. Fifty—and slowing down. A hard-fought fifty. No gainsaying it. He had gotten a hand-hold on a rung or two: from self-taught immigrant to executive, and in a gentile company yet! Proud of himself. And why not! Not totally solvent, but with enough money to send one son to a college. For me he had had advice: Get yourself accepted to City College and maybe eventually you can transfer somewhere else, "I'll see what I can save up." Sighing, he slipped the paper under his arm. "I take it you won't be wanting my further service? I'm excused, your honor?" Laughing, his floridly handsome face suddenly and uncharacteristically coy: a young man making eyes at his girlfriend.

My mother actually blushed.

"Call me when the tea's ready." He played with the top of my mother's feather cut, even cupped the back of her head playfully.

Their little playlet was over. They were, for the moment, content.

And I? I ripped a piece of challah to shreds, dropped each shred into the rich brown pot roast gravy, stabbed the shreds with my fork. So much for total truth in a troubled world! My expression reflected, I was sure, young agony; that would be fitting. They expected that. Hadn't I just broken up with Amelia? My mother took hold of my stabbing hand, stopped it: "For the best, Willy. It'll be for the best."

I nodded. I merely nodded.

After tea, I went to bed immediately and on Sunday stayed in it or close to it most of the day, thinking about what I might do to "persuade myself," as Harry had suggested I do and as my mother had suggested, that whatever had happened was or would be "for the best" . . . if I accepted . . . *things* . . . as they were.

But I wouldn't, couldn't. On Monday I went to the registrar's office and applied for an official leave of absence from school. From there I went down to the book shop and told Mr. Braunstein I had to stop working for a while. I wanted to go away. "So? You knocked someone up? That's it. Because if that's it, I'll help you fix it. You'll stay in school, you'll be here for the holiday season. The holiday season I need you, Willy—" "No, that's not it, Mr. Braunstein. . . ."

When I got home, but before I had a chance to tell my mother and father what I had done, Harry called. He wasn't sure he could see me on Wednesday—"maybe next week. I'll call. But things are going to be complicated for a while. I'm getting married on Thanksgiving Day. . . ."

"Congratulations," was all I said about that. And then, "I've got news for you too." I paused to make sure my mother and father were listening; they were. "I've left school. I've quit my job. I'll be going away, so I won't be able to see *you* for a while anyway."

"You're crazy," I heard Harry saying, and all I would say in

163

response was, "Maybe . . ." before hanging up; I didn't have time for more. I had astonished faces to deal with. I had stories to tell. I wanted to take a trip. I had my own money. I'd worked hard to earn it. Therefore, I had a right to spend it "my way. As long as I don't hurt anyone else. You always said that, Ma. Do what you want when you want . . . as long as you don't hurt anyone . . . because there's no guarantee there'll be another opportunity to do it. Your words . . ."

She didn't deny they were. She went to the stove, took hold of it, surveyed the gas jets beneath the pots and pans, making necessary adjustments: her range of operations, wherein all her hopes, all her opportunities had been, of necessity, transformed into a succession of satisfying meals, year after year, years whose inevitable end crept ever closer with each meal.

And my father didn't deny his words about money: "If you earn it, it's yours, and yours to spend how you decide."

It added up. One principle connected to another principle leading to an action whose consequences were mine to experience, and to live with . . . for better or worse. Standing in front of the refrigerator, I watched my mother putter, obviously pained but resigned; and my father fidgeted in his seat at the kitchenette table, his habitual certainty shaken—but he would, as he always had, trust to the curative power of a good, home-cooked meal. "We'll eat, Ruth. Then we can talk."

We did eat, but we didn't do much talking because before we had finished our fish stew, my brother came in from school and he didn't eat fish so my mother had to warm up a completely different meat meal. There wasn't time for talk. My father wanted to listen to his radio programs and read his paper and be left in peace. "You're old enough to know what you want. Probably you'll be drafted soon anyway." And to my mother he said, "He's a man, Ruth. Not your baby anymore . . ."

That was in 1948. I could have been, but I wasn't, drafted then. Then, I went by Greyhound down to Florida, to Tampa and Sarasota. Through the Everglades on the Tamiami Trail to

Miami and the Beach. Halfheartedly I looked for jobs which I never got. Wholeheartedly I looked for sex and that was much easier to find.

Eventually, out of ideas and money, I headed back home; my welcome was unconditional.

Happily, Mr. Braunstein rehired me. 'Forty-nine by then. Spring. I wanted to, but never did, call Harry. Nor Amelia. I saw Jerry Saperstein once in a while. He had become part of a Brooklyn College group. Gay. Circumspect.

In June of '49 Korea began.

September, I returned to City College and lasted for two semesters before I felt the need for another leave of absence, for another trip to nowhere I knew. Up to Canada for a while. Down to Chicago. I bummed around—they used to call it that, then: bumming around. Or, finding yourself. Or taking stock. Whatever they called it, it finally didn't matter because it ended in "Greetings," and my mother's "I told you this would happen," and my father's "It'll be the best thing for you. . . ."

From the induction center at Whitehall Street in Manhattan I was sent up to Fort Devons for a week, and then there was the troop train down to Texas where I met Samuel R. Tolan. . . .

Tentatively, I ran my fingertips along the curve of the dark surface arching over me. Very close up to that arching surface my aching body went on aching. *Clickety-clack. Clickety-clack* . . . in an upper berth. Being an intimate of troop trains, I certainly knew an upper berth when I felt one.

But what of the intimate who had gotten me up into my upper berth? He who had stripped me down to jockey shorts? What of him? My defender . . . "Di Carlo?" I called out softly.

Hardly a moment passed before his face appeared between the heavy velvet hangings fronting the berth. A dim light behind him from the aisle lit outlines—and his tightly coiled curls. "You feeling sick, Willy?"

165

"Cold. This blanket . . ." When I felt for it, I realized there was none, only a sheet. "Where are we?"

"Somewhere in Alabama. It's about two in the morning. You think you'll throw up some more?"

"I didn't know I had."

"Did you ever." He hoisted himself higher. By then the light played along the ridge of his nose, that slightly off-center bump—and then I saw he was smiling, a sweet smile, angelic, My Guardian Angel. "Maybe if I come up there and we talk, you'll feel better." He hoisted himself all the way up, not waiting to be invited.

Cramped quarters. He did his modest best to stretch the length of the berth, on top of the sheet—but he had on a T-shirt and shorts. Very proper. And properly companionable. We were both thin enough—his thin was supple muscle, compact—to fit together up there. I was mostly thin—and bones. Not the most comfortable package to adjust to in cramped quarters. But he wanted to try. For some mysterious reason he wanted to try. "Are you spinning around?" A whispering, cautious, his words close up, popping into my ear explosively.

"Yes. Like the wheels of the train."

"I'll hold you. That'll help." His breath . . . like nervous wind rushing through stripling trees: jittery, jumpy and, then, quiet, a stillness. He turned me inside his arms. His skin burned. And, through the sheet, I felt the hardness of his prick—and mine. All the parts of us met at about the same place. "I just want to hold you like this. That's all. Okay?"

"Okay." Good thing I felt sickly. Good thing the taste in my mouth embarrassed me. Good thing my mother had taught me not to do things if there's a chance of hurting someone—because even being held the way I was by Anthony di Carlo, even though he had a hard-on, even though he had been playing with me all day long, I didn't for a moment feel he wanted anything more to happen in that upper berth. I could hear his heartbeat: steady, unrushed. He really did "just want to hold" me.

166

And I did just want to be held and to fall asleep again.

Eventually, I did, listening to the *clickety-clack, clickety-clack*, echoing back, but once more taking me ahead to somewhere else I didn't know.

Of the five of us from Fort Hood—not counting no-account Busbee—only Anthony and I were assigned to the same training company, wouldn't you know it. Kismet! as some have been known to say about such mysteries. God obviously wanted it that way. God's Will. That's me. Following, wherever I am sent. A servant. A tool of Fate. God's arrangement, not mine.

Fate had brought di Carlo and me to adjoining cots.

Fate had assigned us to the same workbench once the electricity school lab work began.

Fate gave me a new asshole buddy . . . on the rebound—I was, not Anthony.

We learned little about electricity during the instruction period and even less during the work period because then we could talk openly. He told me; I told him . . . what I thought it proper to tell him, given the circumstances. (We were not, nor would we ever be, sisters.)

Back up in Troy, Anthony had two older brothers, three younger sisters, and Isobel Patton, his girlfriend, who was ten minutes younger than he. Their mothers, sharing the same hospital room, had decided, right then and there, that their children would get married some day, that they would grow up going to the same Catholic elementary school, Immaculate Conception, and to the same high school, Our Lady of Perpetual Sorrows. And that's exactly what did happen, Anthony told me, while we both explored the defective circuits of a jeep radio. We were supposed to find the trouble and correct it. Troubleshooting, that was called. Fortunately, Anthony was one of those people who could do more than one thing at the same time. He could heat a soldering iron and tell me how falling in love with Isobel Patton

167

didn't take any effort at all. "She's beautiful-lookin'. And built. Stacked."

"Do you . . . did you have sex?"

"You're kiddin' me? Sure we do . . . did. A lot. And young, too, because we always knew we'd be married and have kids, lots of kids. . . ." He'd get that far and stop because when he talked about *having kids,* my concerns would direct me back to the color schematic we were supposed to be tracing out. Where did the yellow wires lead? And the red? The blue? The white and the black? Methought he protested overly, and over and over, about the *kids.* Skeptical: I felt that. Not doubting his intentions. Just skeptical, about how the prospects he would face really felt inside him, down "certain fathoms deep," because his behavior around and with me certainly didn't fit the perfect picture his words described. Or, maybe I resented being treated as someone safe, someone he didn't have to "go all the way with" because it was . . . against his religion, and because, after all, even if he *thought* of doing *it,* he hadn't, and, anyway, wasn't he going to marry Isobel Patton? One thing he always wanted to avoid talking about was what had *not* happened on the train. And talking kids seemed to bring him back to that and ahead to what kids meant: a life circling a center he was convinced he wanted. "One thing for sure, Isobel and I, we have great sex. Being married's only gonna make it better. You'll see what I mean, Willy. Maybe you'll get back with Amelia. Maybe you'll get married."

"Not for me. No marriage. No kids. No. I honestly don't feel I want that. . . ."

At such an impasse, we both turned our attention to the task at hand: electricity . . . and the romance of its ebb and flow and how it gets generated in the first place.

Anthony enjoyed lectures about theories. He had wanted to go to Rensselaer Polytech, which is what made Troy, New York, important. He had grown up not far from it—"but Italians, they don't get accepted there much. Anyways, we didn't have money

168

for it. So this here, this stuff in the army—maybe I'll go into electricity when I get discharged. . . ." Having said that, he would pick up the schematic with renewed diligence.

We were taught about resistors and impedance; capacitors and farads; diodes and triodes and amperage and frequency modulation. Day after day. Week following week. And right after night, next to his cot, there I was, listening, while he talked and talked about what his life would be like after the army, what it had been like before the army, but never about *now* or about why he kept us isolated, together, from the rest of the guys. Not that that part bothered me. It didn't; dissimulation did. My cowardice did. Di Carlo immobilized me. I didn't want to do anything. I didn't care very much about anything. I longed passionately for only two things: Sammy and/or discharge.

Before sleeping, I would muse on the possibility of madness, of going on sick call one morning and insisting I be allowed to see a psychiatrist. I would tell him I was gay, that being surrounded by naked men day in and day out was leading me to a nervous breakdown. If I wasn't discharged, no way to know what I'd do, what would happen to me—but, by morning, my musings would mist over. Di Carlo would slap my behind and tell me, "Up and at 'em, Willy"—and so much for sick call.

I wrote long, sad letters to Sam.

Sam wrote back, advising me that what I most of all needed was a few weekends in Atlanta:

. . . *alone, V'lodya. Be wise. Private di Carlo does not sound like Mr. Right. Nor does the psychiatrist sound like an answer: he will once more ask you if you love your mother. You will say yes and he will tell you, that's normal. So, try Atlanta, alone. Sister Sammy knows whereof she speaks. For myself, I go on up to Dallas, alone. I go to the Blue Bonnet, stare into the mirror behind the bar and miss you. I do so very much miss you, V'lodya. . . .*

169

I did go to Atlanta. I went alone. Di Carlo questioned why he couldn't come along. "I do things your church doesn't approve of." "Don't do them."

"Do you realize, Anthony, I'm over twenty-one and, therefore, filled with unquenchable longings?" He enjoyed it when I said such things, camping, just as long as no one was nearby. "Jerking off offers no pleasure. You, I can hear you, jerk off, to visions of Isobel, I'm sure. For myself, I prefer my reality." At such moments, I'd let my eyes play all over his body, especially lingering over his crotch. I enjoyed it when he stripped down to his shorts before lights out and sat along the edge of his cot, lecturing me about discipline of the eyes, knowing that he knew what I was doing—and enjoying it. He did. He would lean back, making his crotch bulge and bunch up. Liked to take my breath away . . .

Musing thus and so, three more months of army time passed by with agonizing slowness, a largo of lost days. Reveille. March to school. March back for noon mess. March back to school. March back to barracks at four. Exercise. Dismissal. Shower. Mess. A movie. The service club. The PX. I went to the library alone. Anthony wasn't much of a reader, although he liked to ask me questions about what I read. I liked to tell him. We were asshole buddies. One thing I didn't miss was Sergeant Heebler harassing me.

Every once in a while we met Youngfelt and Stein. Cartwright, they told us, had failed the first two phases of instruction and had been hopped, skipped, and fuckin' jumped over to fuckin' Seoul. Our strategy for returning to Fort Hood remained constant: I would write to Sam at battalion HQ; he would see to our return orders. As long as we all passed the course, Sam would have no problem. He assured me! "I promise, Sister Blanche, I most assuredly do. . . ."

Anthony and I passed Parts and Circuits without any difficulty. Anthony had trouble with Tubes.

During Field Repair, it seemed like he purposely fucked up, doing cold solders, making wrong-color splices, knowing he was and then immediately leaving our bench to show the instructor how wrong he was. I would try to stop him, but that only angered him. I reminded him what was at stake. He knew. He didn't ever forget that. He didn't think he'd ever forget . . . some things. Like what? I would ask. He always answered it was none of my business. But one look at those serious dark eyes avoiding mine, darting off for a depressing view of a drab Camp Gordon vista, and I knew the business going on behind those eyes did, indeed, involve me. How, he wouldn't say. Not in the barracks. Not on any of our evening travels. I asked. I picked and probed. I decided I had a right. It was all my time he tied up, day after day, like a jealous lover—and then, when it became clear he would fail Field Repair, I felt responsible. He would be shipped out. He'd be sent to Korea. It would be on my conscience.

Instead of going to Atlanta, I asked Anthony into Augusta. My treat. The Hotel Bon Air, out near the National Golf Links. A sophisticated spot, to put him at a disadvantage, to make him susceptible, to get him to talk things out. Drinks first. Dinner. I had even reserved a room for overnight, for myself—or for both of us: his choice to make—if it ever came to choices.

A martini for him.

I stuck to my gin mist.

Five P.M. A Saturday, Janaury 17, 1952. (Yes, I wrote it all down. All the facts, in point of fact.)

We wolfed the first round, and, sipping the second, Anthony's awe, of the old wood along the bar, of the thick carpeting underfoot and the sparkling chandeliers overhead, subsided. He began to stare at me and to talk about Isobel. We were in a dark corner of the barroom, in easy chairs on either side of a low, small marble-topped table. The chandeliers gave off a dim, glowy soft light that seemed to smooth that something off-center in his nose. Close to perfect, his face, but more than that, close to perfect inside him as well. Decent and confused. I might add to the confusion, but I hadn't created it. All I wanted to do was ease things, if I could—but he seemed bent on building the barricade

171

of Isobel higher and higher between us. His third martini and my third gin mist changed that.

He said, "Maybe Isobel and I could come down to this hotel for a honeymoon. Maybe I'll put in for a furlough and get married and bring Isobel back down here. You'd get to know her."

"Why do you want me to?"

"So you could see her for yourself. You'd understand better."

"Understand what, Anthony? Tell me what I'd understand."

"You think you know everything, don't you?" He didn't raise his voice, only his glass. He leaned closer over the marble table, getting himself prepared, I hoped, to proceed—but, as he always did, he slumped back and away.

"I don't know everything, Anthony. I don't know why you're trying so hard to fail radio repair school. Tell me that much."

"What do you want from me, Willy?"

"That's easy enough. A more important question is what *you* want from me?"

"Friendship."

"You have that. Why aren't you satisfied with that?"

"Because of what we almost did on the train." Once more he leaned closer, almost whispering what he went on to say. "It would be wrong . . . it'ud be a sin for me to do anything with you."

"But you keep thinking it, don't you? And you want to."

"That doesn't matter. It'ud be wrong."

"Not for me, Anthony. For me it would be natural." I stopped at that, letting it sink in, giving him a chance to say or do anything he might want to do next.

He leaned back again, away, his gaze shifting to where the bartender was greeting some men and women. Quiet laughter there. A simple scene. Real people sitting down at the bar, ordering real drinks. Free people doing whatever they wanted to do. His face registered all those sensations. And then he said, "Let's have something to eat—we'll split it."

That's when I told him I had paid for a room at the hotel—

"which you're welcome to share. Your decision. But I want you to. I won't deny it."

"Only if you promise . . . not to push me."

"I promise." I trusted to human nature and biology and a good dinner, maybe some wine, some of the old Harlan Royce philosophy about "enjoying what there is to enjoy right here, now" and to "stop thinking so much. . . ."

I kept my part of the promise. I didn't push him.

He pushed. When he stripped down to his shorts and followed me into bed, he pushed right up against me and kept pushing his hard, cotton-sheathed prick into my equally hard, equally cotton-sheathed prick. He held me just as he had in our famous upper berth and pushed and pushed until he came.

So did I.

We didn't talk afterward. We rolled apart. It was a big enough double bed so that if we rolled far enough apart, we didn't have to touch each other. He seemed to want it that way. He hadn't kissed me. I hadn't tried to kiss him. He had held me and pushed. What we had done didn't have to be called "having sex," not officially, not in Confession.

Nevertheless, when I awoke the next morning, Anthony was already in his uniform—and anxious to get going. He always went to church on Sunday before breakfast.

Days we changed sheets we had to roll our mattresses so that they looked like gray jelly doughnuts. Blankets had to be folded—just so—and placed—just so—on top of the mattress. The pillow had to be puffed and centered on top of the blankets. Those mornings were more hectic than the usual shave-and-shit mornings. And it was on that kind of morning of the following week that Anthony turned me from my appointed task to tell me he was going on sick call. He hadn't gone to mess either, it registered, suddenly. He felt sick to his stomach, had a headache, fever maybe.

Jewish mother style, I touched his forehead. Perhaps something subterranean. An ancient force at work down deep inside him—but maybe all that silent suffering had erupted in another way. Yes, he had better go on sick call. I would check on his whereabouts later on, first chance I could.

Which turned out to be lunchtime.

Anthony did not appear in the mess hall.

He was not in the barracks.

I went to the orderly room. The first sergeant would tell me nothing more than that Private di Carlo was gone and that I had better get my ass over to the formation. They were ready to march on back to school.

On sheet-changing days, we were marched after school directly to the quartermaster's supply room, where we would sign for and then be issued new sheets. Endless that line those afternoons.

Freed, finally, I rushed back to the barracks. No Anthony. Okay. So he'd been kept on by the medics. I could check on that. I could find out where he'd been taken. But then I realized his footlocker was gone. His standing locker door was open. Nothing inside. Perplexed, trying to piece it out, I dropped my sheets on his rolled mattress, began to undo my own. A carton of Luckies fell out and down onto my boots: our brand. And also, pushed further inside the uncoiling roll, was a letter:

Dear Willy,

The carton of cigarettes is to replace all the ones I mooched from you. I took them because you liked giving them. When you find this, I'll be gone. I applied for Korea a few weeks ago. I didn't tell you because I didn't want to be talked out of it. I'm glad I did it before the night at the Bon Air. That night made me feel even more I was right to leave. I think we would have gotten into a lot of trouble otherwise. I'll miss you a lot. I'll miss talking to you and watching you listen so hard. I'll never forget that. I'll never forget you. The best of everything to you.

Love, Anthony

My knees gave way. I landed with my head on the exposed springs of Anthony's cot, one hand clutching the carton of Luckies, the other squeezing the coils, trying in that way to control what was about to burst inside me.

Didn't work.

I remember crying. I remember faces coming closer, questioning me, faces I had never bothered to get to know as long as Anthony was there. He had wanted it that way; therefore so did I. But now . . . Anthony was gone. Gone to . . . Troy. To the Trojan War—and it was not, could not, be for the best. . . .

By the next week I had worked my melancholy into a state of preparedness: I would go on sick call too; I would get myself discharged from the army, just as I had mused I would.

When I insisted on seeing a psychiatrist, the medic sergeant said to get the fuck back to my company. Nothing was wrong with me. I wouldn't budge from the waiting room bench. I played out a scene I had rehearsed and rehearsed so carefully, I achieved my goal. The sergeant watched me fall to the floor, watched me roll back and forth. Was I having a fit? Was I an epileptic? He called the doctor. The doctor called the psychiatrist.

But the psychiatrist was no pushover. No army psychiatrist could be. Just being in the army disqualified them from any spontaneous, honest human responses. When I told him my story, when I told him I was gay, he said, "So what? Lots of guys in the army are. They enjoy themselves. Why don't you?"

"You call yourself a doctor?"

"Watch it, Private. You *are* in the army and I am an officer. Unless you get caught doing something on base, you're going to stay right where you are."

"You fuck."

"I'm going to forget I heard that."

"I don't care what you do." I leaned down over his desk. I

175

wanted to make damn sure he had to face me when I told him, "You're an insult to your profession."

"And you? You're a creep. I want you out of here. Right now. I want you to go back to your company. I'll be calling your company commander to make sure you get there. Sergeant! . . ."

I was forcibly ejected.

And when I returned to my company I was immediately called down to the orderly room. The so-called psychiatrist had called. The so-called psychiatrist had advised my captain to arrange for me to see a chaplain—"every Saturday. And I expect you to exercise self-control . . . in the barracks particularly, but everywhere else as well. Do I make myself clear? Any infringement and you will face a court-martial. I kid you not. . . ."

I was called before the psychiatrist once more. He informed me he would not pass on the facts of my outburst to higher levels. He would *neglect* putting anything down on my Form 20. He would conveniently forget the entire incident.

I didn't say thank you. I didn't say anything. I had lost without there ever having been any battle, although the Methodist minister I was forced to see every Saturday thought he was waging a battle . . . for my soul, he said. When he decided to send me to see the Jewish rabbi, I told him it was about time. He turned another of his cheeks. The rabbi would only talk to me about my bar mitzvah and about my parents, my family, and how much they must love me. Would I want to shame them?

I saw him only once. I walked out after his *shame* routine. He never reported me to the company commander, although it was the company commander who drove me in his jeep to the rabbi's office building three Saturdays in a row. (The holy number.) Why he did it would be too bizarre for me to conjecture. I surely gave him no reason to hope.

Of the original group sent to radio repair school, three of us had managed to survive, each in our own way.

The beginning of March, I wrote to Sam about our returning. A piece of his response follows:

. . . I have long since explained your situation to Lieutenant Rod. All is in order. Merely rest your heathen soul in patience because even as I send this off to you, thinking of you and your close call, my Rod and my staff are busily typing your orders. You will have all kinds of pleasant surprises when you receive them, of a magnitude, I pray, which will numb the feeling of Anthony di Carlo's loss. You'll see, V'lodya, a new life will soon beckon. Owen Lawrence Murchison, for one, longs for you. And Sergeant Heebler has long since departed, back to Korea for another tour of duty. Misconduct. He beat up on a young soldier who featured you in the face. The details were, as you might suspect, smarmy. At any rate I'll let one surprise out of my bag of tricks. When you return here, you will be transferred to Headquarters Company. Lt. Rod feels as I do: you belong with me. Love in the highest, Ah—men . . . Sister Sammy.

Yes, my travel orders ordered me back to Fort Hood, but, first, they also ordered me home to Brooklyn for two weeks! My very first furlough! Sammy! Sammy! Sister Sammy for star! If only I could have thanked him . . . in the manner I more than ever wanted to. Perhaps when I return to the Fort, perhaps then, after my so long absence his fondness will have grown accordingly. Perhaps he will have a change of heart . . . more likely not. Whether I will it or won't it I will probably never be his Will-hee? Won't-hee? the way I want to be. . . .

Still leaning at Sam's window looking out, I feel the weight of my shoulder bag dragging me down. Or is it the weight of all those years filling my head? In any case, I need a chair. I need to break the spell Sam has locked me into. I need to say something about *now*, to say anything that comes into my head, to say the first thing: "How did you get those geraniums to grow so tall, Sammy?"

"They do it naturally. Those are regals, honey. Queenly plants. I just trained them to hug the synagogue wall. For moral support, doncha know." He smiles, pulling me closer once again, not letting me turn away, obviously not wanting me to. So my mind, held in thrall, returns to those geraniums. The mind, oh, the mind . . . it was on Mother's Day I arrived back in Brooklyn to begin that long-ago furlough. Mother's Day . . . geraniums . . . we always gave my mother geranium plants for Mother's Day. . . .

Coming in from LaGuardia Airport, I ask the cabbie to stop at a florist.

When I get out of the cab in front of our two-story, I see my mother at the upstairs window. She waves. I cradle the geranium plant, drag my duffel bag along.

I struggle up the stoop. The front door opens. My mother takes the plant. She is crying, happily so. My father reaches around her to take over my duffel-bag strap. I hug them, kiss them, move us all inside the vestibule.

Going up the stairs, I lift the bottom end of my duffel bag, my father pulls at the strap. "What have you got in there? It's heavier than you are."

"Dirty clothes."

"For me," my mother says, "to go with my geranium." But she is laughing now, studying me, assaying the damage the army has done. "You are thinner, but that I'll change. That I'll change in a hurry. Everyone's coming for dinner. All the things you like you'll have. . . ."

My sister, my brother-in-law, my two nephews arrive within the half-hour, bearing geraniums.

My brother and sister-in-law arrive soon after. She is pregnant, her dress proclaims, more than her body. "Don't I show? I'm in my fifth month already."

"Not really—but I like the dress anyway."

My brother has a story to tell about why their geranium plant

178

isn't a great one. "In our neighborhood, the florist had none. The guy over on Utica Avenue had this left. I had to take it. How could we come without a geranium, Ma?"

"It's fine. To me it's beautiful." She places it among the other plants over on the wall-long buffet, a piece that matches the dining room table, all of it part of a suite she and my father bought in Macy's when we moved to Brooklyn from Bayonne, New Jersey. While we move to take our accustomed seats, my mother stands before the buffet, her arms opened wide, as if to embrace all the plants there. She sees me watching her. She smiles, turns, heading out to the kitchen to get our first course: stuffed cabbage.

My father is insisting I sit in his seat at the head of the table— "in honor of the occasion, Willy." His seat is the only one of the dining room set with armrests. It has never been anyone else's seat. In my recollection the only person to whom it has been offered is the prophet Elijah, at our seders. My father has me by the shoulders, trying to force me down into it.

I resist, playfully pushing against his now sizable stomach. "No, Dad." All the weight he has gained over the years has gone directly to his stomach. The rest of him is lean, tall and lean, taller than I. But, standing almost eye to eye just then I see that his long, narrow nose has thickened some, that his full lips are bloodier. So is the color of his skin. Or is that the sentiment of the moment? He isn't used to having his requests refused, his orders disobeyed. I have seen his impatience explode into instant rage—but that won't happen now. "No, Dad. You earned your armrests. You worked hard for them." There is nothing ironic in my tone. He relaxes his hold on my shoulders, hugs me close. Sentiment wins out, wells up in sudden tears. It hasn't always been so, although he has never hit me. He has always found it easy to demonstrate affection for me, much more so than for my brother—even then, as I move back and away from my father, I catch a glimpse of my brother's expression. He is watching us, hurt, I sense. My brother has been slapped for staining a tablecloth, for neglecting to replace a roll of toilet paper, for spending too much of his allowance on candy bars instead of saving it up to buy the bicycle he once asked my father to buy for him. I have even seen my father raise his hand as if to slap my sister. It never fell on her either, but it had on my mother, once, only once. One of his instant rages had exploded, unpredictably, near the end of a Friday-night dinner. He had been telling us his opinion of the relative merits of George Washington, Abraham Lincoln, Franklin D. Roosevelt, wanting us to agree with him that Washington was the best of all of them. My mother wanted to clear the table. She interrupted him to say so, and his hand shot up, hitting her. Stunned us all, including him. His expression had frozen, a still point caught between the remnant of his rage and the instant remorse he obviously felt. "You see what happens? Why the hell couldn't you wait a few minutes? Where you in such a rush to get to?"

"Nowhere. I'm tired. I want to finish."

"If you're tired, sit down and listen."

She did. He resumed his monologue, putting his hand on top of hers, squeezing it in a show of affection equal in force to the outburst of his rage; but equally caught up in his words, proud of them and of his knowledge. He had taught himself all he knew, and he knew a lot about a lot of subjects. He could debate politics, history, economics with his college-educated children and hold his own. He enjoyed that. He enjoyed debating and winning, except, as on the occasion of that Friday night, when, winning, he lost our interest, and our respect. We were watching my mother. She stared down at the tablecloth. She would stay put until he was finished. So would we. She had taught us early on to excuse his rages and appreciate his love. She, not he, had told us all about the pogroms he suffered in Minsk; about his having to leave school in America during the fourth grade because his father died suddenly and his mother, his younger sisters and brother needed food; about his working at two, sometimes three jobs, during the same day . . . and there she comes, my mother, bearing a platter of stuffed cabbage. I take the seat my sister places behind me at my father's left.

As my mother serves me, her smile, her pleasure over my being home brings tears to my eyes. That kind of love, so easy and renewable and there, always, is just what has been missing for so many months now, even more so since Anthony's departure. I look up at her, wanting her to see I feel that same kind of pleasure and love for her. She nods—and then she leans away to serve my nephew.

I think of Sam then, for no clearly discernible reason except that I wish he were there to share these . . . offerings of love.

But what would he make of stuffed cabbage? (My mother's was a memorable balance of sweet and sour, with lots of prunes and raisins.)

And what would Sam make of my father, who, in a trice, would be asking him about Electra and asking how Sam's father had managed during the Depression and the dust-bowl years.

Matzo balls Sam would like. His mother made marvelous dumplings. My mother's matzo balls were legendary, gossamer light. She gives me extras even before I begin the soup, "so you'll put on weight faster. No one else be jealous. There's plenty more of them for anyone who wants. . . ."

And plenty more roast chicken, potato kugel, tsimmis.

"Leave a little room, William." Oh, the sound of that *William!* That is the balm of Gilead . . . but so are the apple cake, the honey buns, the lemon meringue pie: only the peaks on Mrs. Tolan's pie are a match for my mother's.

After cake and tea time, my sister-in-law inches her chair back from the edge of the table; all the better to cup the bottom of her stomach, to raise the contour of her future birth into the family's present view. She sighs, for one and all to hear.

My mother asks her would she like to nap? Or, perhaps, she would like to take a walk around the block?

She shakes her head no to both suggestions. She really wants

181

us only to take note of what she will soon be giving to our family.

She is on the other side of the table, between my brother and brother-in-law. I smile warmly, I hope. Pregnancy is, I'm sure, a blessed state, but hardly unique to my sister-in-law. As long as the baby is healthy, is what I always say. And, personally speaking, I am happy for all concerned. I am happy to be uncle to as many children as my sister and brother-in-law, my brother and sister-in-law shall create. I feel no anguished urge to become involved in the process. It occurs to me, sitting there, surveying the smiling faces of my young nephews and my sister-in-law's stomach, that there are—will more than likely always be—a sufficiency of fathers. Me and my minority are no threat to the survival of the species. And, at any rate and at twenty-two, I am still in about the seventh-month madness of creating myself. The recent experience with the psychiatrist, the unsettled sensations caused by di Carlo's secret departure, the unchartable, deep-down longing for Sam—those and many unspecified, sudden encounters with unpredictable feelings indicate I have miles to go before I can begin to know who I really am. Anyway, since Amelia, neither my mother nor my father has brought up the subject of marriage. For a soldier, my father would likely say, marriage isn't even a question. Therefore, fatherhood doesn't enter the picture. Fatherhood isn't necessary to prove my manhood. Soldierhood proves it, one-hundred-percent proves it. And, anyway, if anyone seated at that table thinks other than that of me, I feel secure no one will say so (not in 1952 they wouldn't). Each look at me, each smile offered what I had never lacked from any one of them—unconditional love. For that, I knew I was blessed. Others have not been so fortunate. Filled up with so much food and all that love I float lazily on the waves of good feeling. No Sergeant Heeblers, no kike curses, no troubles in mind threaten for the moment.

And two weeks of the same lie ahead. Perhaps, if I move ever-so-carefully, hand-over-hand, I might just squeeze through a hole in my head to someplace hopeful, to someplace I had never traveled before . . . perhaps—but just then my mother stands up, readying herself for clearing, the fingers of her outstretched hands wiggling: Give me your plates, they say; my kingdom for those plates. Waiting, her gaze shifts to all those geranium plants on the buffet, shifts back again to the task at hand: my father is offering her his plate. Her fingers stop their wiggling. She stares at them, at my father, at all of us seated around the dining room table. She smiles. Silent, all of us, we are watching her, waiting for her to continue, before we go on to do whatever it is we will be going on to do. She knows what she has to do next. The moment records itself on my memory: the red geraniums, her smile, the offered plate—which she takes hold of then. . . .

On my side of the table my sister rises to help collect and scrape. My nephews are released; they lean against my chair on either side, asking me to tell them about the army.

My father wonders if maybe I and the boys will go outside with him for a few minutes, sit on the porch maybe, say hello to some of the neighbors because "they're always asking me how's the army treating you. I'll show you off to them. . . ." Me? Show me off? I feel touched because I also feel how heavily my army-issue uniform hangs on my sticks-and-bones frame. Now, if Sam were here . . . but if my father is proud of me . . . so be it. "Sure, Dad . . ." I take hold of my nephews' hands. . . .

Each day of that furlough I made another sortie into my past, hoping thereby to prepare a way ahead when—and if—I regained control of my life. When I owned my own life once more, I promised myself to make it work better than the past had worked. I went to see Mr. Braunstein who was still bitching, only now he was bitching about how Times Square was no more the way it used to be, "Soon there won't be readers left anywhere, Willy. It'll all be Empire State Building salt-and-pepper shakers. . . ."

183

From San Remo, my favorite bar in Greenwich Village, I telephoned Harry Royce—just for the sheer agony of it. He was at his old number, and up to his old tricks. He was more than willing to meet me, would rent a hotel room to do so. I said no. I told him I had only called to see if he was happy. "Happy? Are you drunk, Willy? What's happy? Are you happy in the army? You and your happy!" I told him I was still going to try to become so, and then I told him, "Good-bye."

Amelia was more difficult to track down. A mutual friend from City College remembered she had married. Berini was her name now. Her husband taught at City College, in the English Department. When I got her on the telephone, she was surprised, amiable, crisply so. She wanted to know about my "hypothetical man . . . the man in New Orleans? Do you still see him? Do you still . . . love him?" I told her the truth. I told her I would be going back to City College after my discharge. "Perhaps I'll take a course with your husband." She wasn't much amused.

With Jerry Saperstein I went out barring. Instead of a man, I met a woman who liked to go to bed with gay men. I was dressed in civvies which meant she wanted me for myself alone and not my uniform. If she didn't care, I didn't care. If it worked, fine. If not, so be it. What could it prove anyway? That sex is, after all, sex? When you get right down to it? And that love is something else? Anyway, we fucked freely and we had fun. Her touch was gentle and reassuring; her body was small and trim and reminded me of Bernice Rosenbaum's . . . in the breasts. She didn't sing.

So, that too came to pass: *It*—a number of times that furlough. And, as I said, I did enjoy it. To my taste, it was no better than, nor worse than, with a man. Different, of course. Yes. Easier to fake, for her, for me—as long as I stayed hard. I did. I was young enough.

The bloom, according to my mother, came back into my cheeks. "You see what good food can do?" What I saw was the same old angular gaunt look looking back at me from the mirror on the wall.

On the day of my departure, the Mother's Day group reassembled to take me out to Idlewild Airport. My duffel bag contained everything cleaned and home-scented. It bulged with tins of pinwheel and chocolate chip cookies. Exerting myself beyond caution—perhaps I'd collapse—I slung it onto my shoulder, which impressed my nephews, although what they had come to see especially was the moment I would board the airplane, a new Constellation.

Not too many tears were shed, my mother feeling my fate had "turned a safe corner. Unless, God forbid, they'll start yet another war."

"God won't forbid it. Rest assured of that," my father assured us all. "Truman dropped atom bombs, so the next war will have to be something bigger and better to kill with. It's all money."

"I don't like it when you talk that way in front of them, Sol." My mother pressed her grandsons against her, trying to cover their four ears at once.

"Like-shmike. The truth is the truth. Eventually even they'll have to know it."

No gainsaying that. Nor did she try, knowing that no airport, no public place would intimidate my father, if provoked. She led herself and my nephews further up the ramp leading to the plane. We followed.

Hurrying, other passengers stepped around my convoy.

I hung back, reluctant, even as my sister and brother-in-law, my brother and sister-in-law, my nephews had their way with me saying good-bye. My mother and father linked me to them, on either side of me; I heard myself saying—"less than a year. That's all," trying to steel them and myself. "Before you know it, it goes by. Less than a year and I'll be back home. . . ."

But, sometimes, departures turn out to be rehearsals for ultimate loss. What if, before the year . . . what if . . . fear froze me between them. My father's strong hand pressed against the hollow of my back. My mother's small fingers lifted my chin. Their youngest! Their baby son . . . grown up! A time of their lives done with, gone, finished. In my father's eyes: That's the way life is. In my mother's eyes: Nothing to do about time passing—but smile she did. She kissed me. So did my father.

I forced myself to move off. Like it or not.

At the exit, I stopped to look back. They were waving. I waved back until the flow of people blocked my sight of them. So did tears blur them—and then someone shoved me on my way outside to where the airplane waited.

Without realizing I was climbing I started up the steps. A new Constellation it was—but it would be taking me back to Sammy.

CHAPTER
4

"**O** my dear, O my dear," the return to Texas: the fucking westering sun, the heat, oven dry, causing the water in my eyes to steam.

The Fort Hood bus idles while I step down its few steps dragging my duffel bag behind. I will never lift it onto my shoulder with virile soldierly abandon when expected to . . . or ordered to. I have learned the pleasures of little, secret rebellions: the bus groans, waiting—and then grinds through its range of gears, rolls away, blue-black exhaust fumes briefly obscuring the western sunglow. Here I am, back to my home away from home . . . and then, as if he has never left off looking through it these past six months, there is Sammy opening the screen door of battalion headquarters, stepping clear of it, shading his eyes to make sure it's me.

Yes, honey, it's your Blanche-d Willy, I would like to shout out, your sister, home from the sea. Not that I would, of course. And, anyway, there's no time because instantly Sam bounds across the street to greet me all very man-to-man-like, whooping and hollering and back-slapping and whirling. So awesome an expenditure of energy when a simple kiss would have said so much more! "Soon as that bus stopped, I knew it. Had to be. Spent all last night worrying after you. You are officially AWOL, you know. Where *did* you spend last night?" Sam relieves me of

187

my duffel bag, makes familiar with my elbow (that, at least that much), readies me for movement.

"I only did what you instructed me to. I flew into Houston, went out to Ellington Field for a hop. There was none until this morning so the air force had to put me up for the night. A very crowded transients' barracks. A pigsty, 'doncha know.' And this morning's hop went to Waco. I've been hitchhiking down here all day long. Frankly, if I'm AWOL, I don't give a damn. This is not exactly Tara. It's only for you I came back."

"Well don't you worry none. I've taken care of everything, you can rest assured. These days, there's little I can't do." He offered his sleeve for close-up viewing. From shoulder to elbow, chevrons, a stack of them and rising above them a base of smiling semicircles.

"Why you sly-boots you. You never even wrote me."

"Just happened last week. I've been rushed into the rank of sergeant major before my time. Colonel's choice . . ."

We had arrived at the front porch entranceway of the very first barracks building across from battalion headquarters. I looked up the cinder street, far up, to where Dog Company lived, and beyond to the very last one in the row, across from the motor pool: my tank runneth over.

"You are here now, Willy. With me." He didn't carry me over the threshold, only my duffel bag.

Ah, my strong, green-eyed sergeant major, my sister Sammy for star, lead me wherever, I will follow! I will step out smartly. Just then I followed him into the dusk-dark, false-cool downstairs of my new home.

Some of the drowsing, done-for-the-day troops lifted heads, some lifted eyebrows, one even limped a wrist, I thought. It was an odd sight: the sergeant major carrying the duffel bag of some no-account private first class, carrying it right past their surprised faces and on up the back stairs where some more drowsing troops took note of our passage. Nary a murmur. Sam's expression said, just let any one of them dare to and he'd lay 'em to whaleshit is what he'd do. He'd have 'em on a Korean levy so fast they'd be dizzied by the speed of it all. Yes, indeed: commanding, that jut of chin, that breadth of shoulder, those chevrons.

I followed him to what I took to be my cot. A coveted location: the first cot to the right of the screen doors leading out onto the balcony above the entranceway. Sam's cot was just across the aisle from mine. "My latest promotion entitles me to a cadre room. I refused. I always want to be among the troops."

On the top of my rolled mattress were sheets and what looked to be a new blanket and certainly that had to be a freshly laundered pillow. "Land o' Goshen . . ."

"Chokes you up, does it? Well, I have a friend in the supply room. An Arnold Duberman. From New York, as chance would have it. He's in the cot next to mine."

I unrolled, thinking: Sister Sammy . . . smitten by Semites! Aha! Sam dumped my duffel bag onto the mattress. I had miles to go before thoughts such as that could be thought through. Besides, just then, my knees sagged, and with them went my spirit. I felt for the edges of my mother's cookie tins. Back in Brooklyn they'd be sitting down to dinner about then. I longed so for what I had recently left: some unquestioning, unqualified love. Sam saw. Sam read the runes in my bloodshot eyes. He moved me from the cot and out onto the balcony, out into the glowy evening light, getting me to lean up against the balcony railing—and him, just, grazing his arm and his lovely leg. Nothing pushy. Nothing obvious to the naked eyes looking up and over from the steps outside the rec room. Those guys didn't care. Idling, smoking, while the glowing light darkened into night. Sam searched the sky for a sign, I imagined. So did I. Something dramatic. Something to welcome me back. A comet. A falling meteorite, deep in this heart of Texas. Nothing doing. " 'Those girls aren't out tonight,' " he whispered for no one's but my ears. And then, more silence.

I languished, lazying lower over the railing—and I had my cot still to make up, my duffel bag to undo, my life to bring back into some kind of focus before reveille the next morning. "I better get on with unpacking, Sammy." But I didn't stir.

Neither did Sam.

We stared out. We watched while the wind started up, raising eddies of dust.

And then, there came a soldier, in helmet liner and fatigues, who waved up. "Arnie." Sam waved back, straightened. "Come on in, Willy. Meet him. And be friendly. He is not . . . I repeat, not . . . a friend of Dorothy's."

No, he was surely not a friend of Dorothy's. His best friend had to be himself, what with all his smiling and preening and posing when all he had to do was extend his hand to shake mine. Really! A little much, I mused, nevertheless admiring his gladiatorial stance. I am no prig. Handsome he was, yes, and aware of his effect. But ingenuousness did not suit him either, which is what he wanted me to warm to. I didn't. I aimed for indifference, while I studied his intent.

Sam began filling in the facts. Arnie lived in a place called Riverdale. "Do you know it, Willy?" "Yes." Arnie had gone to a school called Fieldston Academy. Did I know that school? Yes. Arnie had gone out to Hollywood to try to break into the movies. . . .

"I didn't know that."

"No. Of course you didn't know that, Will-hee? Won't-hee?"

"What did happen to you out there, Arnie?" I ventured.

"I ended up with the clap. . . . Ha, ha, ha." He actually clapped his hands with each *ha*.

But beauty can get away with such nonsense. I could see that in Sam's beaming pleasure. Infatuation flushed his skin, boiled his common sense. Not that Arnie wasn't prodigious. He was. No gainsaying that. Lovely, piercing blue eyes. Soft spills of light brown silky hair—once he remembered to remove his helmet liner indoors. A square shield of a face, with each feature settled into imperturbable harmony. I'd bet my life on the im-

190

perturbable fact of that face: It had no Achilles heel. So, yes, I was jealous, and also annoyed, because I was expected to stand around and admire Arnie while he ceremoniously stripped off his fatigue jacket and pants, his boots, his socks, and then I was literally pushed down onto Sam's cot and expected to make small talk while Arnie proceeded to do his evening exercises. Why, Miss Ida Flare, she had gone stark raving mad over this . . . this . . . Jewish gladiator from Riverdale.

Squat jumps and sit-ups. Strainings and gruntings and then a set of push-ups. Seemed like a never-ending thousand I was being asked to endure.

No. Never. I bent around Sam's transfixed admiration, beat it back across the aisle where I belonged.

Truculent? You bet.

And *triste*? Very *triste*—particularly at that moment, as I opened a tin of my mother's most prized pinwheel cookies: each alternating circle of vanilla and chocolate had crumbled; not one cookie remained intact. What further disillusionment would follow? I scouted the few faces left in the continuing floor show. I saw torpor. I saw boredom. I saw indifference. Oh blessed state! Would that I might wait out these remaining months in such a state. Only discharge could set me free. . . .

I settled my books into the bottom corner of yet another footlocker. I covered them with clean khaki socks, re-rolling them because my mother's way was not the army's way.

Truculence deepened into melancholy; melancholy plummeted to despair. No certainty sustained—except being gay. That was all I knew for sure. That steadied me.

That helped. That one fact . . . a *yes* to hang on to. The rest was—always will be—filled with too many unknowns for a body to worry himself over—as Harry would have said at such a juncture of thoughts. Harry lightened my despair. Harry laughing *with* me. Harry calling me from his western window. Harry holding me, bearlike, consoling, direct. From behind the locked gates of *done with*, Harry, lit up for a moment, reminding me of

191

myself *then*, watching me begin to arrange the pieces of myself for *now*. Out of change comes . . . change—and after change comes whatever consolations console one along the way, even an Arnold Duberman. No harm done.

Sam managed to suspend his admiration long enough to hie me over to the Queen Bee for a homecoming float. "I mean, honey, I can't follow him into the shower room, now can I? A sergeant major? Unseemly—and I have a thousand things to tell you, you alone. For you have been sorely missed, my lady—in spite of whatever evidence you have witnessed to the contrary. Arnie, I look at. Merely that. You, I see."

We stared our fill of each other freely. The Queen's neons flickering; the soft ice cream machines humming. Nearby, a beery bunch made raucous counterpoint: nonsense sounds on the breeze. They could not see us touch fingertips between the barricade we made of our float containers. I more than welcomed their modest whoopings. They would pay us no nevermind.

Sam leaned back, lit up, launched his telling: "First things first . . . Lieutenant Rod re-upped in order to be shipped out. Didn't want one more day of Texas," a quicksilver leaning toward me, in *sotto voce*, "nor of me. Not that I ever gave him cause for concern. Cross my heart, honey. He was not in my stars. He was not it at all." He leaned back again. "But he recommended my promotion. Went to the colonel and told him I was indispensable." Another leaning in, lowering, "Me, honey . . . your Sister Indispensable." And back. "Imagine. Serious stuff, this responsibility. . . . Mama was duly impressed. She's been asking after you. Wants you up for a visit." A hungry drag on his cigarette. "Owen is gone from Electra. Sent to Geneva, Switzerland . . . that far away . . . by Oveta. To study the piano with the best that money can buy. Owen's learning how to finger his passages proper. So says Oveta, but . . ." a lunge forward, "Owen wrote me that his piano teacher is one of *us*. They are living together. An older man. Distinguished and settled-down, doncha know . . ." A slower motion backward, in case some more needed to be whispered—but then the beer group readied itself for departure. So did some stragglers over closer to us. At last we were left alone. "Thank the Lord." Sam lit another cigarette. "About wore myself out rocking back and forth. Can't take as much of that as I used to. Don't want to have to. . . ." A deep, deep drag on his Lucky. "Oh, this life, honey! This tangled web of things! And now, this rank. It has given me pause. It most assuredly has. It has got me to reconsider most of what we are forced to do—and then there came your letter from Georgia telling me what you had gone and done. Well, I liked to worry myself sick over it. You came within a hair of total ruin, Blanche, honey . . . the thinnest of hairs. Did you realize it? Did you think what might have happened to you? Done in the name of love? All for the love of a soldier . . ." he mused out loud.

"No. Not for love. I didn't love Anthony. I . . . did it for myself. To prove I could. To prove I owned my own life, even in the army. I am not Harry Truman's slave, not his to dispose of however he wishes. Neither are you. None of us are. None of us has to be."

"There are laws. *They* make them. Not us. In their eyes we are unnatural. We are sinners. Perfect for drafting and killing off . . . in the name of God and country."

"I'll proselytize. I'll fight against dying for flags. For fags, I'd die. There'd be some sense in that."

"Blasphemy, honey. You are talking New York, commie blasphemy."

The Queeen's neons flickered. Almost lights out and I had miles of mundane matters to set in order before I slept. My cot to make. My clean clothes to stow away. My cookie tins to cradle. An Arnie Duberman to place in the proper perspective next to Lieutenant Rod . . . and others. No doubt there would be others, myself not among them. Never. Never the way I had imagined it. That much seemed clear enough. But, looking up and over at Sam just then—he had turned reflective, was staring intently at the tip of his cigarette thinking thoughts he would probably never share with me—I knew I would keep on trying, right up until discharge, to throw him into a bed of peace. That too seemed equally clear. Wearily, my head lolled back. Poles apart, Sam and I. "Star-crossed" lovers but, even though we had come to this moment at the Queen Bee by chance—a touch, a graze, a cruise—we *had* come to it. It mattered to both of us that we were together.

Just then the Queen's lights went out. The soft ice cream machines ceased their humming. All I heard was the music of the spheres . . . and Sam's breathing. Under cover of the darkness, Sam reached across the table to take hold of my hand. "How happy I am to have you back with me, V'lodya. I have missed you sorely."

After my furlough, army time felt like being in an airplane trapped in an endless holding pattern—except, of course, I knew there would be a landing.

Being in Headquarters Company helped some, even lending status to so humble a soldier as a Howards. I was assigned to maintain the colonel's electronic equipment, wherever it existed. For that I was promoted to corporal, and when the colonel reviewed his levy-decimated battalion, I sat in his jeep fiddling with the dials of its radio. If he ordered his tank out of the motor pool in order to go into the field to oversee maneuvers, I too surveyed the scene from his turret.

According to Sam's report the colonel was more than pleased with my performance. He instructed Sergeant Major Tolan to keep Corporal Howards off any new levies for Korea or Europe. " 'Those New Yorkers' . . . he did not say 'New York Jews,' Willy. A colonel has to be careful what he says. He said. 'Those New Yorkers have got brains *and* balls, big balls.' That's exactly how he put it. And I'll bet you do too, Willy, have lovely big balls. Don't you?'' That kind of talk Sam reserved for the bar at the Blue Bonnet. Since the colonel had also excused me from having to stand Saturday-morning inspections, Sam and I could always count on hightailing it up to Dallas, weekends.

Or Austin. Once in a while San Antonio. Only once down to Houston. Dallas, of course, was the most congenial, even with Arnie Duberman dragging after us. My "tin can," Arnie Duberman. Sam felt obliged to teach him some life-preserving hitch-hiking tricks. So, with Arnie in tow, when we got to Dallas, we would start our drinking on neutral territory, usually the Diamond Horseshoe Bar opposite the Adolphus Hotel. After all Sam had saved me from, the least I could do was let him lust with his eyes after Arnie to his heart's content because soon enough Arnie would get frightened off. As soon as Sam's gin-loosed heat showed itself, Arnie would decide it was time for him to head for *his* bar near Neiman's. He'd met up with a model there— "a hot lay, and beautiful. She'll be there waiting for me. You guys take care. See you tomorrow. Same place. Same station . . ." What Arnie knew, he new. He didn't want to talk about that. Neither did Sam. I did—but out of respect for Sam, I never insisted. Instead, I followed my heart to the Blue Bonnet.

Throughout that summer and on into the fall, I sat by his side, loyal, faithful, sipping gin mists and ginger ale chasers late into the evening, suggesting every now and again that perhaps a meal might be in order. Not seriously suggesting it, just testing to see whether or not he was in a drinking way or a cruising way or a sleeping way. And when we had drained our arrival bottle, the first one onto his feet, steadily onto his feet, would go off to get a fresh supply. Behind us the bar would jam up against our stools, bodies pressing in, and around us, the jukebox doing the music from the *Moulin Rouge* or the theme from *Ruby*, our eyes meeting in the mirror behind the bar, Sam's lips forming the words, Blanche, honey, mine answering, Stella for star, and, sometimes a hand would take hold of my privates and fondle them sweetly, sometimes I would see a hand do similar things to Sam's. Sweet, sweet sensations . . .

And when it was last call we would order a last setup. I would lean in closer, hoping that way to corner him, to cut him off from anyone else's longing.

And, after we drained the last of our gin and ginger ale, we would take to the street, joining yet another wild Saturday-night Dallas already in progress. We whooped. We hollered. We hoisted our brown paper bags up toward the sky: a prayer for a bed of peace. So did the cowboys in their starched dungarees. So did all manner of others, sisters some, some in uniforms, some in civvies, all of us heading for that magnetic north pole of everyone's desire: the corner outside the Baker Hotel and diagonally across from the Adolphus: the heart of downtown Dallas. I would cling to Sam's belt loop as he maneuvered for a leaning position behind the pipe railing so we could watch the cruising cars go by.

Go by they did indeed. Around and around and around the cars came by, their drivers split-second-searching among the crowd for a pair of eyes to connect to. A miracle, those meetings, what with all that screaming, all those empty bottles being flung into the street, all those pressing, swaying, groping bodies. But, always, someone would sure enough push free, would mosey off down the block, would find the car that waited moth-like. Homing-pigeon-like. Horny at one, two A.M. Slowly the ranks would thin out. Cars would speed off into darkness, searching for a somewhere to stop long enough for the cramped, cold comfort of a backseat blow job. That corner outside the Baker Hotel was no country for old men when Saturday-night Dallas during the summer of 1952 turned into Sunday morning. I know whereof I speak. Sometimes even I would connect. Sometimes Sammy would.

But sometimes, earlier on, I would suggest we cease and desist— "get up early, treat ourselves to a major breakfast. Now, how would you like that, honey?"

Some Saturday nights he liked that idea. Some Saturday nights when we had had the sense to secure a hotel room beforehand, he liked the idea very much, especially if it had gotten to be two A.M., with a chill in the air and he dressed only in his sergeant major's uniform and me in my corporal's. "Must have a care, V'lodya. Must not desecrate my country's honor, honey. . . ."

Those Saturday nights I would lead him back to the Southland Hotel where we had registered our single room with its double bed under the name Kowalski, Samuel R., sometimes William B., but always drunk, and, therefore, always extra cautious if Sam was in his sergeant major's stripes; first he, then I, a few minutes later, would go on up, not wanting to call attention to the fact we were together. For shame! Perish such a thought!

Sometimes he would fall upon the bed so drunk I had to undress him. In the darkness I did so, but all very properly. All very sisterly, tender, modest, respectful.

Sometimes when I followed him up to the room, I found him already under the top sheet, smoking, reflective, staring off into the darkness, his face coming into focus slowly, lit up intermittently by the glow of his cigarette tip. I especially enjoyed those nights, watching him as I undressed, stretching beside him beneath the top sheet, waiting for him to decide which story he would tell me next.

Sometimes he would sigh and settle deeper down, turning to say something like, "Blanche, honey, we are so lucky to have each other for sisters. . . . When I think how lonely Deron Johnson used to feel . . ." Or it might be Owen and Oveta he settled on. Or Miss Amanda and the Electra Free Library. Or it might be about someone new, someone he had never pulled from his bag of secrets before; it was someone named Barnett Peterson, the night I'm recalling for you, just now. "Barnett Peterson? You mean I never said that name to you before, V'lodya? Now, however did I neglect that . . . first man I would say I ever truly loved . . . truly . . . loved." And, having begun, he would have to raise himself higher onto his pillow, enough light in the darkness to see the sharp, strong angles of his face; cigarette

197

light, focused, pin-spotting his eyes as he dragged deeply, deeper even than memory, to the quick blood current of being on which everything else we are, or get to be, feeds. "Barnett Peterson . . . I called him Barney. He didn't look like a Barney . . . and that's why I did it. He liked it too. Seventeen, V'lodya. That's all I was. But tall for my age. . . . One Saturday afternoon, late, I just happened out from behind my cash register at the A and P—just been paid, doncha know—and so I headed for the highway. Don't ask me what ever prompted me because I can't rightly tell you. I do not know . . . but anyway, I just lifted my thumb and the next thing I know I'm in Dallas and I'm standing at a urinal in the men's room at the Greyhound terminal . . . the very same site of our famous meeting, and, honey, I went there because I did have to piss something fierce. Cross my heart. Seventeen pisses when it has to piss. . . . Saturday night by then. No different from Saturday night tonight, let me tell you, except at seventeen I'm a lot less acclimatized. Not innocent. I never was . . . innocent . . . so I'm standing there pissing, just staring down at my steady stream, but I'm seeing everything. Brown bags opening and closing every which way. Want to or not, my eyes have to travel. Tedious, that morbid stream of piss—and you know how they have that strip of mirror running the width of the urinal wall? You know how, want to or not, you just have to see things? Always wondered who thought up that strip of mirror. Had to be a friend of Dorothy's. Certainly one of *my* friends because from the next urinal I spy a pair of dancing eyes and beckoning me to stare over and down to see what's what with him. Well, what was what with him was he was simply fondling himself, that's what, V'lodya, honey. Playing with himself . . ." And how Sam laughed over that, laughed and lit up again, lost in his story, dragging on his cigarette as if that was the way he could get right down to re-seeing every remembered detail.

"Playing with himself. Mesmerized me, his prick did. A lovely size. His eyes talking to me, so brown, deep. His face . . . a little boy's face. The smoothest of skin. Flushed. Heated. Like after a

long run . . . playing with himself but not getting hard because
he doesn't want me to do anything except follow him out of the
men's room. I can tell that's what he wants. It's all in his eyes
by then. You know we know these things. Who knows how, but
we do. And when he's sure I understand, he stuffs it back inside
his very starched jeans . . . with difficulty stuffing it back inside,
let me tell you. Vividly, I remember that. Vividly, I remember
following him out onto the marble madness of Saturday night
inside the Greyhound terminal. He goes to a bench and I follow
. . . the very same bench I was sitting on the day you and I began
our beautiful friendship. And I was sitting there that morning
for a reason too, V'lodya. I was sitting there trying to resurrect
Barnett, trying to flesh out the memory of his little boy's flushed
face, and how his eyes darted and how his coal-dark hair would
slip down the center of his forehead no matter how he tried to
push it back up into place and how his flushed lips opened to
tell me—what else?—that of course he had never done such a
thing before as he had just done with me. Smartass me, I nodded, not believing, but not caring, one way or another, to tell the
God's honest truth. Only he did care that I should believe him
because it *was* the truth and what he'd done he'd done because
he felt compelled—his very word . . . *compelled.* . . . Compelled
me right on up to his hotel room he did. Over to the old Jefferson Hotel near the depot. Said he went there because the train
from Tulsa put him in near it. Said he's from Tulsa and worked
down near San Antone. Said he's a cowboy . . . in point of fact.
Well, he surely was saddle lean. He surely used every muscle on
him. Not a bit of him in excess, let me tell you. And hot? Heat
takes on a whole new meaning. On fire. Seventeen, honey.
Seven fucking teen. And when we got down to doing it, doing it
right off in a masterly way . . . on the spot, because, to tell you
the truth, at seventeen, what did I actually know? Not much. I
knew jerking off with Deron. I knew fucks with Oveta. I knew
Owen's mouth sucking on it . . . but not much else, so I don't
know where all that knowledge came from with Barnett. From

199

Adam's rib, I suppose, because I did things as if I'd been doing them all my life. . . . Maybe we're all born knowin'. Maybe it's always there, waitin'. . . . Anyway, we thrashed and heaved and came so many times—I can't remember how many—and doing it all night long, sleeping and waking until it turned morning light and he had to catch the train for San Antonio . . . 'O my dear, O my dear,' what a leave-taking that was. . . ."

Sam lay back, sighing. He lit another Lucky, the match flare revealing an unguarded instant of sad serenity only a finished memory can free.

Some drunken nights he would stop his story at such a place, choosing to pick up its threads when the telling might be more entertaining. But the Barnett Peterson story, once begun, was beyond Sam's customary control, which is why he had held it a secret for so long even from me. "I just knew it would all come spilling out all over the place, Willy, honey. No stuffing it back inside. Just the hottest kind of love, Barnett Peterson. Young hot love. Left its mark on me for life. I try never to think about it, let alone tell it. . . . And the saddest part of all is I mostly saw him five times, maybe six times, a year after that first night. Whenever he was on his way from Tulsa or to it. He'd write me and we'd set up something in Dallas at that same hotel . . . but in between times thinking about him never left my head. I'd be running somewhere wild with Oveta and Owen or I'd lollygag over a poem or I'd sit through a Bette Davis, show after show, at the Shadowland Movie Theater making believe Barnett was next to me. Finished off high school in a haze of hallucinations. Didn't have clue one what to do with my life so I began working full time at the A and P just to fill up time until I would see Barnett again. Waiting was what I mostly did . . . waiting . . . for Fate to take charge. Which it always will . . . sooner or later. . . ." Sam stubbed out his Lucky, sat up, drawing his knees up under his chin, his arms wrapping them tight. "The spring of 1949 was the last time I saw him. Soon as Korea began Barney was drafted. He made it as far as the Yalu River. . . . Just twenty-four years old, V'lodya. Twenty-four . . . and the way I found out was his mother wrote to tell me. Barney had asked her if anything happened to him she should be sure to write his very best friend down in Electra, Texas . . . so she did just that. Wrote me and told me how he'd died. A mortar . . . blew him up . . . into little pieces. . . ." Tears stopped him. His arms came loose. He slid back, sobbing, rolling away from me at first, and then back, reaching out to take hold of my hand, to hold it inside both of his, steadying himself that way, connecting himself to me. "What is the use . . . of talking, V'lodya?" He pulled me closer.

I leaned my head onto his chest, with care, hoping he would welcome me there, hoping he would realize I only meant to comfort him, to calm him, just that. Truly. That was all. But hope never knows its place. Locked up longing and love—yes, love—and horniness and tears and drunk, they know better.

I pressed harder. I couldn't help myself. I inched up higher. Not with stealth. No thief in the night. I wanted him to know what I was up to, what I couldn't help myself from wanting, not anymore. It was that night or it was never. I was hard. I was needy. And I did love him. And what I felt was going to fire his feelings for me. I was sure of it. How could it be otherwise? Compassion was in my fingertips touching his chin, ever so lightly touching and smoothing. And passion? It was everywhere. It was shooting through me. So hot. Longing. Lusting. Loving and in a way that had nothing whatsoever to do with loving Harlan Royce or Jerry Saperstein or Anthony di Carlo. Sam was the way of my life, the way I wanted it to be. By then I had about crawled on top of him, sure that he was going to want me too.

But, of course, I was not it. I was not it at all.

He managed to lift me enough to slip out from beneath my hot, hasty hands. He eased me back, distancing me, sighing, sitting up, but holding onto me. "I'd do it, Willy, if I thought it would lead us anywhere good, anywhere better than where we are. But it won't. If anything, it'ud lead us to a greater loss.

We've arrived at where we're best off . . . Blanche, honey." He drew me close again, in control again, of himself, and, as always, of me too.

Let me tell you, in case you've been fortunate enough never to have felt it, rejection hurts. Repeated rejection hurts repeatedly. How long it would go on hurting I couldn't begin to think about that night. Sitting up in that bed feeling sorry for myself, I could discern no shape to anything, certainly not the limits of my emptiness. Everything would fail, now that I had failed Sam's feelings for me. I had betrayed him. I had even been ready to commit an act of incest. For shame, Howards! It was the drink led me to it. It was feeling . . . hopeless . . . about everything, even about Adlai Stevenson's losing the 1952 election. Even that! My first presidential election . . . by absentee ballot: a bad loss, Adlai's—and now mine, an unequivocal loss. "Mortified, Sammy. I am. I'm sorry. I was being selfish. I . . ."

"Sorry, honey? Don't you be. I'll probably end up being the sorry one. . . ."

After that Saturday night in Dallas, whenever Sammy and Arnie and I hightailed it off of Fort Hood proper, I never again sought anything more than sisterly solace from Sammy.

As our revered Carson McCullers might have put it . . . Not much more is there to tell you about those two years Samuel R. Tolan and William B. Howards came, by chance, to befriend each other in that friendless Texas of the earliest fifties except how and where and under what circumstances that time and their friendship came to an end. . . .

In point of fact, Sam's passage through Fort Hood's separation center preceded mine by two days. We had worked out a plan— or, to be precise, Sam had. I let myself be cajoled into accepting it. "Why rush back to Brooklyn, V'lodya? Lord knows when you'll come back down here. Let's us just take to the open road for a while. Get the lay of the land again. See what freedom tastes like. You've got nothing you must do right away. Neither do I. We'll hitchhike somewhere. Maybe go Greyhound down to Mexico City . . . or Cuernavaca. Something's going on down there. I feel it in my bones. . . ." Walking back from the Queen Bee for the last time, we threw caution to the winds, walked arm-in-arm, asshole buddies about to be separated. . . .

"Okay, smooth talker. You win." First telephone booth we came to, I called Brooklyn collect. My mother answered. My description of what I might just do after discharge did not fill her with very much joy. Disappointed was what her "Oh" sounded like—and something else too, something worrisome in it. Worried about me? Still? After two years in the army? At twenty-three? And she's still worried about me? Ridiculous. "Come on, Ma. I'm here. I might as well take advantage of that fact. I'll be home soon enough and stay for a lifetime."

"How soon is 'soon enough'?" I remember her asking, as if her life depended on her knowing, knowing exactly.

"I don't really know, Ma. Do I have to tell you right now? Tonight?"

"No. Of course not." I remember she breathed deeply, too deeply for something not to be wrong.

But I didn't want to hear that, not that night. I wanted to follow Sam to Cuernavaca . . . where something was happening. . . .

"Where? Spell it for me so when your father comes home from work, I can tell him. He'll be so jealous. Just mention a trip to him . . . but you know all that already, William. . . ."

I spelled it for her, becoming more and more exasperated with each letter. After all, for two years my mother and father had gone on living their lives without my assistance, so why should I have to feel guilty about taking another few weeks—or even a few years, if it should fall out that way—away from them?

"What's wrong, Ma?"

"Nothing is wrong. You just go on and have a good time. Remember me to your friend. Just, please, write us, so we know where you are, in case . . ."

"In case what, Ma."

"In case nothing. I have to go. Something's burning on the stove. Just be well. Take care. . . ." Not even a good-bye, or love—so I knew something had to be very wrong—but that night I was not about to think myself into the glooms. That night, arm-in-arm, Sam and I walked back to the bare barracks in the separation center where, in side-by-side cots, we went to sleep. I dreamed of release.

The next morning Sam left for Dallas where he would wait for me at the Blue Bonnet.

On April 26, 1953, I had my last breakfast in a mess hall, went immediately to the barracks for the final physical exam. The psychiatrist didn't ask a single question. Nothing amiss. DIS-CHARGE was stamped across my records. A salute, my happiest, my smartest, for a Captain Anonymous who then handed me a check, separation pay, a check for the biggest amount of money I had ever held in my hand.

And then I stepped backward, back across an imaginary line, to freedom, to the place in my head where, two years before, I had left off living the life I chose to live, the life I thought, until that other day, I had owned.

All that was left was my duffel bag. I lifted it with the greatest of ease. A steamy morning it was, but no matter. Near the rail-road siding where it had all begun, I hailed a taxicab to take me out onto the Dallas Highway.

Time was moving backward, but to another beginning.

And it was only a matter of minutes before a sleek, brand-new maroon Mercury stopped to pick me up. " 'I have always depended upon the kindness of strangers.' "

"So have I," he answered. He was no stranger. He was a friend of Dorothy's. Not my type. Beefy, although sweet. He drove me right up to the door of the Blue Bonnet.

Sammy was there.

We went up to Electra for a few days, to get our bearings and eat a few solid meals, and to "let freedom's shawl settle its folds around us," as Sam so quaintly put it.

204

We would travel light, just our army-issue backpack. Via parcel post I sent my duffel bag up to Brooklyn: gone, another symbol of my servitude.

We zigzagged our way down the length and breadth of Texas, on principle zigzagging: no trace of straight left in us nohow, doncha know. We wore civvies. Mine, my old faithful undergraduate chinos; Sam, freshly starched jeans.

One night we spent in Austin, out near the university.

Then down to Houston. And over to San Antonio for a few nights of fun in the shower room of the YMCA.

And then we floated free down to Laredo, crossed the border there, bought some Bacardi rum for ninety-seven cents a bottle, sipped from it all the way down to . . . Monterrey, as it turned out.

There we switched to tequila and checked in to a picturesque hotel named the Zua Zua. It fronted a plaza named the Zua Zua. At dusk we went out hunting—in opposite directions.

South of Monterrey the road rose into the overhanging mountains higher and higher, in ever tightening spirals, into ever sharpening hairpin turns. Or so it seemed to us, becalmed as we were on our bus by equal measures of rum and tequila. We spoke to each other in Tennessee Williams. We watched the bus hang out over nothing as it turned, rising higher and higher.

Once, at a rest stop in a town called Hidalgo, we pissed at a trough which had written on the facing wall one word of graffiti: *Recuerdo*. For the remainder of that journey, whenever I drifted in and out of sleep I heard Sam whispering, *"Recuerdo . . . recuerdo . . . recuerdo. . . ."*

On the morning after the second night on that stinking bus the road suddenly seemed to level off. We came out onto a plain. Far off through the haze we saw the outlines of Mexico City.

In the Mexico City of 1953 the very poor were everywhere the very rich went. There was no in-between. Rum erased that painful reality. A room at the Hotel Geneve, with hot and cold running everything, was essential.

We went to the Palace of Fine Arts to see Riveras and Siqueiroses.

We walked the Chapultepec Gardens.

We ended up on the San Juan de la Trene. We would allow ourselves two nights. No more than that because we would surely sink out of sight on the third night. In matchbox bars with mariachi bands playing different songs in different corners we got drunk beyond the telling of it. The altitude, I thought, the thin air; the wild free fall, the chaotic freedom, the gin, the rum, all of it threatened to do me in. That was not it, not for me. Sam seemed to deal with it without a care. The first night he even saw me into a cab, told the driver where to take me. Happily I went. I slept a light-headed lovely sleep. *"Ich träumte von bunten Blumen/So wie so wohl blühen in Mai"*: it *was* May, and I dreamed I was carrying a geranium plant all in bloom to my mother for Mother's Day. . . .

The following morning I woke refreshed. Sam over in his twin bed never heard me stir or shower or go out or come back.

But, by that evening he was ready all over to begin again. He took me to a clean, well-lit, mucho macho cantina he had been taken to the night before by *"un hombre,* doncha know. Said *hombre* told me it was the place to go during the after-work drinking hour, if you catch my drift."

I caught it, I could see for myself. Six P.M. and packed. An entrancing place it was indeed, with a long, gleaming, waxed wood bar and gleaming, well-dressed businessmen everywhere one's eyes chanced to look. A gleaming double row of them stretched the length of the bar and all of them very properly lifting bottles of Dos Equis, as if on cue, while the other free hand fumbled inside a pocket, playfully cupping and lifting privates: an offering of testes, or so it seemed to my wondering eyes. And, at my ears I heard a mumuring, mesmerizing sound, a low-down lazy, slow-moving sound, *"Mi corazón, . . . mi cor-*

206

azón . . ." while up above ebony blades of ceiling fans stirred the smoke-filled air slowly, ever so slowly. Light-headed still, I steadied myself against a handy wooden wall.

Sam handed me a Dos Equis and sidled off, disappearing behind those rows of raised arms. *"Mi corazón . . . mi corazón . . ."* came from the jukebox. So did the sounds of strumming guitars. The beer was cold, satisfying, soothing. Now, if only I could find me a *mi corazón* for the night . . . Dazed by it all, I drank deep draughts. Delirious, I thought, but wasn't that a hand handing me another bottle of Dos Equis?

Yes. The hand was real. So was the smiling face facing me. A warm, open, winning face, with a forehead framed by coils of dark wavy hair. A handsome face. He nodded. I nodded. He even bowed. So old-worldish. So elegant. So much easier to call my attention immediately to his hand inside his pocket lifting, offering his cock and balls: the signal. Will-I? Won't I? How efficient. Not a wasted motion. How . . . healthy.

I smile. I nod again: Yes, indeed, I would very much like to "ronda at the old posada" with him as *mi corazón* for the night. *Porqué no?*

Preliminaries concluded, he asks in English of easy grace and style if I have a place to go—"because, unfortunately, I have only an hour, little more, before I must return"—*a mi casa* . . . "to my wife."

"Oh," I say first, and then, "*Sí. Sí.* I understand." I will throw caution off the Mexico City mesa. I have hundreds of wild oats to sow. I don't want them rotting on the vine—if that's what wild oats do. For now, it's lust. For this night this is Mr. Right. "Do you know the Hotel Geneve?"

Does he know it? "A good hotel. Yes—and I am Pedro."

I'll bet, but if he wants to be Pedro, it is perfectly all right with me. I shake his offered hand. A strong grip. I tell him who I am. I tell him, also, that I must seek out the friend I came with— "I don't want him to come in on us unexpectedly, to interrupt us. Interrupt?" I repeat, checking to discover, to make sure, his intentions are the same as mine.

They are. "Yes. You go. I secure us a taxi, Weel-yum? Yes?" *"Sí,"* I say, insisting on Spanish, doncha know. When in Rome . . .

I spy Sam. He is deep in conversation with his own *corazón*. When, and if, he misses me, he will understand. And, anyway, I see that Pedro, out in the real world beyond the glass doors of this lovely barroom, has a cab waiting. When I arrive at his side, he tells the driver, "Geneve," so I know I will be safe. If life is all risk, this one is well worth taking; happily, I will eat a peach with Pedro. And, settling in, settling closer to him as soon as the cab revs up, speeds off, I whisper, *"Mi corazón . . ."* realizing that Pedro expects a whisper. Out in the open air, on the open market, Pedro's manner is businesslike. Any lapse of my behavior would scandalize him.

In point of fact, we are an incongruous pair, me in my college mode, he in his fastidious three-piece. Pedro is perhaps thirty and sleek. He is deliciously oiled and alluringly scented. His beige silk-worsted suit has been fitted tight, revealing a modest bulge of muscle, a full puff of privates. Cunning, all that, and his many-colored silk rep tie, the bright colors on a field sorrel, soothingly green, his white cotton shirt shiny: pima, I presume. Exotic as he is. All the way from the Nile, his pima cotton.

At the hotel he pays the cab, telling me he will follow me to the elevator. I should not look back; he will be there. Have no fear. He will attract no attention. Impossible. Heads turn as he pats the top of his lustrous hair, as he strides with manful grace just a step behind me. "A thing of beauty. . ."

Once inside the room, Pedro, accenting our need for speed, strips, never once stopping to preen or pose, even accomplishing the practical: he pulls back the bedspread before extending himself on the top of the fresh sheet. He stretches luxuriously so that the dim light of the bedlamp will pinpoint the high points

208

of what he knows to be an uncommonly well-molded body. All the parts have been harmoniously assembled.

As I undress, assessing the prize I have won, he smiles, pleased that I am pleased, and pleased with me. Scanning the merchandise being offered, he then welcomes me down beside him, his fingers instantly busy, tip-tapping their message of pleasure all over the bare skin of my anxious breast. Like castanets his fingers . . . *Ai . . . yi . . . yi! Olé!* He reaches across me to switch off the bedlamp, stays put there on top of me.

Skin to skin.

Oiled and scented and slippery. *"Mi corazón,"* he whispers, and, for that moment of darkness in that nondescript hotel room, instead of laughing, I believe. I make believe I am his heart—at least for as long as it takes him, takes me, to come. The smooth tufts of his slowly circling fingertips convince me nothing else will matter for a while. In the grand scheme of things, this is it. More even than a touch of Harry, this night.

Pedro twists and rubs and sucks and pokes and probes. Considerately. Gently: a gentleness inspiring my gentleness. Sweet simple sex, and everything reciprocal. Back and forth.

An hour or so.

And a half hour more . . . and then he says he will shower. He will have to leave for home. It is after seven by then.

"Yes," I say, but unwillingly, holding on, "I know. You warned me in advance. Go shower. Use whatever you need . . . my cologne . . ." But how can he use Old Spice? His wife will surely smell the difference, will surely sense, when she touches him, the loss of sheen on his luscious skin.

He is prepared. He has a vial of Vetiver. He names it for me. And another vial of rose oil. "I carry them . . . for just such happy moments as these."

Thoughtful, this Pedro. Kind, memorable. He will be. I have no doubt of that—but I have another kind of doubt. I ask him,

"Why are you married? Why did you find it necessary to marry?"

He checks his wrist watch. Yes, his eyes seem to say, there is time. He is fully dressed and buttoned. He sits at the edge of the bed. Thinking, he runs his smooth fingertips up and down my bare back. My question tests the depths of his goodwill. It was foolish of me to ask it just as he was ready to, had to, leave, but he is obviously a decent man. He wants to say something, wants to explain. He feels that the flow of my feelings is real enough, is genuine. So was his—which is why I felt I could ask the question. In that wordless language, we have understood each other perfectly. "This," his fingers lift and stop above my skin, "has nothing to do with that." Slowly he moves his arm in the direction of the hotel window. "This is private between us. With my wife it is private too. In my country there are many like us. Many have a son and a daughter as I do. I want them . . . and my wife. I do not have to tell her about this. But I do not hurt her in any way. I do not keep anything else from her. I do not keep myself from her. I love her. So far this . . ." his fingers resume their smoothing, "makes me no trouble. And in the future . . . I do not worry about that for now." Once more his fingers stop. His expression tells me he is considering whether there is more he can say—but he has to go.

He stands, slapping his thigh, "So . . . adiós, Weel-yum." He strides to the door; mucho macho his stride and his warm smile. He is satisfied. So am I, mucho satisfied. He waves.

I wave back.

Pedro bows, steps out into the hotel corridor with care, cautiously. Reality awaits him. The coast is clear. Ever so quietly he closes the door and is gone.

I lie there. For the moment, all appetites are sated. Languor in my arms and fingers, my legs, feet, toes. No need to push up and be off. No cot to consider for reveille. No motor pool. No tank to climb into. No colonel to service. No books to hide in my footlocker. Nothing . . . I stretch, shudder, collapse, ready for sleep, a dreamless, Samless sleep.

                              *   *   *

Cuernavaca was stuck in Sam's mind. "We have an appointment there, V'lodya. I just know it. I feel it in my bones. Trust
me? One more time?"

Why not?

The bus we took down there was an unpromising setting for
omens. Squalid and smelly and barely serviceable, it took the
hairpin turns at a crawl.

Sam led us to the main square first of all, to assess the action
to and fro. *Paso doble* to the right; *paso doble* to the left. I saw
nothing arresting. Mangy meats on skewers. Mangy, unpruned
heavy hanging trees—and then it began to rain. Ah, Cuernavaca,
cruel.

The only sign that perhaps our luck hadn't finally deserted us
was that we stumbled into an inexpensive pension very near
the square. Sam suggested separate rooms. They were cheap
enough.

They were on the second floor, and from the veranda outside
them we leaned against the railing to study the courtyard down
below. Vividly green. Lushly overgrown. Lizards skittered for
cover. The rain had steadied to a downpour. Great globs of it
beat loudly on the yucca fronds. On the palm leaves. On the
ferns and cacti. Like the beat, beat, beat of my heartbeat, the
rains came. "Look homeward, Angel," I thought, but didn't say.
I didn't say anything. Neither did Sam. We just stared down at
the rain beating against the green growing things in the courtyard.

Eventually we roused ourselves. We walked out to explore
and found a cantina nearby where we could sit, protected
from the rain, and watch it splash into the basin of a non-
working fountain in the courtyard. We drank Bacardi rum all
afternoon.

And back at the pension we drank some more Bacardi rum,
bottles of which were less than one dollar. Imagine that! We sat
outside our rooms drinking, watching, listening.

Outside another room further down the veranda a middle-aged

                                 211

woman drank from her bottle of rum. At her feet a young girl played with a doll. The woman was all done up in a peasanty tunic over a long full skirt, but she was unmistakably American, with hair frizzed a very dyed red. Sam asked her could we join her. "Yes, indeed yes. Please . . ." She was from the States, from Massachusetts, "I'm so hungry for talk from the States." Sam asked her how long she had been staying in Cuernavaca. "Not staying . . . living. Have to . . ." One question was all she needed; she told us the rest without being asked. Back home, in Boston, she had been someone's mistress, "Someone well enough known so that when I became pregnant and didn't want an abortion, I had to be shipped out. . . ." Her daughter was seven years old; Lili was her name. Lili looked up at her mother. Her mother had begun to sing, too loudly, "'The song of love is a sad song, Hi Lili, hi Lili, hi lo. . . .'" Clearly, Lili hates her mother, hates her for a lot more than the song she continues to sing. Sam joins her. He's drunk. So am I. So is Lili's mother. She leans forward to smooth Lili's blond hair the rain has curled into tangled strands. Lili shivers, her hate too much to handle.

Or am I imagining it? Am I so drunk I'm beginning to see things that aren't there? Lili and I watch Lili's mother and Sam lean closer together to sing together "'Hi Lili, hi Lili, hi lo. . . .'" I lift my bottle of Bacardi and realize with a sudden sobering degree of certainty that if I take one more sip, I'll throw up. I don't want to do that. I also don't want to sing, which is what Sam keeps urging me to do.

I nod no, and no, and no, and then I hear myself saying, "This is not it. This is not it at all, Sam. . . ."

I remember managing to get up, managing to find my way to my lumpy bed in the dark of my room. I remember spinning in the darkness. I remember feeling lonely and alone. I remember thinking I had to stop the rum, stop the spinning, stop this following after Sam. . . .

The next morning we hung low over the veranda railing and I

212

told Sam I thought it was time for me to hightail it back up to Brooklyn. I would return to Mexico City. I would use most of what was left of my severance pay for an airplane ticket.

He didn't seem at all surprised. He nodded more than he said anything. We watched the rain for a while. I asked him what he thought he would do.

For a time he would stay on at the pension, as long as his money lasted, and wait for the next thing—"for some kind of . . . vision. You seem to have had yours all of a sudden. . . . In any case, likely we've gone about as far together as we can . . . at least for now we have. . . ."

CHAPTER
5

The hand I am leaning against at Sam's back windows is the hand on which I wear my Omega. Its ticking fills my head, distracts me from the miracle of how Sam's garden grows. Five P.M. back in New York. Usually, Victor would be about ready to telephone me, at the apartment, or out at the house. But today? What will he do with that habit today? And where will he go when he leaves his office? Aye me, I sigh, musing so, for those concerns are for now none of my business. Sam is—and before he can stop me this time I plunge into my shoulder bag, pull from it a fifth of Johnny Walker Black. "Happy house. Happy Birthday. Later you choose a place for dinner. My treat."

"Thank you ever so, Blanche, honey. I think a drink would do us both a world of good. You look a mite peak-ed. So why don't you sit yourself over to the table. I'll get us some glasses." Into his faded eyes some green fire flickers. In a bound he makes his way over to the wondrously waxed wooden cabinets above the sink. His handiwork, no doubt.

My shoulder bag, if not my mind, lighter, I heave-ho away from the windows, from the comforting view of the synagogue wall. Weary, I am that, and wary too. Yes, because the management of the mind at fifty is always uncertain, unpredictable. All sorts of siftings and fugitive wisps therein; fragments of old now-useless feelings, fossil feelings preserved in the remembered fuzz of a root beer float. And faces and places and phrases, remembered pictures always escaping from cramped cubbyholes, always working loose, sticking out of cracks and fissures, always so sharp-edged, sharp as a knife, those memories of another time. Times with Sam. Times with Victor—and where is my Victor now while I am here seeking the comfort of a comfortable chair?

A straightbacked chair with arms. It gives. It supports.

And the tabletop underhand? It soothes with its cool smoothness.

Before sitting—his chair is sister to mine—Sam pours what strikes me as an overdose. He raises his tumbler. The Scotch trembles in it.

In mine too.

"A toast, V'lodya . . . as you used to say it: To whatever consolations console." He sits before he chugalugs.

Challenged, I follow his lead . . . in the manner of our Blue Bonnet days. For old time's sake, doncha know. But my stomach is an older stomach—and it is empty. It growls. My eyes fill up with tears.

And so does Sam wince, I notice, managing nevertheless a brave smile. "Lovely. Just what we needed. Settles the nerves so. And Lord knows I was nervous . . . all these years since Cuernavaca. More than half my lifetime. Just whooshed on by . . . my life . . . and done so differently. Still . . ." he pours again, a modest amount, but the floodwaters are rising; the dike will burst, ". . . do it one way, do it another, no matter. Same time gets used up." He sips.

I sip. I feel a great flush rush to the surface of my skin. I feel heat beneath my beard. "O my dear, O my dear . . ."

"Do you still *recuerdo* it all, honey? Do you remember the San Juan de la Trene? and all those *mi corazóns*?"

"As a matter of fact that is exactly what I was just remembering . . . but you always could read clear to the bottom of my mind."

"Then. Not anymore, I expect. Soon as you boarded that bus for Mexico City . . . we stopped. You just left me there alone. Bereft is how I felt. . . . Never wrote you that in my letters, though. No point . . ."

"You didn't try to stop me either. All you did was dangle your bottle of Barcardi . . . by its neck. That was good-bye. You even walked away from the bus before it pulled out of the square."

"If you'd stayed, things might have been different." He hasn't heard me. He doesn't want to. "We could have traveled on to someplace more to your liking. We could have gone anywhere then."

"No. We couldn't have. My mother was dying. Remember? I wrote you? Three months after I got back to Brooklyn she was dead. She knew it all along, knew it that night I called her from Fort Hood. Remember that night? I called to tell her we were going to travel around for a while. 'For how long?' she asked me. 'How long is long?' she wanted to know. . . . Even if I'd stayed in Cuernavaca, Sammy, I would have gone home for the funeral. I never would have left New York after that. There was City College. She never wanted me to leave it. If I had listened to her, I never would have been drafted."

"And then you never would have met me . . . but, if you had stayed in Cuernavaca, you never would have met Victor, would you?" His eyes, I see, are now after mine: their target.

I look away first, glancing over at the brown, side-by-side GE, and then to the mullioned panes of the back windows. The sunlight has grayed. Clouds are scudding. I must force my gaze back to a present sticking place, to some bric-a-brac on which it can land heavily. Instead, it is drawn to Sam's stomach. An overflow. Straining the buttons of his cardigan. Pressing the edge of the table, impinging its bloat on the flatiron firmness of how I remember him. He sees the object of my attention. He is not amused.

This time my flush is embarrassment. I find myself sipping too fast and too much, sloshing the excess stinging Scotch through the crevices the years have worn between my teeth. I should apologize. Age has, after all, withered me too. There is the obvious matter of my frizzled gray beard and my thinning gray hair. Flyaway hair . . . fly away, fly away home to Victor, hair. . . . And what of my eyes? Surely a match for his bad ears. Quite chopfallen, both of us. I am as new to him as he is to me.

He lights a cigarette, subjecting me to some up-close, fierce scrutiny. "Stopped smoking, I suppose."

"Yes. Victor did, so I did. At the same time. That helped."

"Helped what?—no, nevermind that. Scratch that. And grass? To accompany your Scotch!"

"Victor doesn't enjoy it. No point doing that alone."

"If most things you do are alone there is."

Angry: he is clearly angry . . . with me. I've betrayed him by staring at his stomach too long. But, surely, there's no gainsaying its size. As plain as the nose on my face.

"Changed some, haven't I?" His chin lifts challengingly.

"We both have. Living will do that . . ." I want to ha-ha-ha, ho-ho-ho and a bottle of Barcardi's. I want to say, You went your way, I went mine, and after twenty-seven years of doing things differently, differences are bound to pop up, doncha know. Not necessarily for the worse, not necessarily for the better, just . . . differences. *"N'est-ce pas, Sammy, honey?"* Perhaps a foreign tongue will neutralize the tartness between us, get us marching ahead, out of this no-man's-land between the trenches of then and now. Or perhaps we have no present interest in each other, only the past? No new *links* to link us together? No grand allusions? No strong, subterranean feelings left? No "talk" left in "those turning eyeballs"? The sunlight streaks the tabletop. Dims. Disappears . . .

"There'll be fog soon enough," he says coldly. I have slipped from the center of his target—for now; but I sense the specter of an unpredictable return. Slowly, portentously, he offers his profile, readying himself for something solemn, "Fog comes fast in San Fransisco . . ." but he's reaching for more, revving up, ". . . given me the arthritis, especially in my knees. Cramps my style. Cuts down cruising time . . . not that you would know much about modern techniques. Out of practice, aren't you, honey? I've had to keep up . . . to survive, doncha know. All very specialized . . . wrinkle bars, fat bars, leather bars, back rooms . . . everything's up-to-date in San Francisco. New York, too, of course, but you . . . you're stuck at the letter V. I remember I wrote that in one of my sassy letters some years back . . . while you were stuck at the letter V, I would be searching for the next letter of the alphabet to love—I saved all of *your* letters—"

"And I saved all of yours, Sammy."

"Honored, I'm sure. Embarrassed too. All those lovers I've documented. In the sixties alone there was a Don, a Rick, a Larry . . . then Edward. Lovely Edward. Lasted right up until that famous love-in . . . in the Golden Gate Park. That would have been in sixty-eight. Allen Ginsberg came to that . . . and that was also the afternoon I met Hardy. Hardy was from Pretty Plains, Kansas. Can't ever forget someone from Pretty Plains, Kansas, can one? And he was some pretty, let me tell you. He didn't last long, fortunately for me because his father came looking for him, to take him back home. Turned out Hardy and his father had been making it from when Hardy was eleven, which was right after his mother passed on. Hardy featured her. I saw photographs of them side by side. Duplicates. And that father? Ferocious, honey. A quintessential bull-eyed block of a man. I was fortunate to get myself free of all that without a mortal wound. I do remember writing you about that unsavory episode—but letters are pretty compared to reality. . . . Anyway, right after Hardy I managed to find a Zack. Threw myself on him . . . and then onto a Peter and an Amos. Amos from Beersheba. Looked like you. He was the only one who lasted any respectable amount of time since then, and about then's when I wrote you wondering how you were able to stay stuck on the letter *V*? Don't you just sometimes hanker after some passing hump, honey?"

"Indeed, I do."

"Then what?"

"Mostly I let it pass right on by. My future's not in pursuit. Victor and I . . . that's been our way. Every couple that stays a couple . . . has to work out their own way."

"And Victor's happy about the arrangement?"

"So far as I know."

"But you're not certain?"

"Not one hundred percent. Conditions are always changing. Even now . . ." I paused. I was running out of steam. Arrived sooner than anticipated, my moment to break down, open up, tell all. Sam was even waiting, expecting something. No matter what he said, he still could read my mind. Lots of "trouble in mind." A trainload of trouble, and twenty-seven years filled with days I could detail. Mundane details . . . a richness of mundane details about Victor and myself that would positively *un*rivet his attention. So where should I begin? At what beginning? He already knows most of the facts from my letters, even knows details about that day before the night Victor and I actually met. . . .

"Even now, what, honey?"

"I . . ." I falter, unsure, my uncertainty coming at me like a one-two to the solar plexus—and I see that Sam will wait no longer.

"Victor wants more? That it, honey? Makes you jealous, doesn't he, when he does the hankering. You always did get jealous. Anyone came between us. I do remember. . . ." His elbows on the table, his raised palms turned up to receive his chin, he remembers. He's revving up again, waking up in another time, "You used to get red all over . . . I never ever will forget that night in the Blue Bonnet we saw Lieutenant Rod . . . my rod and my staff . . . you positively glowed, V'lodya, and you were right.

219

I did so ache after him, but I acted honorably. Can't gainsay that, honey. When I left the bar I was preparing myself for the misery of a lost love. I felt so noble and selfless. It was only the purest kind of chance I bumped into him on the steps of the Adolphus. Just magic is what it was. Happens every now and again . . . and just think what it led us to? I'm alive and you're alive. . . ." He paused to pour, and then he settled back in his straightbacked arm chair, sliding down some, giving up the battle it was to suck in his gut. There it was: round and fully packed. "So wharnow are we, Anna Livia? Is it full circle we've come? 'Could it be you and me?' Still? I mean, who could ever have foretold we'd meet like this in San Francisco? I would have thought New York. I even toyed with that idea. Seriously . . . I truly did. Thought of moving to New York. I wrote you and you were ever so encouraging but then your mother was dying and then you met Victor and then it was one thing after another . . . my father dying— that was in 'fifty-five and all I was doing was hanging around, going up to Dallas when the spirit moved me, feeling I had better get myself doing a lot more of everything or I'd never get to do anything at all. Nothing more than drink myself silly in the Blue Bonnet waiting for some vision to propel me the hell out of Electra. I'd sit at that bar thinking of you and say those lovely Walt Whitman lines out loud to no one at all . . . 'I do not doubt I am to meet you again, I am to see to it that I do not lose you'— except one night someone sitting next to me recognized them, a someone who just happened to teach English lit up at the University of Kansas, in Wichita. . . . I followed my heart to Wichita . . . where I was happy for a time. . . . Mama did fight me. She surely did. But I knew it was then or it was never and I told her if I did not go to college I'd kill myself. I meant it too because by then there wasn't a person left in Electra for me to care about. First Miss Amanda died and then Owen and Oveta moved over to Europe permanently, to Geneva. . . . Murchison Manor's been converted into a condominium apartment house, Willy. Can you imagine that? But back when I was thinking of killing myself

Oveta just up and sold it. Owen wanted to study the piano seriously. Found an elderly Jewish gentleman, a Holocaust survivor, to teach him. They became lovers. Oveta would write me how they used to play Schubert and Mozart four hands and how she'd go to all those spas, getting her blood shot into the air to purify it the way they used to do the water in the reservoir back in Electra. She kept wanting me to follow them over there, wanted to keep me, but what she really wanted was to save me from myself. Wanted to get me going somewhere, anywhere, up to Wichita or to Europe or to New York to you . . . and Victor— which wouldn't have made any sense. So I chose Wichita instead of death. Lasted there for two years. About all I could take of my professor. Nineteen fifty-seven by then. Maybe 'fifty-eight . . . whenever it was your father did in fact kill himself, Willy. Did it the same way I always planned, except it struck me so odd an Eastern man like your father would ever think to do it with a shotgun. Would have been more appropriate for a Texan, doncha know. Double barrels in the mouth . . . squeeze off the triggers with my bare toes . . . oh, Willy, I am a fool. Forgive me going on like this." He reaches out to pat the top of my hand, to stop its nervous smoothing of the tabletop. "It's just we've got so much catching up to do. All we know is from letters and you . . . you seem so *penseroso*, honey, so I thought I'd start out talking. I'm alone so much these days the opportunity to talk carried me away and back, way back. Back and forth. My head's spinning—or maybe it's the Scotch that makes me so digress. Probably it's everything all at once, all this one-on-one . . . that's a sports term, honey. Can't rightly remember which sport, just at the moment. I watch them all on telly. Rather do that some nights than cruise, what with all those hunks jumping around hugging and grabbing ass and then if they take you down into the locker room, well, then heaven takes on a whole new meaning. I love looking. I always did . . . in the men's room of the Greyhound . . . in the shower room of our barracks. Remember how I'd follow Arnie Duberman into the shower room and you'd

221

have one of your jealous fits—" He stops short suddenly, sitting up, staring at me, as if remembering he means to be as angry as he was a few minutes before. And again I am at the center of his fixed stare, its target. Above the rim of his glass, fading green fire flickers; he shakes the amber ice: a warning. "Changed some, haven't I, honey? But make no mistake, I still see that hot water running off Arnie Duberman's sweet prick as if it were today. And Barnett Peterson playing with himself . . . those pictures . . . those are real. So's the lust that goes with them. Inside me I'm as young as I want to be when I remember them—and others. Those half-naked men on TV . . . they just get my motor running, nothing more. Of course, your motor doesn't need any spark. Too busy fucking and sucking with Victor to need any visual aids, I expect. No spurs necessary. No surrogates. No fantasies. Not even a dog!" Challenging, imperious—his chin lifts in its "old high way" of lifting.

But keeping it so requires some extra effort. A pathetic tremor tattletales just how much. That chin wants lowering. It wants to nuzzle, rest, in the nest of his cardigan's floppy collar. Yes . . . and there it goes, down—and out go the green flickerings.

"We did have dogs, Victor and I. Three of them. A mother and two daughters. From different litters. Dead now. All of them . . . of natural causes. As surrogates, dogs don't last, not as long as children do."

"Say what?"—but he has heard me all right. Just doesn't want to follow my train of thought. On another schedule, his thoughts. Something devilishly lascivious flashes out from behind his half-mast lids. "Tell me, Willy, have you and Victor done threesomes yet?"

"Yet? Is it inevitable? But, no, Victor and I still like it one-on-one, as you do. We're the same generation, Sammy. The three of us."

"But however do you avoid boredom, Blanche, honey? Been a problem for me. The novelty wears off, doncha know. Familiarity . . . makes me go limp."

222

"For me it does just the opposite. Not every time, I admit. The earth doesn't move every time we have sex, but, in balance, the balance is favorable. More movings than not, over the years. Conditions keep on changing. So do we—which is how the familiar helps us continue as a couple. The more we change, the easier it is to continue."

"You are talking riddles, honey . . . and I am talking the plain, honest-to-goodness truth. The familiar is a cage. The unknown sets you free."

"There's an inner unknown too, Sammy, and only familiarity leads you closer to that . . . not that it matters, I suppose. As you said, go one way, go another, in the end it's all the same. You come to the same place. Alone, together, gay, straight . . . with or without a 'painted paradise.' Therefore, as I always used to say—and still do: Whatever consolations console . . ." I lifted my glass of Scotch. "Life's a vale of tears with some high-ground smooth patches every now and again. That being the case, and as long as you don't hurt anyone or deprive anyone of their right to be different, I can't see why my way of life should matter to anyone else. Lord knows, I try, Stella. With Victor . . . I try. For twenty-seven years I've been trying . . ."

"And failing? Isn't that why you are so *penseroso?* Been having to try so hard just to continue? That it?" Zooming in, offering his good ear, Sam is on the attack. He's leaped right into the center of my scudding thoughts. "You're the one's doing all the changing? And Victor's not? I'll just bet that's the case."

I fall back, weary, dazed. I need a Red Sea miracle to save me from drowning.

Expectantly . . . expecting what? . . . he waits for some word from me.

I sip some more Scotch, hoping for a shred of self-composure to return. Instead, it gutters, nearly gone. I stare off to where I know Sam's garden will keep on growing, to where I see the fog settling down in earnest now. We are really in the dark, Sam and I.

But Sam, I also see, is rising, and all in a rush he comes to rest behind my chair, his hands taking hold of my shoulders, his fingers massaging a new message into my skin, stirring fossils of feeling down in my deepest deeps. He leans lower, his cheek coming to rest firmly on top of my flyaway hair, his hands holding me against the back of the chair. "Never fear, V'lodya," he whispers, "we've got another chance. We'll just leave Cuernavaca together this time."

The silence lengthens. Somewhere far off, in a room I haven't been to yet . . . Sam's bedroom? . . . I hear a clock ticking. My mind is shooting ESP arrows eastward. Tardy by far too many years this lifting me bodily, this urging me up to turn and face him, to receive his kiss: futile. But in his lips he's packed all our remembered past. Once upon a time he was . . . once upon a time I was . . . and now, at this moment, we are the only ones who know what we used to be. All of that his fingers are trying to touch back into living, into feeling. They seem to be everywhere at once, stroking the back of my neck, tracing the edges of my ears, skimming my lips. He nibbles at my earlobe, breathing into it. Even his prick is swelling. He rubs up against me, pushes gently, slowly, and from side to side: an old rhythm, an old tune he never wanted to play on me when he had all those opportunities years before. He could have played a symphony on my bare skin back then. Now all I hear in his dit-dotting fingertips is tattoo. Taps. His eyes are even closing.

Mine stay open. Those fossil feelings aren't catching fire. Nibble at my neck as he will, nothing stirs. No faking it, either. He never did with me, then; I won't now. No need now, no matter how *penseroso* I may be, no matter how hard I've tried and, perhaps, failed with Victor. No. Done with, that time of my life, the time of wanting green-fire-in-the-eyes Samuel R. Tolan. Yes, that much has changed inside me. And *that* Sam Tolan, the one who touched my romantic-agony young life into living, is only a picture hanging on the wall of my mind: a still-life memento. Next to it hangs one of me; Sam then; myself then.

Decisively, he takes hold of my elbow in just the same way he always used to whenever he wanted to get me going to some place of his choosing. Gladly, then. Now I want to stand my ground because now he wants to lead me from the kitchen, probably to that other room I haven't been to yet, the room where the clock is ticking louder and louder. "It still could be, Blanche," he whispers insistently, breathing the words into my ear, "it could, Blanche . . . you and me. I'm alone. You will be . . ."

I stop.

His eyes open. The me he sees seems to startle him.

And so does my answer, "Are you suggesting incest, Stella, honey?"

The loop of memory he has been caught up in loosens its hold. He moves me to arm's length, studying me, letting the silence lengthen. With his free hand he begins to smooth my flyaway hair. "Sorry, honey. Just the widening gyre, doncha know. Wanted to leap across it, back to then. Wanted to try. Never know unless I tried." He draws me back, back inside an embrace, now all very sisterly-like, warm, comforting.

And that's when the telephone rings. So shrill. Rings a second time. We move apart. Sam has begun to realize that he will have to answer it. His phone, hanging on the wall of his kitchen, is right next to the door leading out into his beautiful backyard garden. "Why, hello," a bubbly bright hello; he has recovered from his reverie, he's even smiling. "Yes he has arrived indeed . . ." He points the receiver toward me. "Long distance wants you, honey. . . ."

225

EPILOGUE

A swarm of gnats buzzes close, hovers briefly before us, swerves, a collective change of mind suddenly sending it lower, almost down onto the still surface of the lake. The water shivers. The swarm flies up and away from the center of a ring of quickly spreading circles. I follow its flight with exaggerated intensity. Victor doesn't. Uncharacteristically, Victor wants to resume his questioning. The gnats were an unscheduled interruption. "Did he? After I telephoned that afternoon? Did he try anything again?"

We have come down to the dock for a homecoming sit-out at dusk. Victor's suggestion, even before I unpacked. He would make drinks. He would bring them down there. I should just go on ahead. I did, but instead of our chaises, I chose the thorny, bare planking above the three steps leading down into the lake: a not-so-cozy opening between the stairposts. In the past, sitting there, upright, had meant hard-core business. If reason failed, well then at least we would have the stairposts to fall back on for support. "After you telephoned that afternoon . . . Sam redoubled his efforts. I let him. I let him lead me into his bedroom. I figured, why not. Better later than never."

"Bullshit."

"Bullshit . . . but what if it were the truth, Victor? Why should it matter?"

226

"It shouldn't. . . ." He sets his drink down next to mine: the line of scrimmage. He leans back against his stairpost, looks away. All during the drive out to the house from the airport we had avoided tender topics: a pact, sealed with a kiss and a handshake; no tough talk until the lake. He had talked spring things instead, about the lobsters and local clams, the tender soft-shell crabs—"maybe we can get some tonight for dinner. Asparagus is over. So are the strawberries. Just about. Lousy crop this year. Too much rain . . ." I asked about Aaron. "Worse, fast. Your letters perked him up. He decided you were having a terrible time, therefore you would come home for sure. He doesn't want a call tonight. Tomorrow . . ." I asked about my sister. "They're all fine, except she thinks something's not right with us. I didn't deny it . . . but when I told her you were coming home, she thought that was a good sign. I agreed. . . ." I asked about the museum. "We're about to display the Southwest artifacts exhibit for the summer. It should be good. These last few weeks I worked overtime getting it together. Kept me occupied. . . ." That topic threatened our neutrality pact, jostling as it did the sorest subtexts of our separation: Sam, Dallas, the Adolphus. I didn't ask any more questions. Victor turned his attention to the road, to the thickening Friday-afternoon traffic on the Long Island Expressway. We arrived at the house just in time for the sunset. . . .

"So? Was Aaron right? Did you have a terrible time with Sam?"

"No. Not terrible. Sobering . . ." As usual, my "Why should it matter?" had come too soon. But his questions, his willingness to ask, the busy beat of his eyelids told me soon, soon, he'd come back to it, just give him a break for now, couldn't I see he was trying? I could—and I would pull back. "Actually, after that first afternoon we fell into our old habit of sisterhood . . . for the last time, probably. We went barring a lot, to the Castro. There's a wrinkle bar he likes. He's made out there. And a leather bar he goes to for laughs. He enjoys the costumes. He's not an S-and-M

227

type. A few times I went to his shop to see his work. His heart is in his carpentry, and in his garden, but he's not a loner. Acquaintances kept dropping by. He does pot with them, gives them drinks and munchies. Sam still has his way. People stick to him. The way they do to you. They don't to me . . . 'they flee from me that one time did me seek' . . . professional hazard. I've turned into a graybeard loon . . ."

"Does that mean you didn't have sex while you were out there?"

"Yes . . . but I did come close. A sweet young man. He reminded me so much of you the night we met. Tough and tender and so unaware of how good-looking he was. Sam kept pushing me to take him home."

"Why didn't you?"

"He looked too much like you. . . . As soon as I said no, someone else was on his trail. No harm done."

"Not to him, Willy."

"Nor to me. I still like my sex to have a future." Another swarm of gnats buzzes before us, blurring our view of the western shore. Neither of us raises a hand to brush it away. They are on their own. They will . . . or they won't. Whatever Mother Nature fancies. Her inscrutable message: imperfections. Gnats in May and June . . . and ticks and termites. Mosquitoes in July. Flies in August. Hornets, bees and ants all summer long. Some years, hordes of hairy gypsy moths. Some years blight on the tomatoes. Some years the corn won't come to a plump ear, the russets taste like sponge, the bay scallops are scarce. Some years . . . more down days, day after day. And some years more up. Down and up. Up and down. The rhythm of change, year after year: the constancy of change the only constant to count on, that and . . . imperfections. The simplest facts of life, those, the same in each and every, whether hetero or homo, and whether *they* like it or no: our shared fate. Life . . . change . . . love, if you're lucky . . . imperfections . . . death. For one and all . . . and gnats . . . and waterbugs. Just now they are skittering quick-

228

silver lines of light below us on the darkening surface of our little lake.

Over in the western sky the sun has sunk beneath the line of trees: on its way to Sam, leaving us its glow. A fiery glow, setting fire to the string-of-pearl clouds at rest above the tree line and to the surface of the water: a mirror reflection . . . the glow, the trees, the clouds, the dusk-blue sky, up and down.

Victor reaches over our line of scrimmage glasses, takes hold of my hand. "It matters . . ."

"What does, Victor?"

"That . . . you came home."

"Oh . . . well, it wasn't my idea to leave. You made me feel that I should. You made me feel I'd lost the battle I didn't even know I was fighting with you. What's a cattleman in the grand scheme of our lives, I thought. You thought otherwise, so I went. I went backward, looking for myself, looking for who I used to be . . . before you."

"Does it matter anymore? Who you used to be? After so many years?"

"It does to me, Victor. Just as artifacts matter to you. Change explains us, especially us. Our beginnings were not exactly auspicious. Remember?"

He remembers all right. I can feel him remembering: he lets my hand slip slowly through his. I can see him remembering: his eyelids begin beating faster; his head tilts as if he is listening for a distant sound at the center of the evening's hush.

A faint breeze starts up, clicking the heavy leaves overhead, shirring the water before us. A flock of swallows, dipping, twisting up, rushes by. A chipmunk darts onto the dock behind us, dashes off into the brush. Far off I hear a dog's tireless bark. And then a train whistle, the 7:40, according to my Omega. I smooth its face, cup it for comfort. Staccato stabbings begin a pick, pick, pick in my heart. A piece of the past opens up . . . and then there we are, walking toward each other. "Remember that night, Victor? In June, too. Twenty-seven years ago . . . but you weren't so

229

quiet that night. A torrent of words you were. You remember, don't you?"

"I do. . . ."

My mother was having a "good" day, the first since her operation, the first since I'd gotten home from Cuernavaca. She had even asked me to help her out onto the porch after breakfast. "Maybe today you should take a day off, William? Why don't you call one of your friends from before? Maybe go to the beach with them. Evelyn is coming with the children later. Your father can take care of me until then. So why not? Go ahead. For my sake, go. . . ."

So, I did—but alone. None of my friends from "before" would have helped, only Sam. *Before* was done with. I was an army *after*, the only one among my before friends, and the only one now facing a mother's premature and inevitable death. One good day didn't mean recovery. She knew it. I knew it. We all knew it. But we all acted *as if* it wasn't the truth. We saw the sunken corners of her mouth . . . and tried to get her to eat a little more, to take another bite. She had gone for radiation treatments, but the cancer had already spread into her lymph system.

I decided on Riis Park. A perfect beach day. Sunny. Not too warm for June. It would be crowded, a Saturday morning, but it was early enough. I hoped the gay section still existed there because that's what would help: stretching out on the sand among my own kind for a few hours. Let my mind go slack. Let the strain of yet another dissimulation—the ultimate one, about death—ease some, loosen: a lollygag.

On the bus, on the subway, I conjured up pictures of Sam.

I placed him next to me on my army-issue blanket. I felt his bare arm graze against mine. Playing with me. Always rubbing my dying hope to hot desire. Our eyes closed, we heard the lazy waves slap up onto the shore nearby, heard the harmless open-air laughter, the campy sibilance of nearby sisters. Fear and trembling ceased for a few hours under the sun.

I lolled. I lazed. I went into the ocean. Lolled some more. Lazed. Listened to whatever the breeze blew by: ". . . the William Tell. Just opened . . . well, of course it's gay. Would I send you to a straight place? Would I let you be manhandled, honey? . . . you would accuse your old mother of such villainy? Well, I never . . . You might as well try it. Worse you couldn't do. . . . It's on Fifty-third, right off Third. . . . Decor? You're asking decor? It's your basic mafioso, dark and dirty. . . . There's only one San Remo. . . ."

About two I strolled up to the open-to-the-air cafeteria in front of the bath house for a coffee and some shade. I cast glances far and near. They landed lonely among the plastic bric-a-brac. I called home. Everything under control, my father assured me. I could hear my mother telling him to tell me not to worry, tell him he should go out afterward, ". . . tell him, Sol. Tell him to go do . . . whatever . . . whatever he wants. . . ."

No doubt about it. I had gone to Riis Park fully prepared for some whatever. She had seen that when I kissed her goodbye. There I had stood before her, my Macy's special, prearmy ivory linen jacket slung over my shoulder (a favorite, lucky charm cruising jacket from my Harlan Royce–City College–Amelia–bookstore period), and wearing a fresh white buttondown, a red and brown silk rep tie, undone, but slid through the collar funnel, and a faded but freshly laundered pair of khakis. Why such an outfit for the beach unless some whatever was on my mind? And why my toilet articles reticule if not for use after the beach in the bath house? She knew. She had kissed me and told me, even then, "Go, do . . . whatever you want, William. . . ."

So about four I went to the bath house, clutching my locker key conspicuously—no takers—to shower, a lengthy shower, bemused as I was by the passing parade of bare behinds. I shaved fastidiously. I slathered my stick of Old Spice deodorant with abandon, splashed its companionette cologne all over my arms and legs. That stung. Sunburn: a vivid red breaking out even as I stared at it.

On the subway into Manhattan my skin stiffened. Beads of hot sweat rolled down my forehead, soaked my shirt, wilted my will for any whatever. As the train passed through the Clark Street station, I felt unexpected tears spring into my eyes. For shame, How-itz! I should be home. I should get off at the next stop, Wall Street, get on the next train heading back into Brooklyn. Wrong-headed, How-itz! Selfish to go out on the prowl for an anonymous hot body when, at home, another body was wasting away. I shivered with shame. Alone in the subway car I pressed the heels of my palms into my eyes, hoping to press back the tears that wanted out. No. No. No.

But, then, a *What!* What would it change if I were to go home? Nothing at all. Would it stop her from leaping out of sleep, screaming, angry, embarrassed that she had awakened my father and myself, but grateful we were there to hold onto her hands until she fell asleep again? No . . . and by that time I would be back home anyway—probably before that—and ready. Truce for this one night; my body pleaded its case. It was needy. How could a little bit of temporary relief hurt anyone or anything in the grand scheme of how fucked-up everything in the world seemed to be? It couldn't. It wouldn't. Mine was a little enough life not to matter much . . . little and lonely . . .

When the train emerged from the tunnel and the doors opened at the Wall Street stop, I stayed seated.

The William Tell's air conditioning comforted some. At seven, no overload of cigarette smoke. Too early by far. A sparse crowd was on hand. I ordered a Schlitz, dedicated it to Sam, chugalugged it, thirst from dehydration easily overtaking nostalgia. Texas, the army—perhaps even Sam—would soon belong to *before.* And then what? What would come after her death?

The second Schlitz I nursed, musing along the edge of my unknown verge, longing for a brown paper bag, for a gin . . . to do

232

me in. But I would have to forgo Gordon's for the unseeable future. When the inevitable occurred I'd have only GI Bill money as a cushion. No extras. No gin. No playtime. I'd be back at City College, maybe back at Mr. Braunstein's souvenir bookshop. I'd be living . . . where? My father was sure to give up our floor-through. No point staying on there. No point . . . no purpose . . . for him . . . or for me. No reason for me to stay in Brooklyn then. I'd move into Manhattan, be closer to school, to work. I'd . . . be alone, live . . . alone. I gulped some beer, peered through the dim light for a friendly face. There was none. We were still only a handful. We few, we unhappy few: much too early to be out seeking solace. And I couldn't—wouldn't—stay out late. Anyway . . . the heat of my sunburn made the thought of heavy contact sex unbearable. Better if I finished my beer and went home. My red reflection in the mirror behind the bar frightened me.

Slowly, wearily, I made my way toward the exit, looking back one last time, to make sure. Nothing doing. The only movement came from the colored bubbles rising up ·the sides of the jukebox. Melancholy dampened the last remnants of desire. I slung my Macy's jacket over my shoulder, jammed my reticule into my armpit. Just not in the cards this night. This night Will-hee won't, Sam, honey, wherever you are. This night Will-hee will go home with the Sunday *New York Times*. He will reach out resolutely, take hold of the door handle, pushing—just as it was being pulled open.

I stepped aside, out of the path of an inrushing string of stalwarts. One . . . two . . . three . . . the fourth glanced up at me. I was holding the door open. I glanced back. A connection, clearly. Lots of talk in his eyes. A second's exchange because there came the fifth and sixth (Aaron! even then a pudge), bumping up against him, pushing him forward. They continued on to the back of the bar, back beyond the colored light of the jukebox bubbles. Dark back there—but I was still holding the door open.

The dusky light from outside blinded me. I let go, stepped back in, searching for the face of my fourth.

He was coming toward me. Had to be me he was coming toward. There was no one else anywhere near me.

The room wasn't a crowded one. We could see each other across it easily. I didn't for a second leave off looking. Neither did he. We kept coming closer. No dallying. No dithering. No doubt in his expression: tough and tender, ingenuously good-looking, a welcoming smile on his young boy's face. No debate in his step, either: decisive, easy, relaxed. A solid, shortish body. Broad-shouldered, he filled his polo shirt expressively. Not a muscle-bulger, but built, built low to the ground. We met on my side of the jukebox, our outstretched hands colliding. We laughed. Every inhibition I had ever felt in every gay bar of my growing up fell away. Instant infatuation instantly freed me. "You first."

"Victor Friedman." He held on to my hand.

"William Howards." Even my fingers felt free, free and safe. "You're Jewish." I laughed again, giddy with exhilaration. My mother would be happy, swept through my head. No mixed marriage this time. He nodded, not understanding, but willing to laugh too. Behind me the door opened, others moved around us. We held on, our laughter strong, shared, comfortable. What I was feeling with such stunning force, he was feeling. No doubt about it. Our eyes beat that message back and forth. Seconds, a minute, no more than that, and the Will-hee? Won't-hee? me I had lived with for twenty-three years sank out of sight, was gone from my face. I could feel it going. I could feel my jacket slipping from my shoulder.

Victor caught it, took hold of my reticule too, and with his free hand touched my shoulder cautiously. "You must be burning up under that shirt. You need Noxzema badly." His touch rushed through my body, alerted every capillary: more was on its way. His hand cupped my elbow; he wanted me to move. He wanted me to follow him—but not back to his friends, beyond

234

them, to the very back of the bar. "I have to talk to you, William . . ."

"Willy."

"Willy . . . I have to talk fast. I have to tell you something, something you won't like, something I don't like. . . ." At the back of the bar, in an alcove opposite the men's room, was a banquette with a row of tiny tables in front of it. On each table was a toy lamp giving off a fifty-cent-piece circle of light. Victor deposited my belongings and me on the banquette, sat down opposite, leaning forward. "I have to tell you before you say anything to me. One of those guys will be coming back here in a few minutes. He saw what happened between us. He tried to stop me from going up to you. I told him I had to. I did. I . . . knew it the second I saw you at the door. I felt . . . sorry for you. Your sunburn . . ." He smiled, faltering, for the first time, looking away embarrassed. The door to the men's room opened, slammed shut: not exactly the setting for the expression of fine-tuned feelings. And then, at any second his friend would be coming back to claim his prize. That was it: they were a "thing" and I had literally stepped into the center of it. Well . . . that didn't change how I felt. It couldn't. It was too late. A second's work, a minute's, no more than that. He looked at me again, serious now. "Whatever you're thinking you're wrong. I'm not attached to any one of those guys. I'm not attached to anyone. I want to be, though. I want that. I know it now more than ever before. . . . I just got out of the army. A few months ago. Two weeks ago I moved down into the city. I grew up in Westchester . . . Scarsdale, but I got a job down here so I moved, I started going out nights, I got mixed up with the wrong group—wrong for me. They like orgies. I don't. I swear I don't . . . but just tonight, tonight of all nights, I said yes . . . and the guy who is going to be coming back to get me arranged it all. He came in from California this week. I knew him from . . . before, from my college out there. He talked me into it. I said yes . . . you don't believe me, do you? Why should you. You don't know me, but

I'm telling you the truth. I am." He took hold of my hand, tugged it, as if to make sure I believed him, a little boy's honest way of coaxing me, come on, come on. . . . "I'm going to have to go through with it. We won't be able to get together tonight, but tomorrow . . . could you call me tomorrow? Tomorrow morning? First thing? I'll never do this again. Never. I swear it. I knew it was wrong. As soon as I said yes I knew it was wrong. Not life-or-death wrong, just stupid wrong, dumb, because I won't enjoy it . . . and now . . . will you call me tomorrow? I want you to. I wouldn't have told you all this if I didn't want it, would I?" He tugged at my hand again, questioning himself as much as me, as shocked by the speed and force of his feelings as I was by mine. "I know . . . I'm happy I met you. It's going to make a difference in our lives. I know those things. I'm a scientist. So? Will you call tomorrow?"

"I will . . . but . . . I may not be able to see you tomorrow. I want to. I just can't promise . . ."

"You won't call. You think I'm bullshitting you." He looked toward the bar. His friend waved. Victor waved him back. "I don't blame you for not believing me. Why should you . . . ?"

"I believe you, it's just that I've got my own kind of problem." I explained about my mother. I told him I too had just been discharged from the army, that I too wanted "to be attached. I know it now, tonight, more than I ever knew it before."

He reached across the table, lifted my chin—and my sinking spirit. "We'll work something out." His busy eyes stopped their beating. He pulled me toward him. I met him more than half-way. We kissed, not briefly, not lingeringly, but warmly, strongly. "Sealed," he said—and then he broke back into another round of rapid words, easier words, though, words to connect him to the real reality he had lived in every day before this night, words about Scarsdale and growing up there protected from the temptations of Manhattan but knowing, every time he did come down with his friends, that that's where he had to get to, eventually, because he knew there was something about himself that was different: "My friends wanted to make out. I wanted to make out with them, with one of them in particular. We never did. I went to college instead. I went far away to college. To Berkeley. And from there, as soon as I was graduated I was drafted. I came out in the army. Over in Europe. In Germany. I had a friend . . . a buddy . . . from Chicago. He took me around. To Paris. To London. To Rome. Even to Capri. I was a . . . number. So was he. We never had sex. I wanted to. He said we shouldn't—but enough about me. Has this . . . this . . . whatever it is . . . ever happened to you before?"

"Not like this. No . . ." I told him about Sam and Dallas, about how different my growing up had been, about how an hour on the subway and there I was, at work, and after work, cruising, ". . . so I found out about myself in a hurry. I found out at an early age I wasn't alone." I told him about Harlan and Amelia and Jerry Saperstein, skimming over the details for now; there wasn't time—and then there wasn't time to tell him any more because there came Mr. California. There was no waving him back again.

Victor began writing on the inside cover of a book of William Tell matches. (Where else?) He opened my palm, placed the matches inside it, closed my fingers over it, covered my hands inside his. "My telephone number and address. Even if you can't come tomorrow, telephone, Willy. I want us to see each other again. You do too. It's in your eyes." He stood up, stood still. A second of silent looking between us—and it was settled: yes. He smiled. "It was your sunburn . . . that stopped me first . . . and your eyes. They're needy. They're honest. . . ." Mr. California arrived in time for that. He laughed, grabbed hold of Victor's arm. Victor shook himself free, stepped around the man— he was a man, more than middle-aged—strode his decisive, nononsense stride back to the bar, charging the center of the string of stalwarts. They regrouped, circling him.

When I saw that they had left, I gathered up my jacket and reticule—those fossils from before—and left the William Tell.

On the subway back to Brooklyn, I memorized the facts scribbled hurriedly on the inside cover of the matchbook, afraid to entrust my future to a possible hole in the pocket of my well-worn khakis.

And when I got home, my mother and father were already asleep. No sound from their bedroom that night, and the next morning brought the beginning of another "good" day. Once again, after breakfast, I suggested she sit out on the porch. I would lower the awning. A strong sun, but a soothing breeze: a fresh green June morning. My father joined us, bringing the Sunday *Times* and my mother's glasses. A perfect morning it would have been to tell them: Mom, Dad, I've fallen in love. I didn't, of course. It was the last time the three of us sat like that together, quietly reading, at peace for an hour.

I waited until nine-thirty before I telephoned Victor. He was up, yes. He'd been waiting for my call, had gotten up earlier than usual to wait for it. The orgy never did take place. "They lost interest when I told them I thought I might have fallen in love. I'd be uncooperative. So, that's that. And, now? What about us?"

"I remember I told them I wanted to go into the city for a few hours . . . to see an army buddy. He'd just moved down from Westchester. I told them I'd bumped into you at the beach . . . a convincing lie, I thought. A lie with some pieces of the truth stuck in it. My father liked the idea of an army buddy: 'At least you got one thing to show for your two years, a friend. It wasn't a total waste.' I remember my mother smiled, but about what I never asked. She sensed something had happened to me, something good for me. I liked believing that. All these years I've liked believing that, that she knew something good had happened to me. How I remember that morning—and that afternoon. We went wild that afternoon. Remember, Victor? We had our own orgy."

"Like the proverbial yesterday I remember it. Twenty-seven years ago . . . it went so fast. More than half our lifetimes . . ."

A breeze starts up, brushes the streaks of reflected light left on the lake. They break into flashing dots, dark diamonds. "What a tangled time our beginning was. Wonderful sex and love and then grief and all those lies . . . one set about Texas we told my family when you came to the house during *shivah*, another set about Europe for your family when I moved in with you. What if they had ever gotten together to compare lies?"

"We would have told them the truth."

"Now you say that. But then, Victor? The McCarthy years? Who told the truth then?"

"At least we didn't hide it from them. When they visited us, they could have asked. They saw our beds together. All your father did was test them to see how soft they were."

"My father was glad I had a place to move to. He didn't. He had to look for an apartment. I was . . . the lucky one. Oh, how lucky I was to have found you . . . just in the nick of time, and in a gay bar yet."

"No luckier than I was, Willy."

"You still feel that? After what's happened?"

"What's happened, Willy? All you did was visit Sam. You got that out of your system—or maybe you didn't. Maybe I'm speaking too soon. Maybe it's me you got out of your system. Maybe you're working your way around to tell me that."

" 'Easy come, easy go.'. . . Remember you used to say that when you were feeling smug and secure. Very butch, very brave back then."

"Not at the beginning I wasn't. I was as frightened as you were, Willy. I didn't know what to do. I didn't know how to keep house or shop or cook or start a joint bank account. Neither did you, so I thought the best thing to do was say 'Easy come, easy go.' But I never meant that. I meant what you said the night you moved in with me. I remember how your father and brother-in-law and sister . . . I guess your nephews must have been there too . . . they all drove you over from Brooklyn. You had all your belongings in two army blankets. Books and clothes and recordings . . . and when they left you stood there between the two blankets and began crying. But I remember when I took hold of you, you also began to laugh. I remember how you cried and laughed and said, 'I now pronounce you man and man.' We both cried then and then we laughed and before you did any unpacking we put off the lights and got into bed and I held you and let you cry it out."

"Some dowry I brought you . . . army blankets, the GI Bill . . . even now I'm always close to being penniless. . . ."

"I'm not, so you're not. For better or for worse, Willy. That's life. Nothing's perfect . . . not even you. Certainly not me. Not even Mother Nature. Here come the gnats again."

Another swarm—maybe the same one—hovers between us, comforting company here in the purple light; something pesky and familiar, something uncertain, unpredictable, just as we are.

"You've changed your mind, Victor? You don't want a divorce?"

"I want us to continue."

"You're sure now? Better try and be as sure as you can be because we're about to turn the corner into the end. This may be your last chance to get rid of me. I'm not exactly fresh goods. I'm used, I'm perishable, I'm not likely to add very much, if anything, to our bank account in the foreseeable future. So, before age starts roping you in, before the arthritis strikes, better try and be as sure as you can be. I won't take you to court. The dogs are dead so there's no custody battle. I can give up my opera subscription. We can divide the books and records. . . ."

"And the house? Our lake? The pictures from our trips? All these years? Can we divide those?"

"No, Victor, we can't. But we can't re-do them either. They stand as they are. Are you sure they are enough to make you want us to stay together?"

"Yes. And you? You should be as sure as you can be, too, because I'm the one who causes the problems, usually."

"You also caused the love."

"So did you. You were sunburned. My heart went out to you. I wanted to be of help."

"I wanted to kiss you, right at the tip of your Roman-coin nose . . . a classic. You were that night, you are now."

"In your eyes."

"Others see you so. Most recently, a cattleman on his way from Albuquerque to Dallas saw you so."

"I can't promise you a future free of cattlemen."

"You never promised me a past free of them. I never promised you one either. I only promised to tell you the truth about how I felt. If the balance between us went bad and stayed bad I would tell you. It hasn't. In San Francisco I knew for sure it hadn't."

"My balance is favorable too. And I promise to make it more so for you. I promise to try not to say *nothing* when you ask me what's wrong."

"I promise to try not to ask you what's wrong when you're studying the sunset."

"You can ask. It's your habit to ask and to talk. It's my habit to look and to listen. I was trained that way. The scientific method. Always on the lookout for artifacts."

"Like me. Before your very eyes I'm turning into an artifact. You can hang me in your museum."

"A prime example of the graybeard loon genus, but not hang-able. Not yet. In thirty years, maybe, when you start wearing dentures and have to take them out to have sex, maybe then we'll face our next crisis."

With a will all their own, my fingers fly to my chin for some combing through the tangle of my beard. "Thirty years," I murmur, tugging, so it hurts, so I know I'm still alive, still hanging on, "I'd like to live at least thirty more years with you. We'll be eighty . . ."

"And we'll probably be down here on the dock, sitting out. Probably you'll ask me a question but I won't answer because I'll be staring out at the sunset, studying it, and then you'll get angry and make me feel guilty. Some habits last a lifetime because they're efficient, even guilt. They get naturally selected, help the species survive." Smiling, he reaches across our now unnecessary line of scrimmage, pulls my busy fingers from my

241

beard. "We're a unique species. We don't reproduce but we don't die out. They can't get rid of us. We're always around. Must be something in our genes, something like spontaneous combustion." He squeezes my hand with a happy young force, a force I remember from my oldest memory of his touch.

And, happily, I feel his force touching off young familiar feelings inside me. The old machine, that complex network of feelings and memories, starts up in an instant. Down in my privates rushing blood tells me I'll be ready. All is in working order.

Victor stands.

He offers his hand to help me up.

A moment of silent staring between us: his eyes asking. I nod yes. Case closed. Settled out of court. Settled . . . for now. Probably settled until the end—as settled, probably, as human beings can ever manage to settle these matters of living and loving and death. Always there's risk, whoever loves whom, Jane and Dick, friends of Duke or Dorothy. But it's the loving that makes all the risks worth taking, that and memory. Love makes old memories reusable now and in the future. Love helps them survive, always intact.

We turn together for a last look at the lake.

Darkness. No breeze. A stillness our deep, rapt breathing fills. We're alone here together under another night's black velvet wonder of sky. But underfoot there is the solid wood comfort of our dock. And there is our house. Victor points to it, his hand at the small of my back urging me to start up to it.

But, first, I bend to retrieve our Scotch glasses: an old habit. It must be efficient. Someone of every twosome has to play Griselda now and then.

We stop to watch the crescent moon just now rising above the chimney. How many crescents hidden inside how many full moons since that soft shoulder near Waxahachie? The flowers have burst their buds. V'lodya has gone to sleep inside Willy. Good night, Sammy for star. . .

We continue on up to the house, enter it without turning on a light, pausing only long enough for me to set the glasses in the kitchen sink.

And upstairs, no light either while we undress.

Victor joins me along the edge of my bed. We kiss, a long welcome-back kiss. Pressing closer, slowly we lean back, his arms guiding me lower, our bodies asprawl across both beds, our legs searching out their accustomed ins and outs, settling into a familiar fit while our old bodies adjust to the sudden surge of young feelings. Blood drums in my head. Well-worn signals switch on once again, opening channels to memories of past performances. My ear pressed against his chest, I hear his heartbeat, and my heartbeat. They're speeding up, pumping faster, faster, rushing us ahead together.

In the darkness my failing vision is no handicap. My fingers know the way. Familiar territory, his skin. Touching here, touching there, they rouse familiar feelings, feelings no less thrilling for being familiar, rising from a source no less mysterious. My fingers . . . his fingers . . . smoothing . . . soothing . . . old feelings, setting them free, sending them deeper down into the unfamiliar, unknown place in him, in me, into that stream of all time always rushing through each of us and up from which new feelings leap into life. Only familiar fingers, fingers we can trust, can lead us there.

I slid lower along the surface of his sweet-smelling skin.

Slowly he turns.

Our mouths meet their separate targets.

We are linked in a circle of love.